Leaving MEGALOPOLIS™

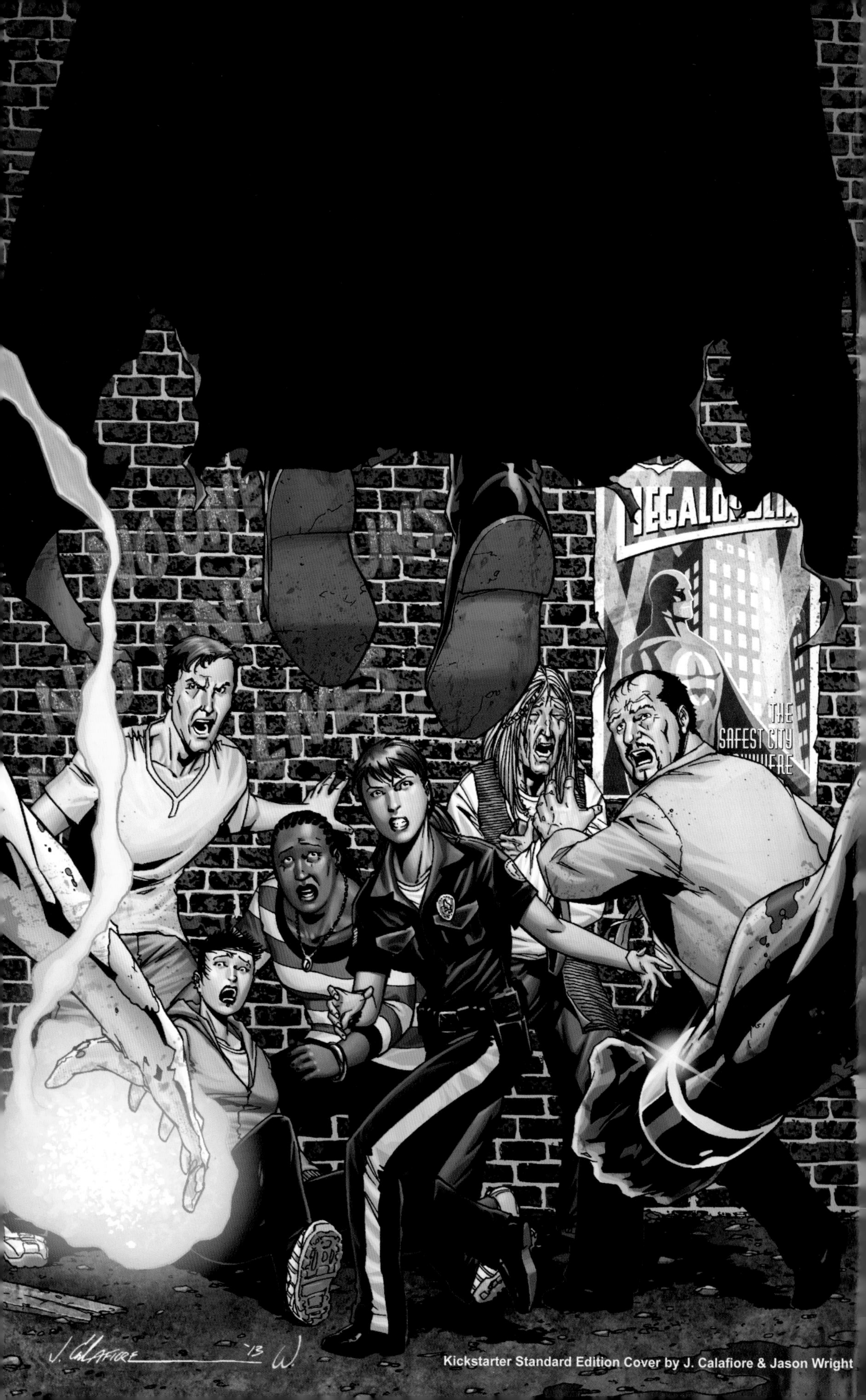
THE
SAFEST CITY

Kickstarter Standard Edition Cover by J. Calafiore & Jason Wright

Leaving MEGALOPOLIS ™

VOLUME 1

by
GAIL SIMONE
&
J. CALAFIORE

colorist
JASON WRIGHT

letterer
DAVE SHARPE

DARK HORSE BOOKS

publisher
MIKE RICHARDSON

collection editor
PATRICK THORPE

assistant collection editor
EVERETT PATTERSON

digital production
CHRISTINA McKENZIE

designer
RICK DeLUCCO

Published by
Dark Horse Books
A division of Dark Horse Comics, Inc.
10956 SE Main Street
Milwaukie, OR 97222

DarkHorse.com

To find a comics shop in your area,
call the Comic Shop Locator Service
toll-free at 1-888-266-4226

First edition: September 2014
ISBN 978-1-61655-559-7

1 3 5 7 9 10 8 6 4 2

Printed in China

MIKE RICHARDSON President and Publisher **NEIL HANKERSON** Executive Vice President **TOM WEDDLE** Chief Financial Officer **RANDY STRADLEY** Vice President of Publishing **MICHAEL MARTENS** Vice President of Book Trade Sales **ANITA NELSON** Vice President of Business Affairs **SCOTT ALLIE** Editor in Chief **MATT PARKINSON** Vice President of Marketing **DAVID SCROGGY** Vice President of Product Development **DALE LaFOUNTAIN** Vice President of Information Technology **DARLENE VOGEL** Senior Director of Print, Design, and Production **KEN LIZZI** General Counsel **DAVEY ESTRADA** Editorial Director **CHRIS WARNER** Senior Books Editor **DIANA SCHUTZ** Executive Editor **CARY GRAZZINI** Director of Print and Development **LIA RIBACCHI** Art Director **CARA NIECE** Director of Scheduling **TIM WIESCH** Director of International Licensing **MARK BERNARDI** Director of Digital Publishing

INTRODUCTION

Anybody can write superheroes. They're easy. Yes, there are varying degrees to which it can be done well, but as long as you bear the basics in mind—superpowers, hands on hips occasionally, noble purpose, sense of self-sacrifice, admirable deeds, etc.—really, anyone can hit the beats to one degree or another.

Writing about ordinary people, though . . . That's hard to do convincingly at all, much less do well. Superheroes are, by nature, visual and expressive and come with their own shorthand (see above). Ordinary folks, built from scratch on the comics page by the writer and artist, they require a little more work if we're to care about them, root for them, invest in them. They have to feel real to us.

Gail Simone and Jim Calafiore make this look simple. Both of them, separately, are exemplary at giving readers dramatis personae with depth and dimension—Gail by never forgetting that even the most minor players in her scripts are complex individuals, Jim by presenting us with characters who have weight, who are vividly expressive and unique and unforgettable.

Together, the Simone/Calafiore team rocks.

Were I you, I'd get comfortable, because if your experience is like mine, once you turn the page, you're not going to be able to stop reading until the end.

–Mark Waid

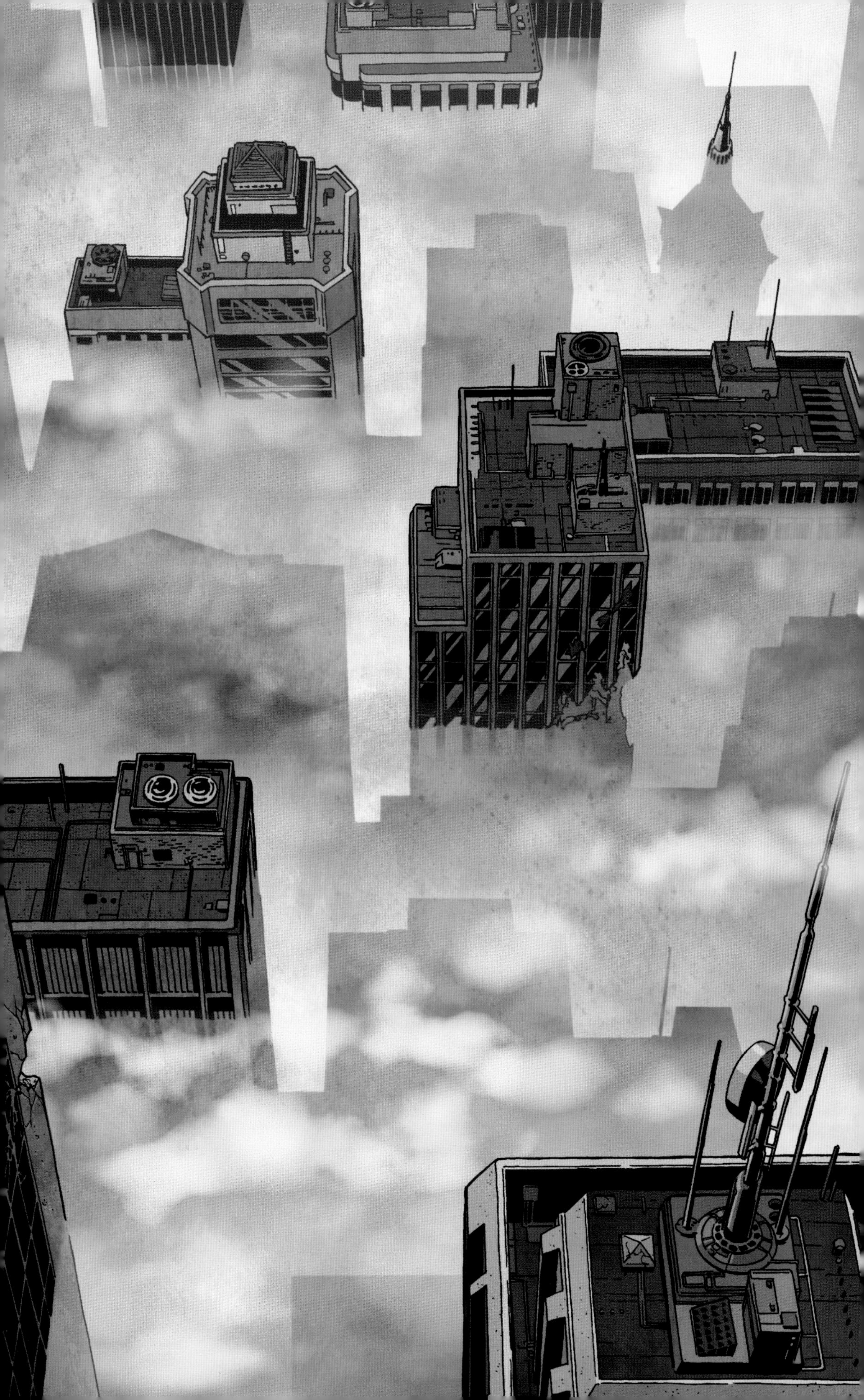

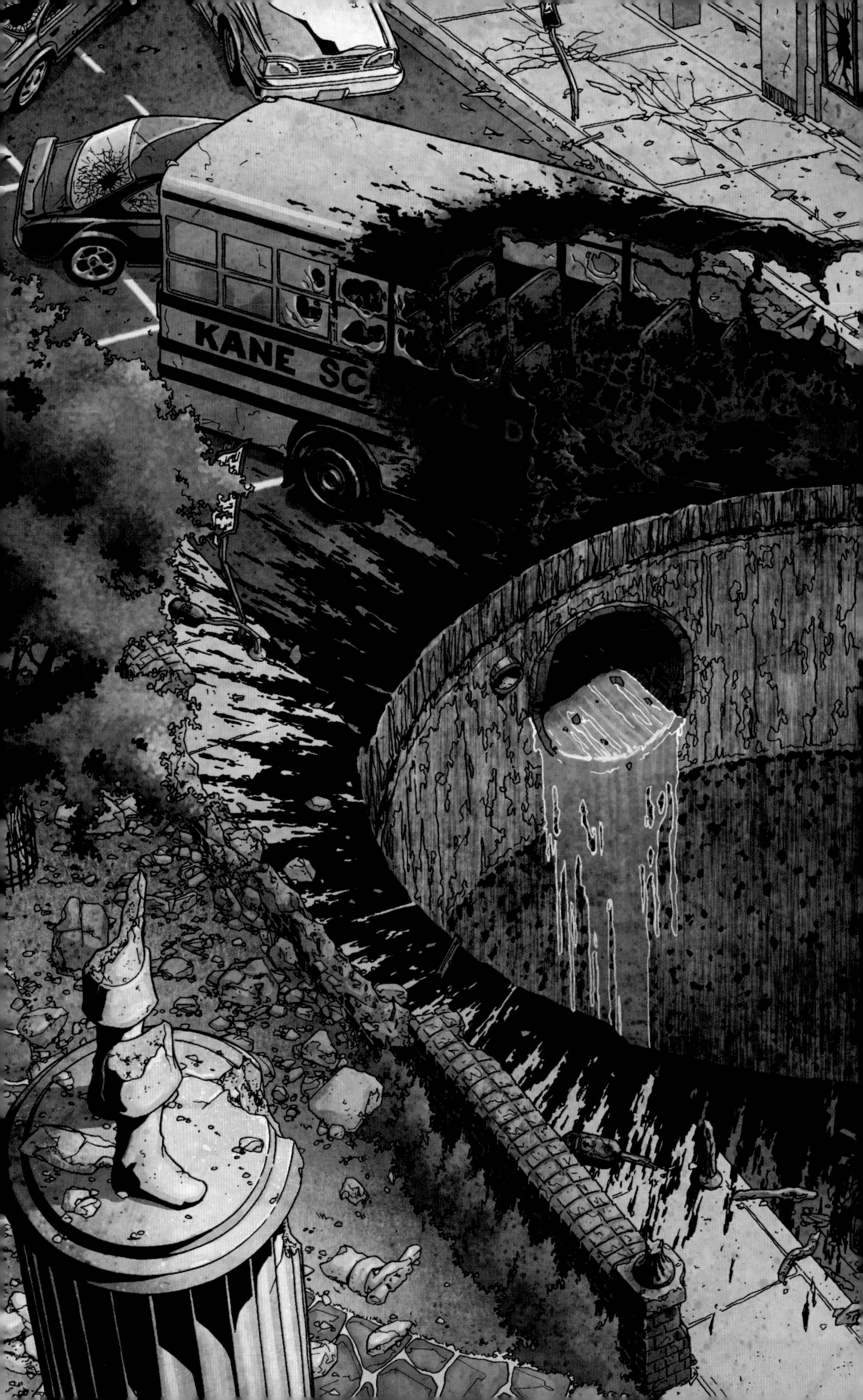
KANE SC

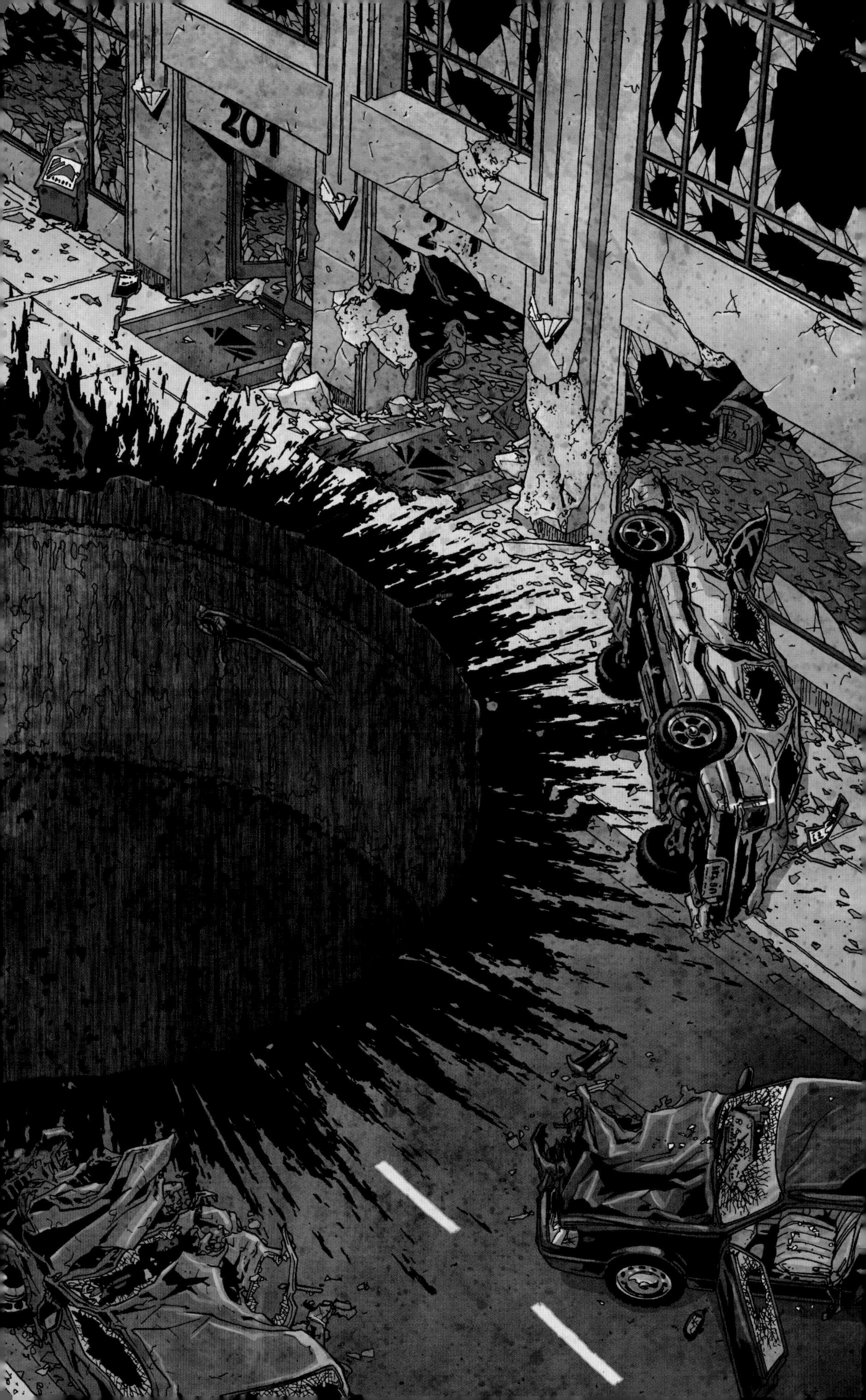
201

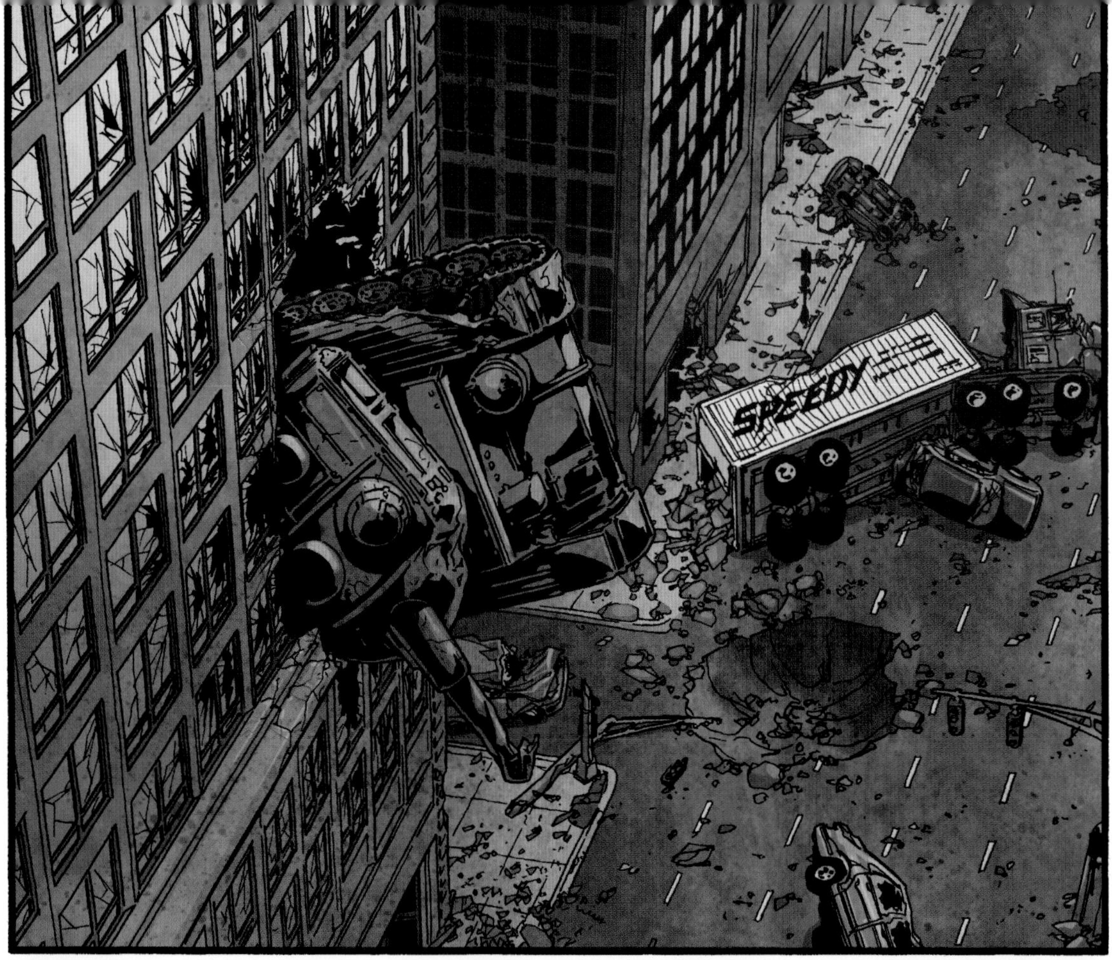
SPEEDY
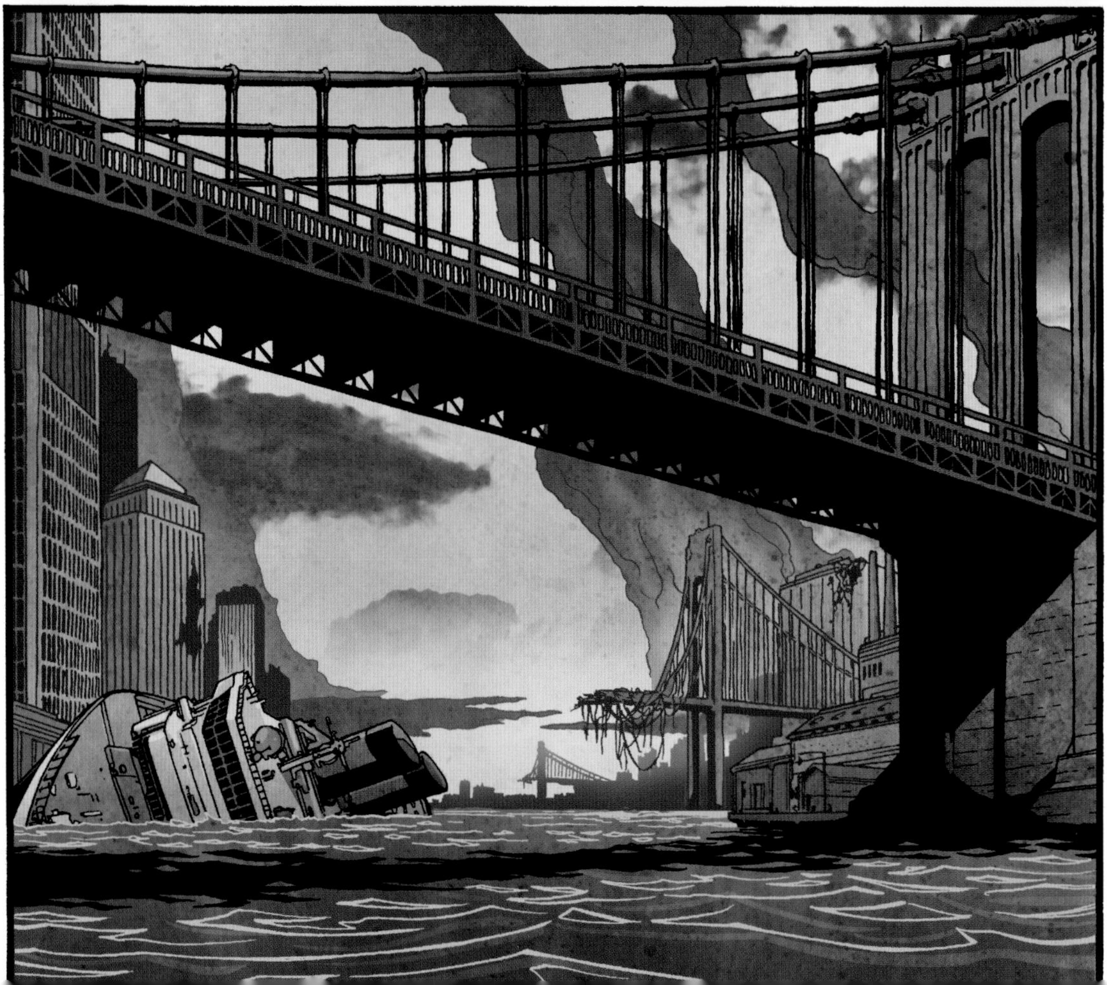

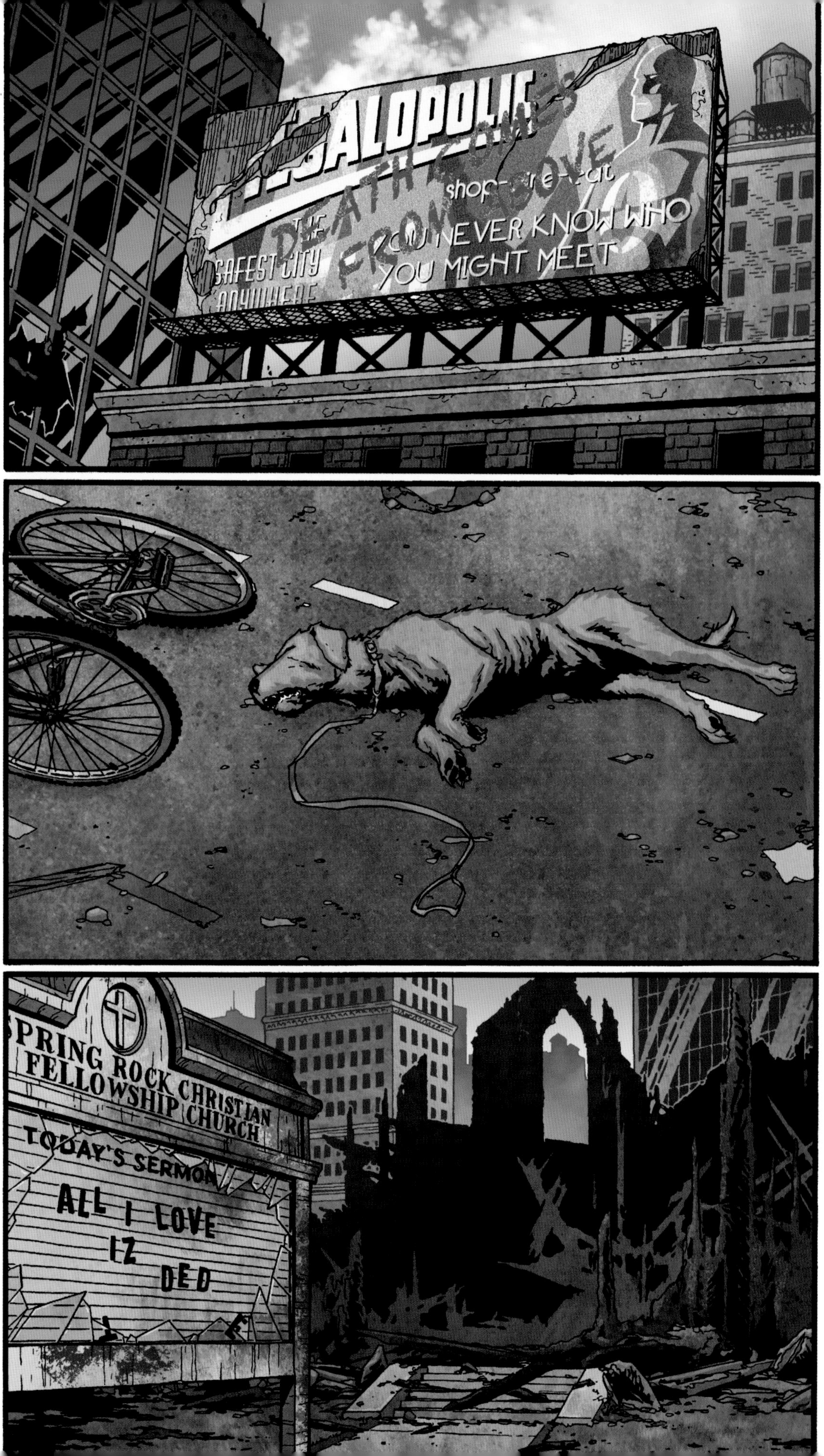

ALOPOLIS
THE
SAFEST CITY
YOU NEVER KNOW WHO
YOU MIGHT MEET
DEATH COMES
FROM ABOVE
SPRING ROCK CHRISTIAN
FELLOWSHIP CHURCH
TODAY'S SERMON
ALL I LOVE
IZ
DED

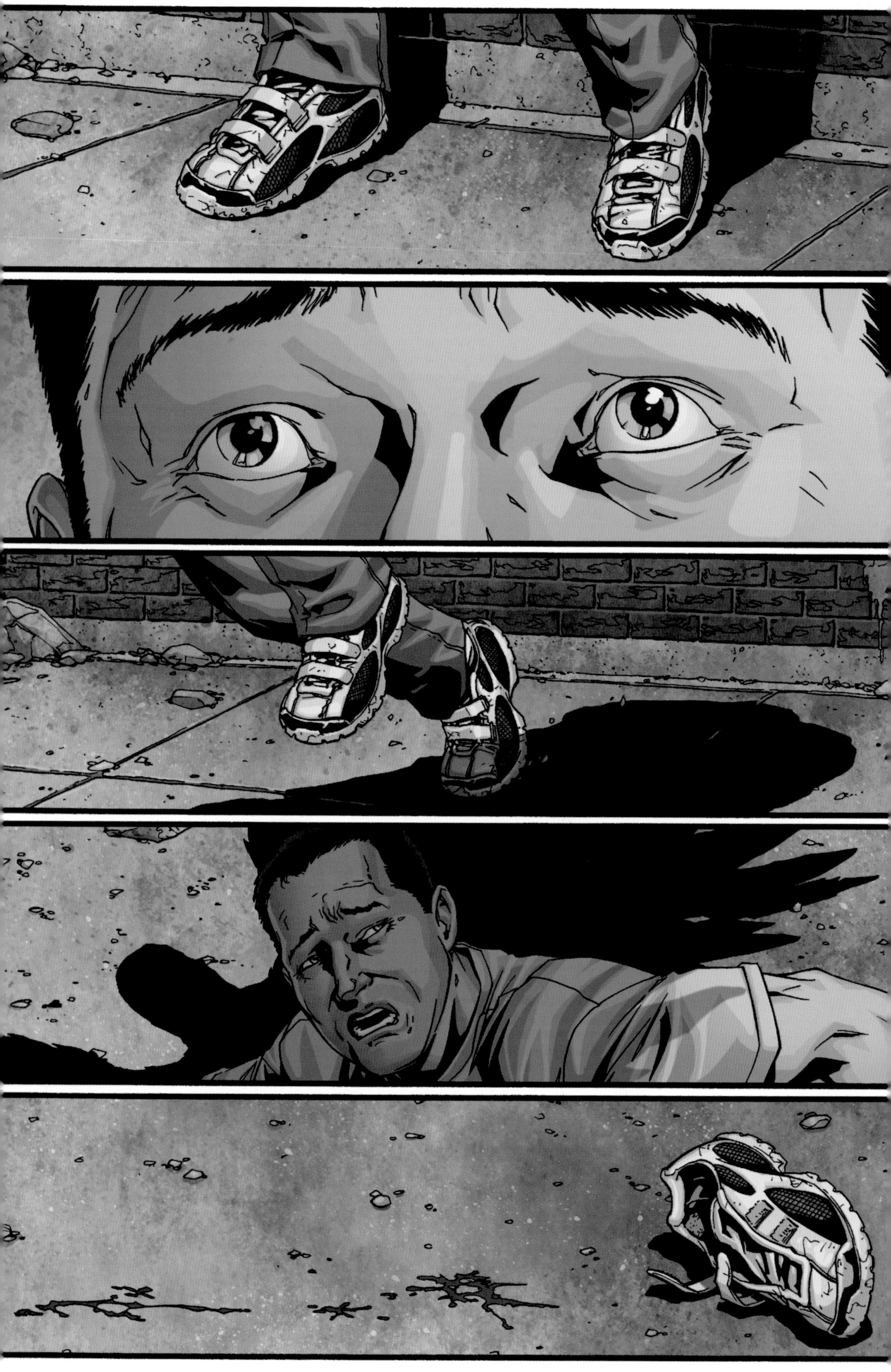

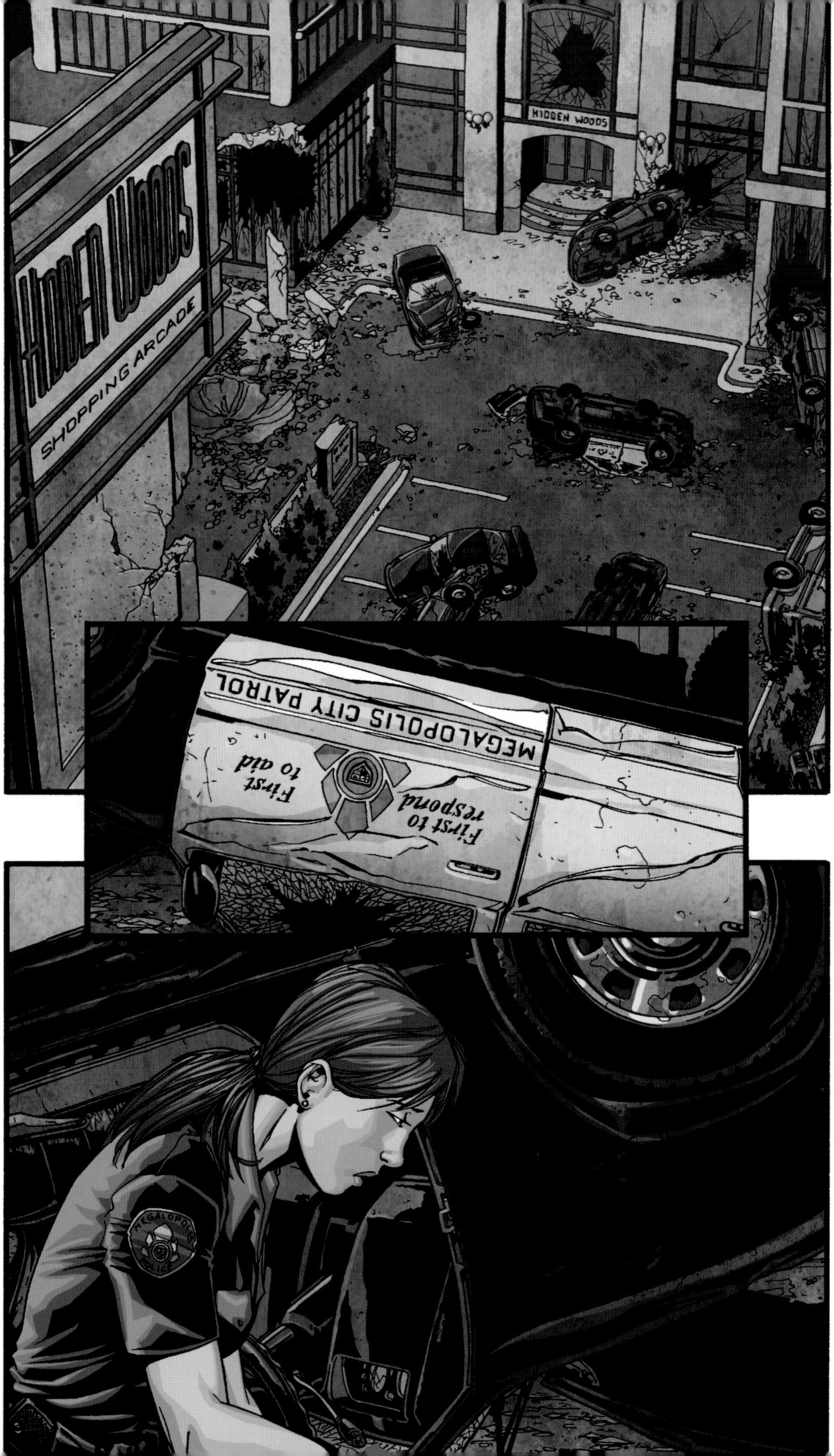
HIDDEN WOODS
SHOPPING ARCADE
HIDDEN WOODS
MEGALOPOLIS CITY PATROL
First to respond
First to aid
MEGALOPOLIS POLICE

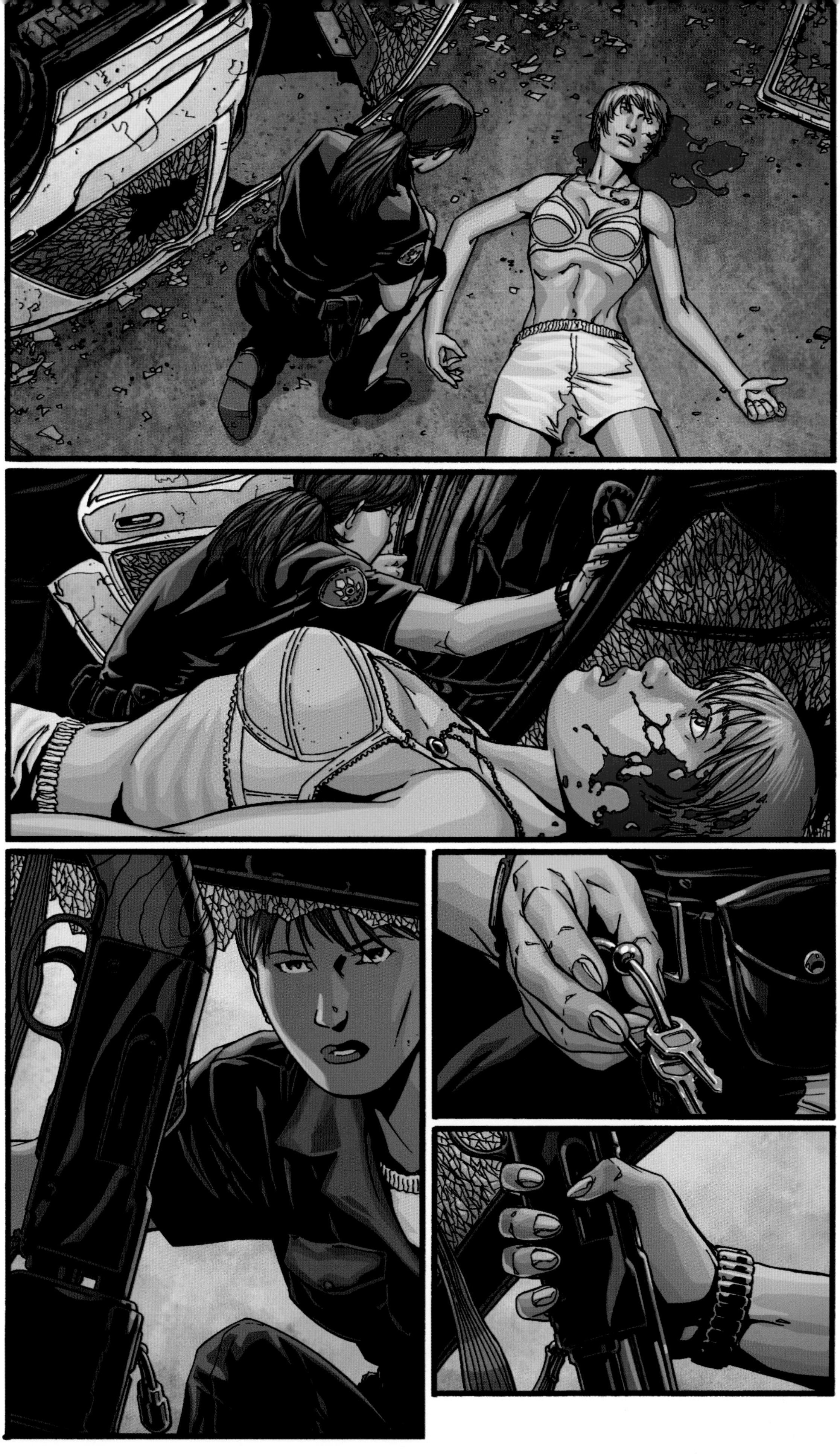

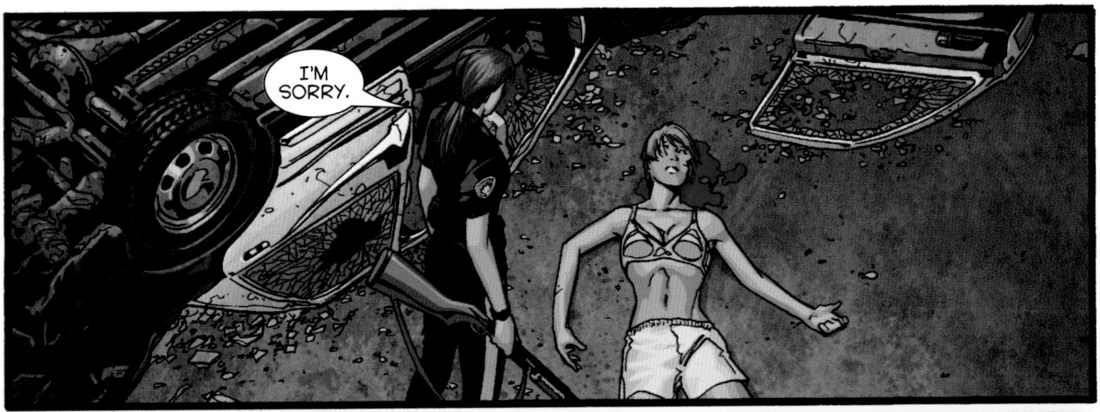
I'M SORRY.

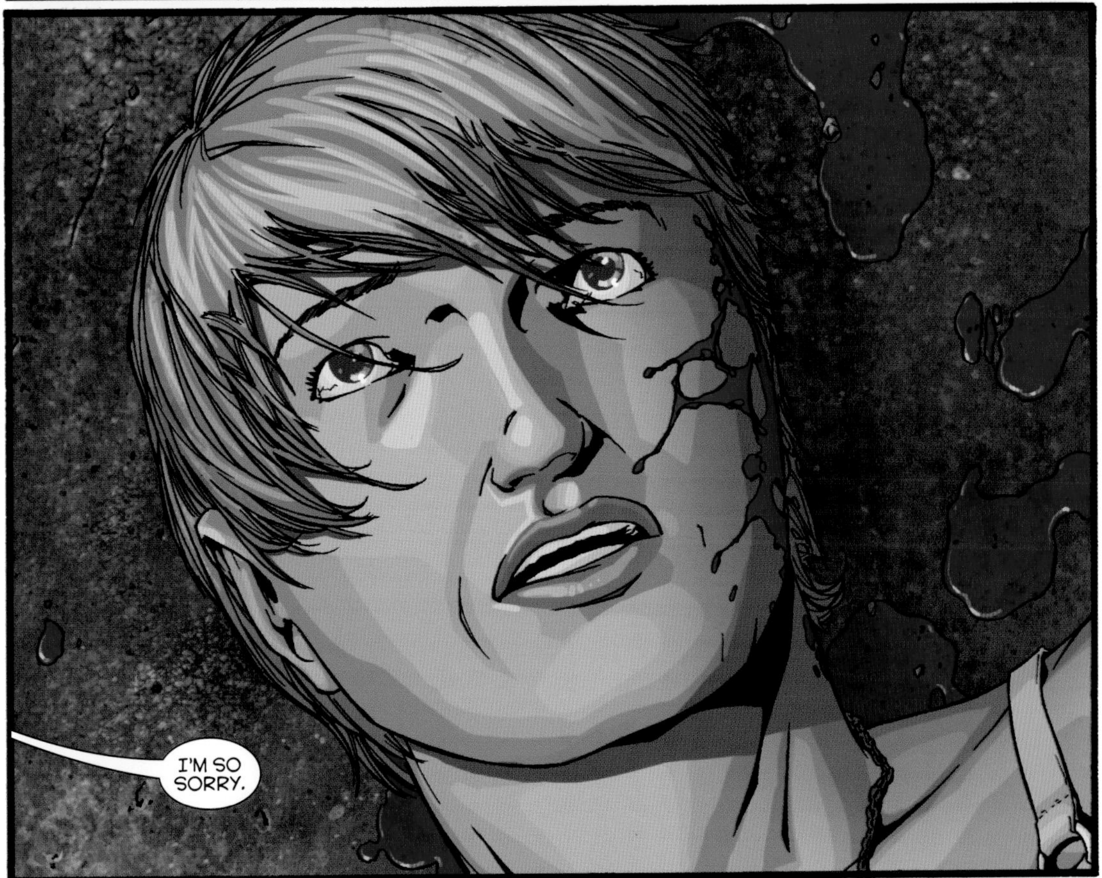
I'M SO SORRY.

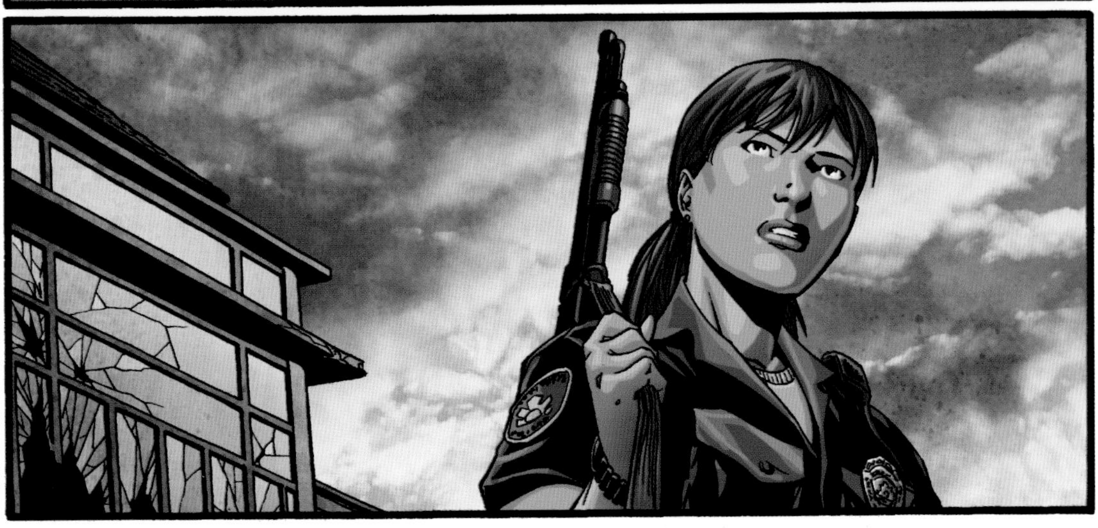

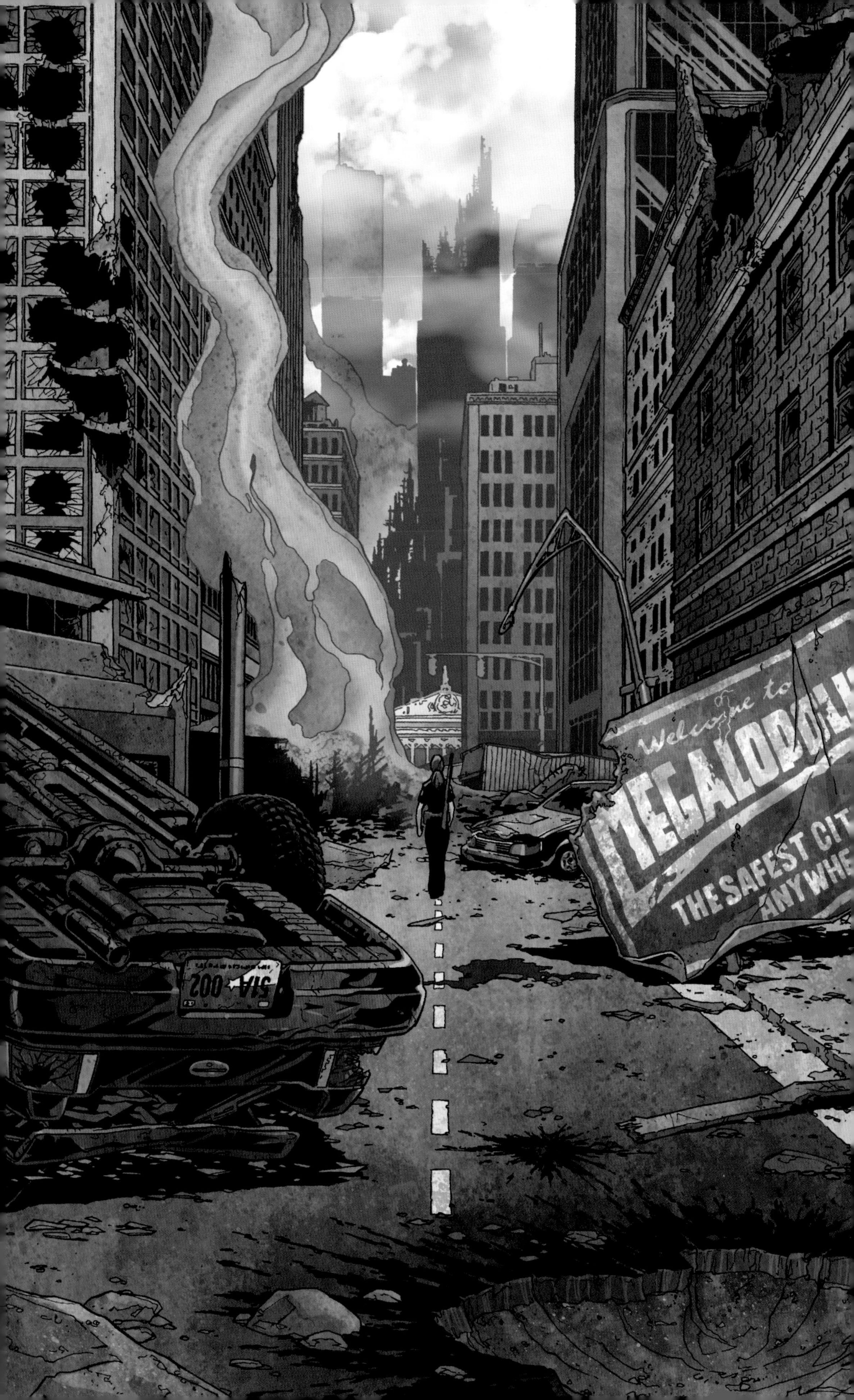
MEGALOPOLI
THE SAFEST CIT
ANYWHE

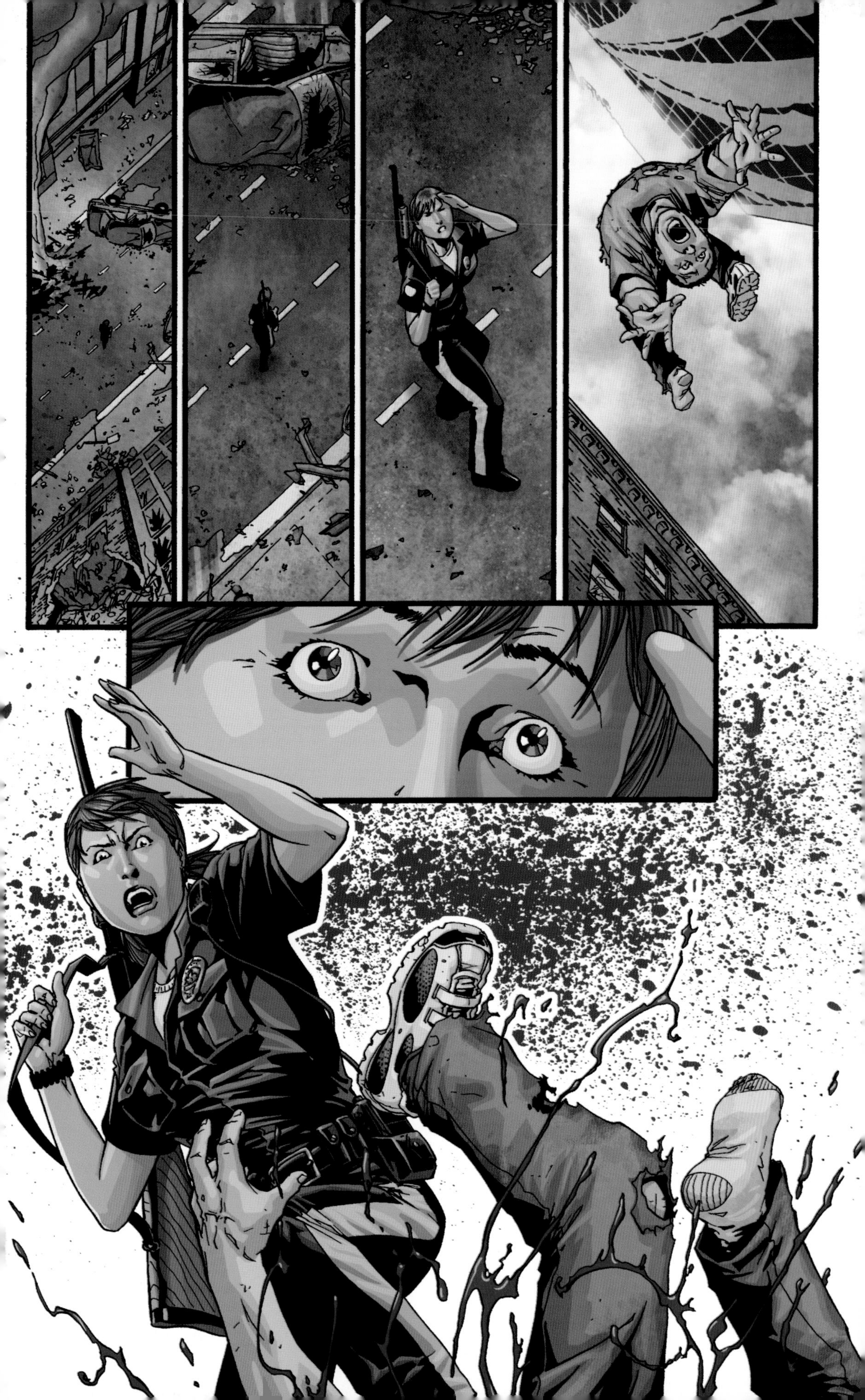

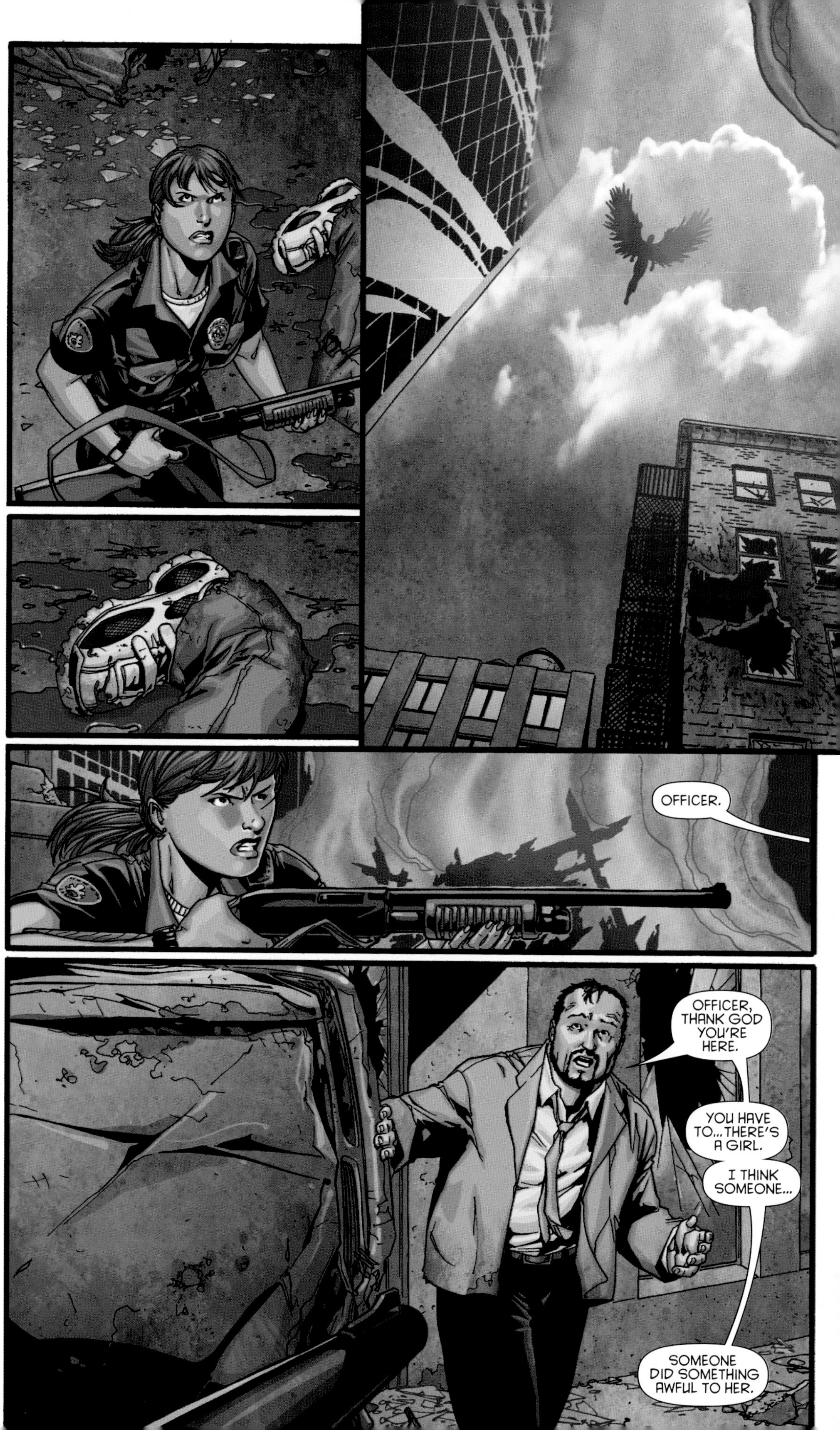
OFFICER.
OFFICER, THANK GOD YOU'RE HERE.
YOU HAVE TO... THERE'S A GIRL.
I THINK SOMEONE...
SOMEONE DID SOMETHING AWFUL TO HER.

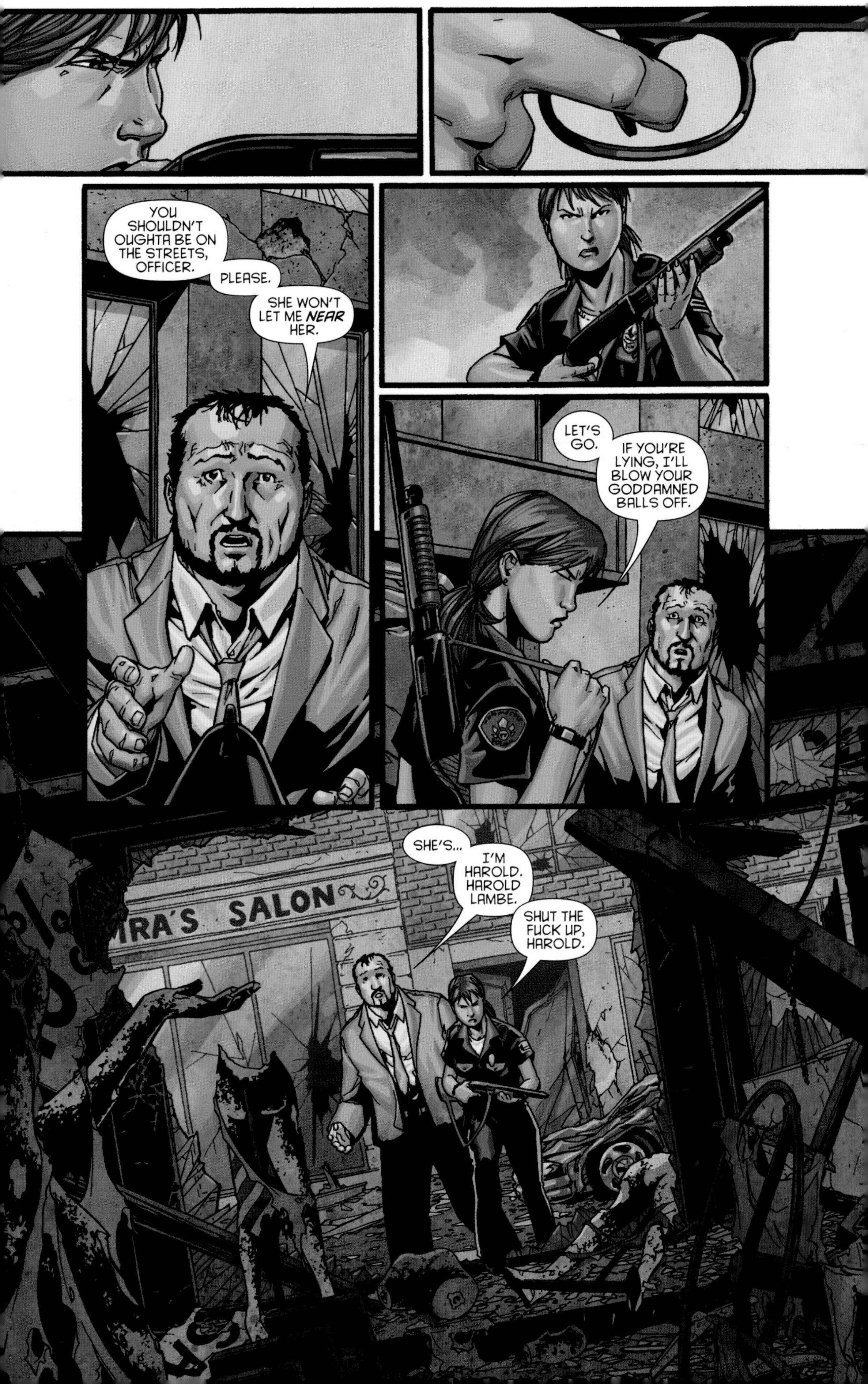
YOU SHOULDN'T OUGHTA BE ON THE STREETS, OFFICER.
PLEASE.
SHE WON'T LET ME NEAR HER.
LET'S GO.
IF YOU'RE LYING, I'LL BLOW YOUR GODDAMNED BALLS OFF.
MRA'S SALON
SHE'S...
I'M HAROLD. HAROLD LAMBE.
SHUT THE FUCK UP, HAROLD.

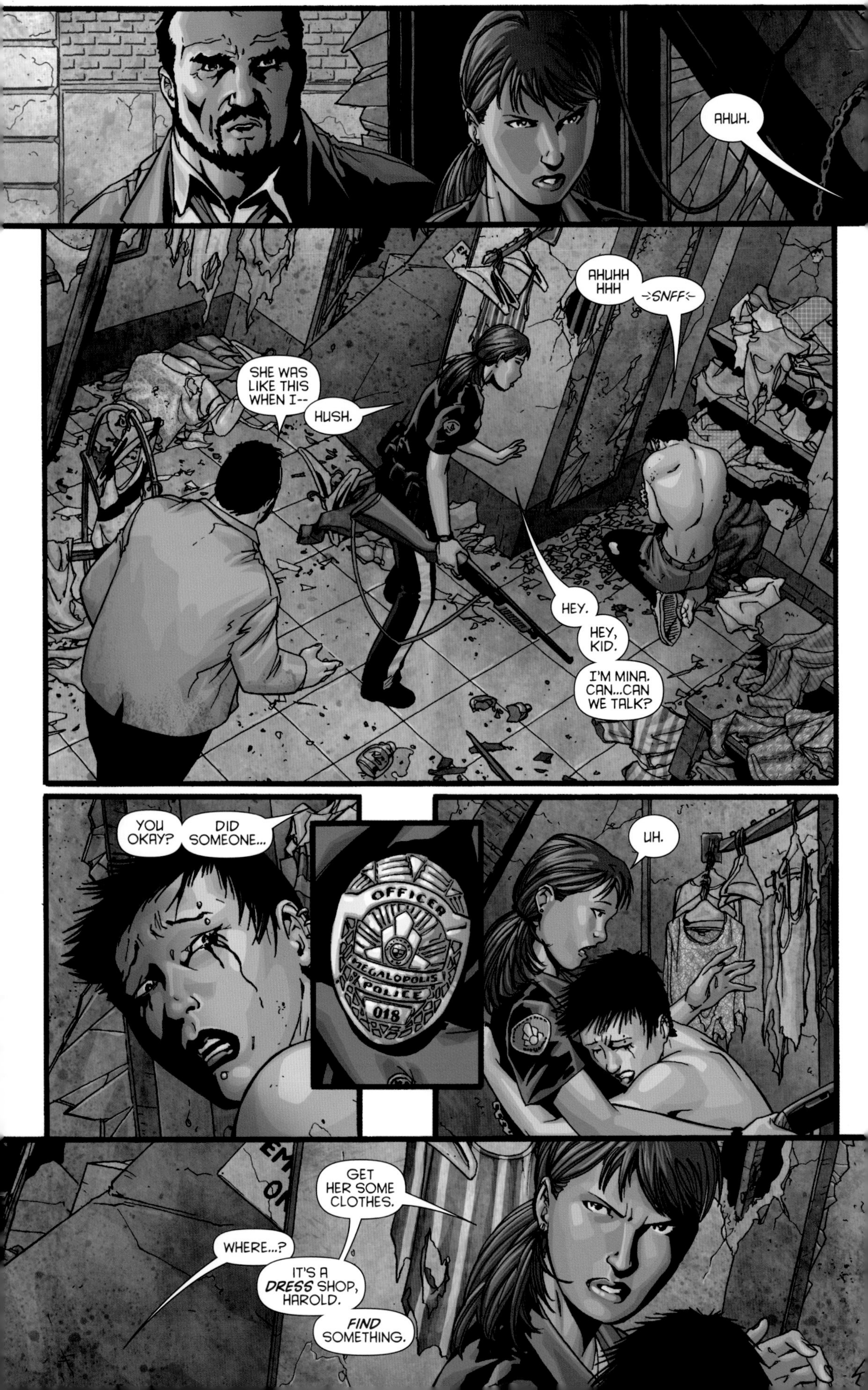
AHUH.
AHUHH HHH
SNFF
SHE WAS LIKE THIS WHEN I--
HUSH.
HEY.
HEY, KID.
I'M MINA. CAN...CAN WE TALK?
YOU OKAY?
DID SOMEONE...
OFFICER
MEGALOPOLIS POLICE
018
UH.
GET HER SOME CLOTHES.
WHERE...?
IT'S A *DRESS* SHOP, HAROLD.
FIND SOMETHING.

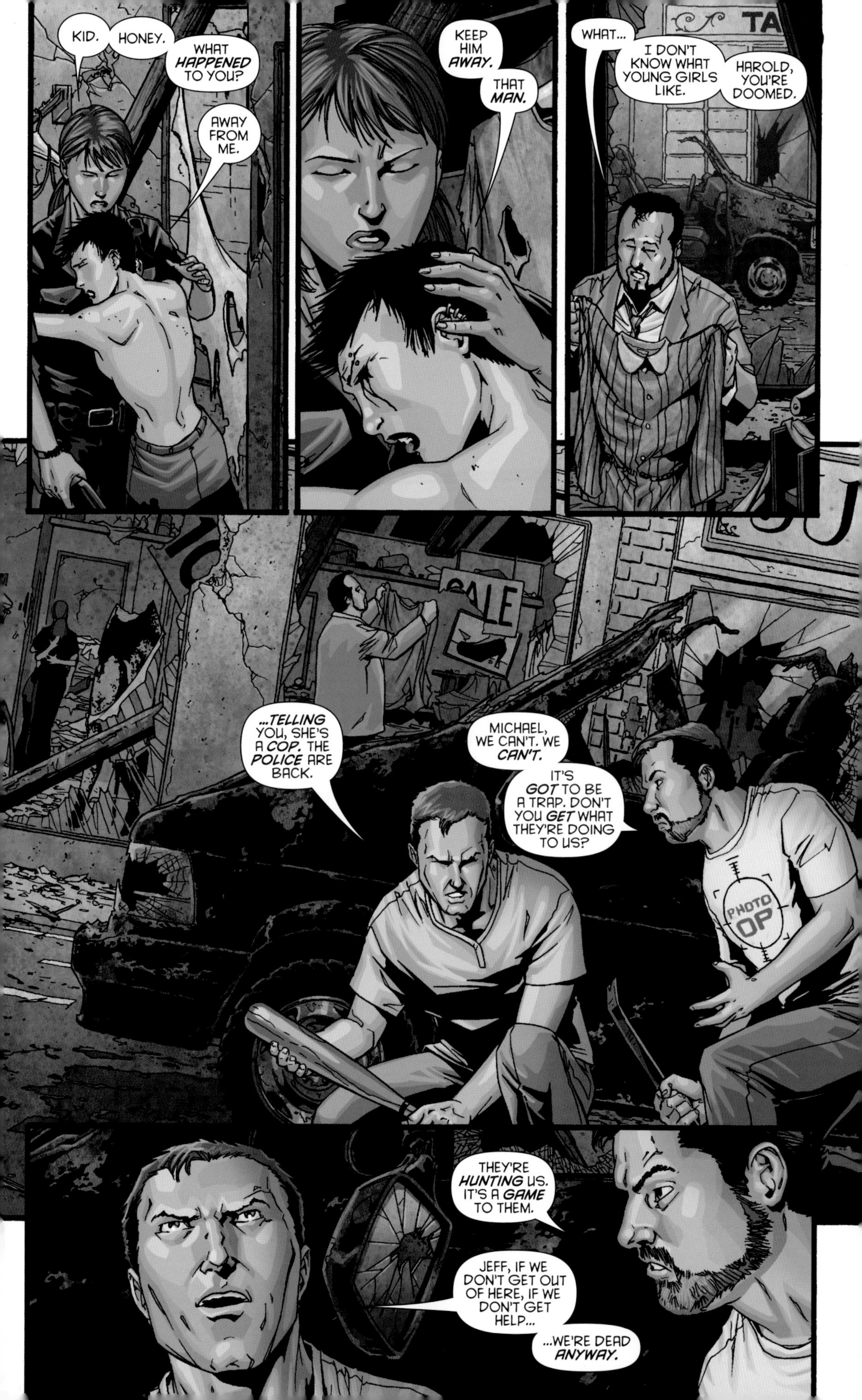
KID.
HONEY.
WHAT HAPPENED TO YOU?
AWAY FROM ME.
KEEP HIM AWAY.
THAT MAN.
WHAT...
I DON'T KNOW WHAT YOUNG GIRLS LIKE.
HAROLD, YOU'RE DOOMED.
SALE
...TELLING YOU, SHE'S A COP. THE POLICE ARE BACK.
MICHAEL, WE CAN'T. WE CAN'T.
IT'S GOT TO BE A TRAP. DON'T YOU GET WHAT THEY'RE DOING TO US?
PHOTO OP
THEY'RE HUNTING US. IT'S A GAME TO THEM.
JEFF, IF WE DON'T GET OUT OF HERE, IF WE DON'T GET HELP...
...WE'RE DEAD ANYWAY.

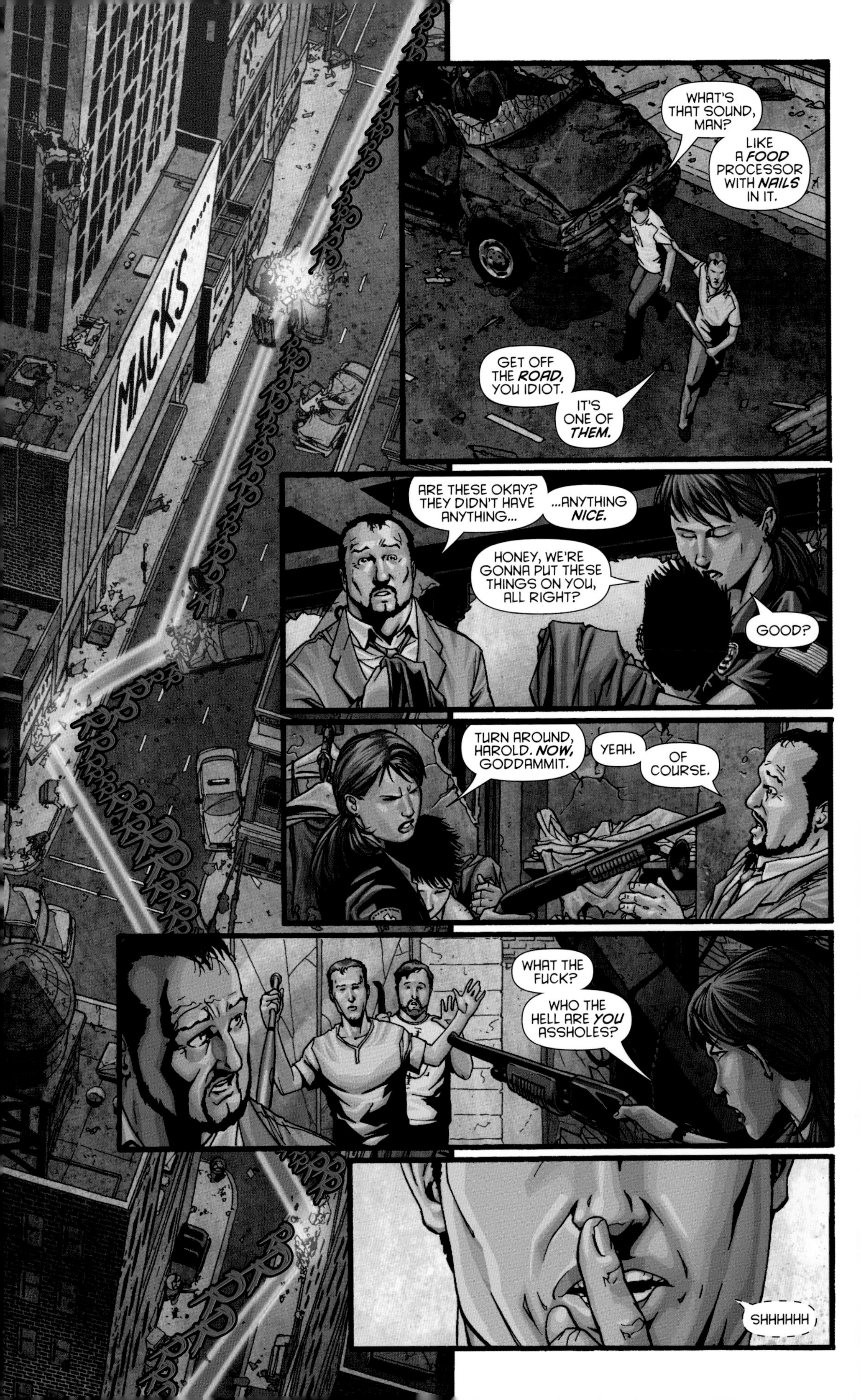

MACK'S
WHAT'S THAT SOUND, MAN?
LIKE A FOOD PROCESSOR WITH NAILS IN IT.
GET OFF THE ROAD, YOU IDIOT.
IT'S ONE OF THEM.
ARE THESE OKAY? THEY DIDN'T HAVE ANYTHING...
...ANYTHING NICE.
HONEY, WE'RE GONNA PUT THESE THINGS ON YOU, ALL RIGHT?
GOOD?
TURN AROUND, HAROLD. NOW, GODDAMMIT.
YEAH.
OF COURSE.
WHAT THE FUCK?
WHO THE HELL ARE YOU ASSHOLES?
SHHHHHH

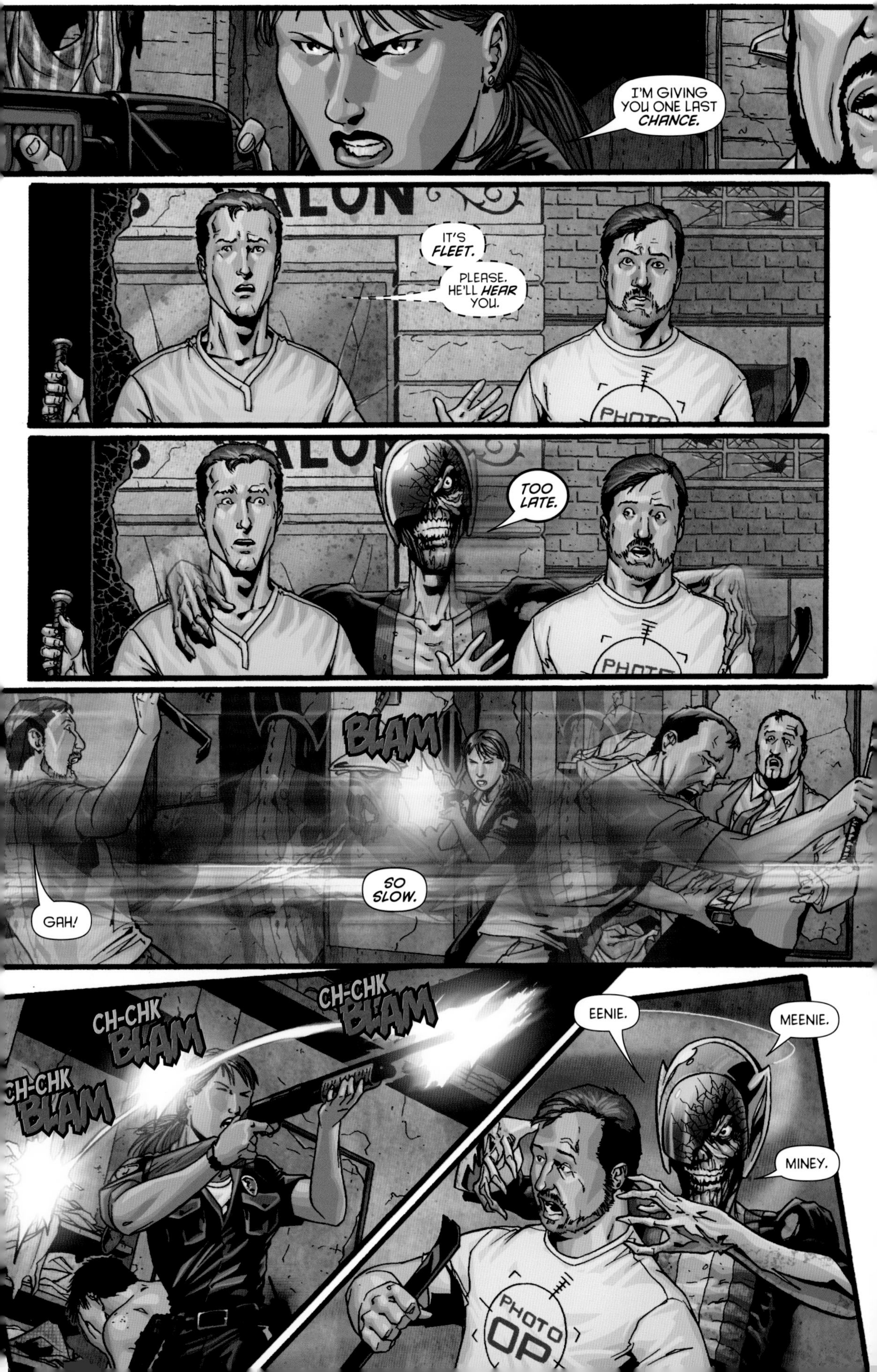
I'M GIVING YOU ONE LAST CHANCE.
IT'S FLEET.
PLEASE. HE'LL HEAR YOU.
TOO LATE.
BLAM
GAH!
SO SLOW.
CH-CHK BLAM
CH-CHK BLAM
CH-CHK BLAM
EENIE.
MEENIE.
MINEY.

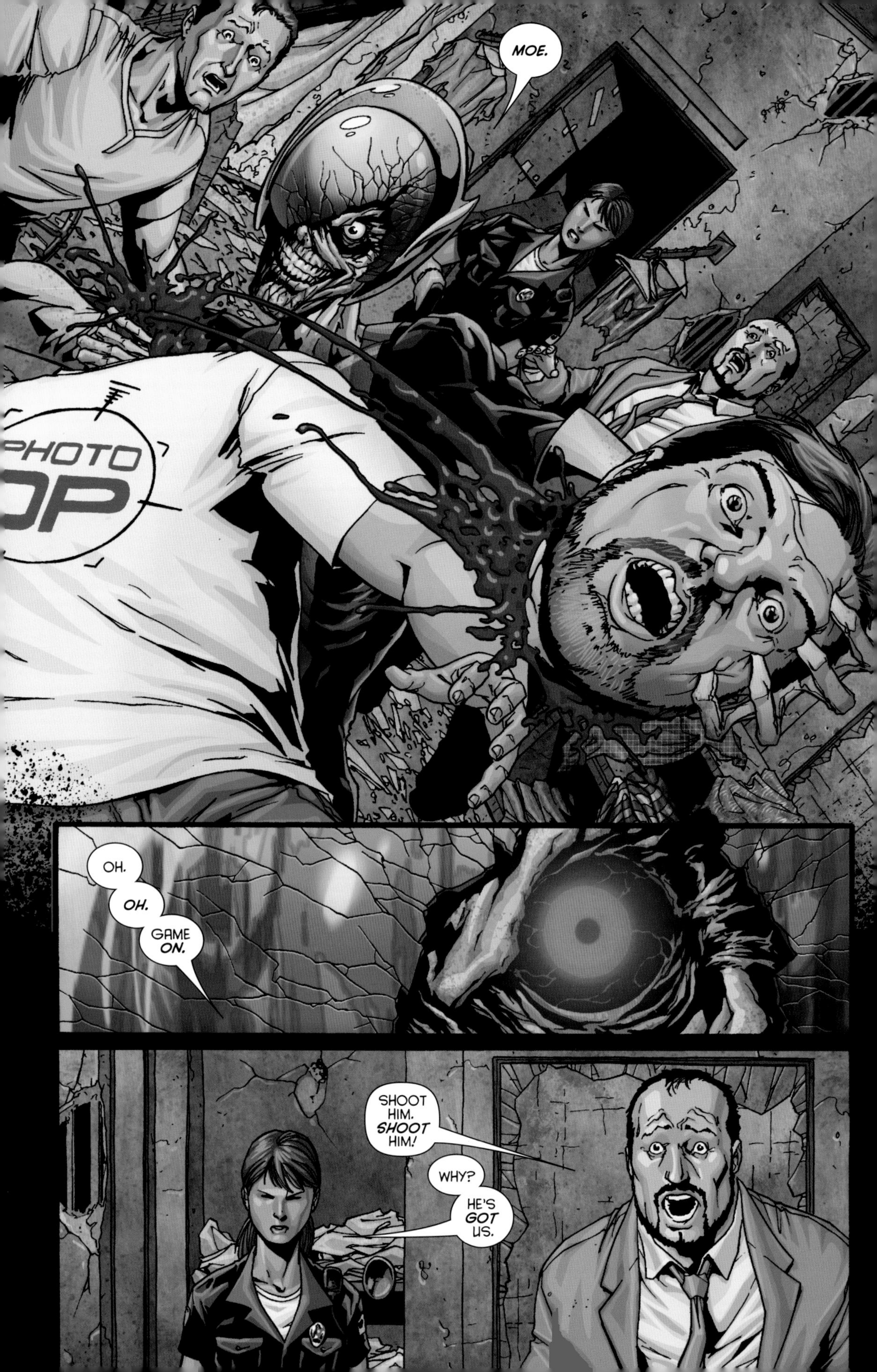
MOE.
PHOTO
OP
OH.
OH.
GAME ON.
SHOOT HIM. SHOOT HIM!
WHY?
HE'S GOT US.

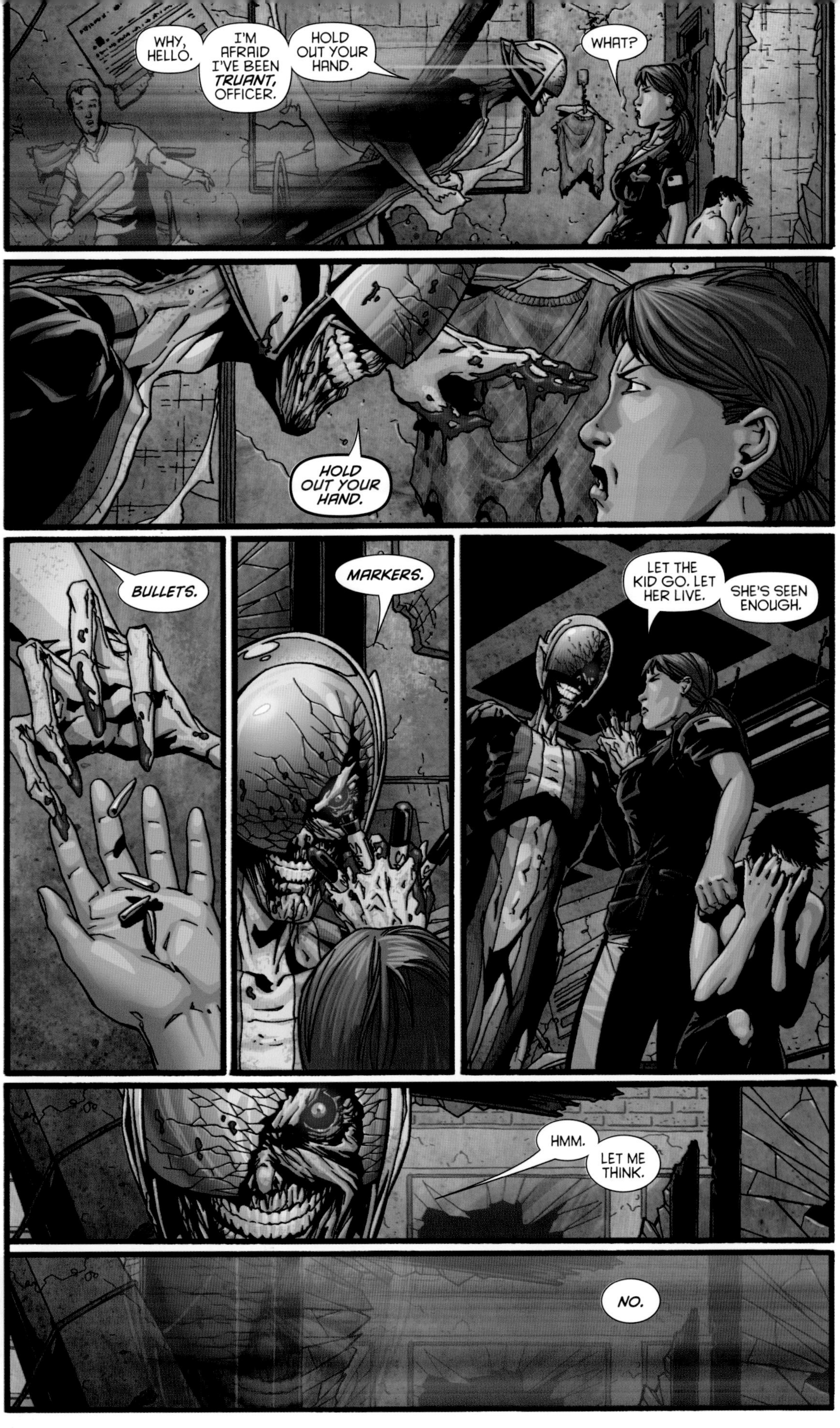
WHY, HELLO.
I'M AFRAID I'VE BEEN TRUANT, OFFICER.
HOLD OUT YOUR HAND.
WHAT?
HOLD OUT YOUR HAND.
BULLETS.
MARKERS.
LET THE KID GO. LET HER LIVE.
SHE'S SEEN ENOUGH.
HMM.
LET ME THINK.
NO.

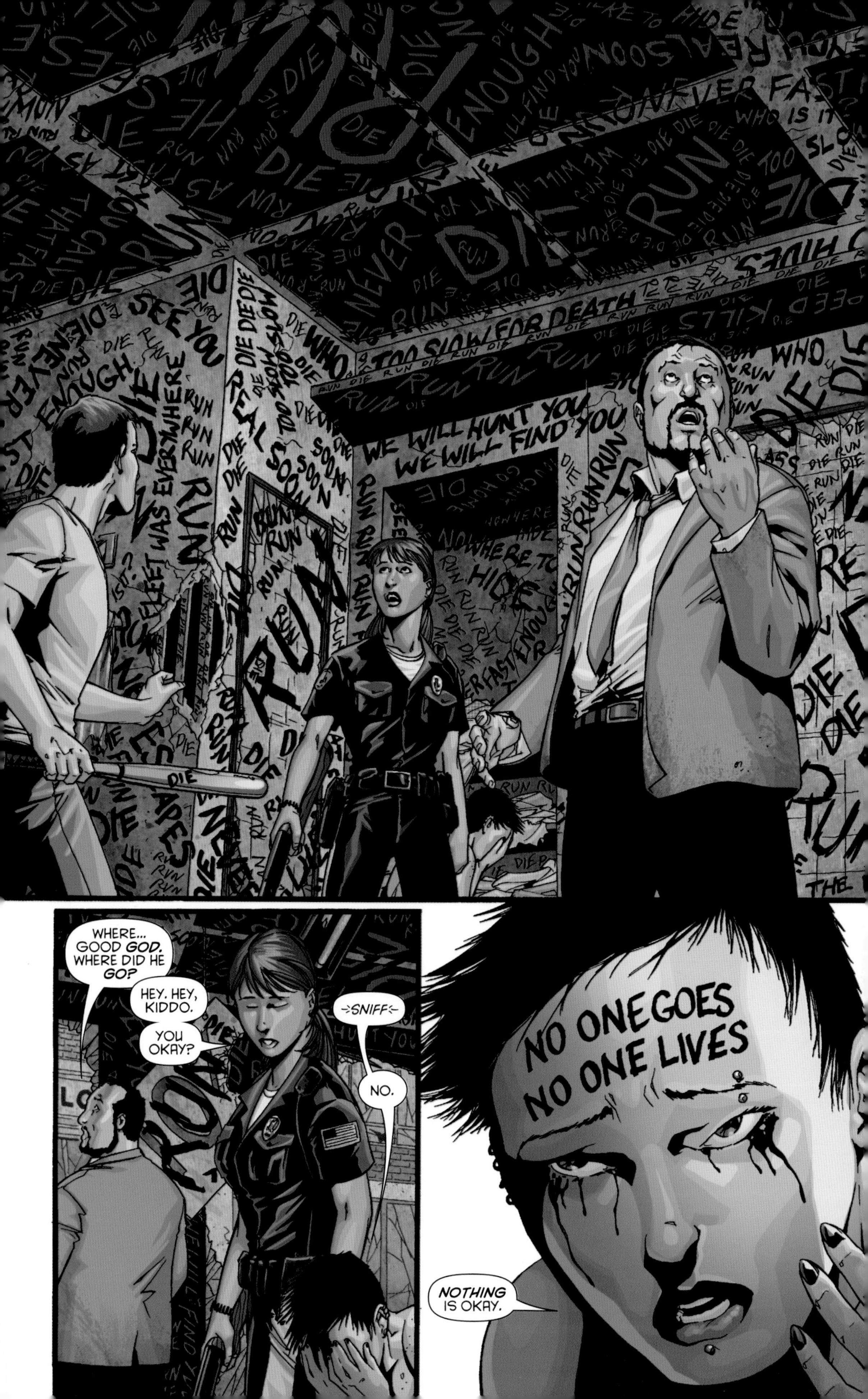

TOO SLOW FOR DEATH
WE WILL HUNT YOU
WE WILL FIND YOU
SEE YOU
FLEET WAS EVERYWHERE
NOWHERE TO HIDE
WHERE... GOOD GOD. WHERE DID HE GO?
HEY. HEY, KIDDO.
YOU OKAY?
-SNIFF-
NO.
NO ONE GOES
NO ONE LIVES
NOTHING IS OKAY.

SENATOR BELL: ...remind the good doctor that this is purely an exploratory subcommittee, not an exculpatory process. While you are entitled to have legal representation, we would like to assure you that it is not at all necessary.

DR. PREINE: Respectfully, Madame Senator--

SENATOR BELL: Please address me simply as "Senator," Doctor.

DR. PREINE: Senator. Counsel assures me that prudence requires his appearance. We are dealing with a massive government failure, and--

SENATOR BELL: I will repeat that this committee is not prepared to discuss your allegations regarding the chain of command. As head of the N.O.A.A., it is singularly your expertise in the meteorological aspects of the event in question.

DR. PREINE: (Dr. Preine pours himself a glass of water; counsel whispers something in his ear; Dr. Preine nods.) Understood. Senator.

SENATOR BELL: What was the first indication that the city of Megalopolis was experiencing an unorthodox weather event?

DR. PREINE: It was the clouds, Senator.

SENATOR BELL: Go on.

DR. PREINE: Well, cloud cover in that region is nothing unusual. But our equipment registered an extreme sulfur content, something like the particle content that would be surrounding four pre-legislation paper processing plants.

SENATOR BELL: Would these clouds be toxic, Doctor?

DR. PREINE: With prolonged exposure, absolutely. Potentially fatal for those with respiratory illnesses. We asked for a full evacuation but were flatly denied--

SENATOR BELL: DOCTOR Preine. I will AGAIN caution you to stick to the questions in your field of expertise and will insist that you do not again stray into unsubstantiated rumor. This is your last such warning.

DR. PREINE: You don't understand. I'm not blaming anyone. We all thought everyone would be safe in the city.

SENATOR BELL: Doctor--

DR. PREINE: All those heroes...that was their home base. Overlord. The Mite Brigade.

SENATOR BELL: Doctor, you don't seem to be LISTENING.

DR. PREINE: We thought the citizens would all be SAFE because of the HEROES.

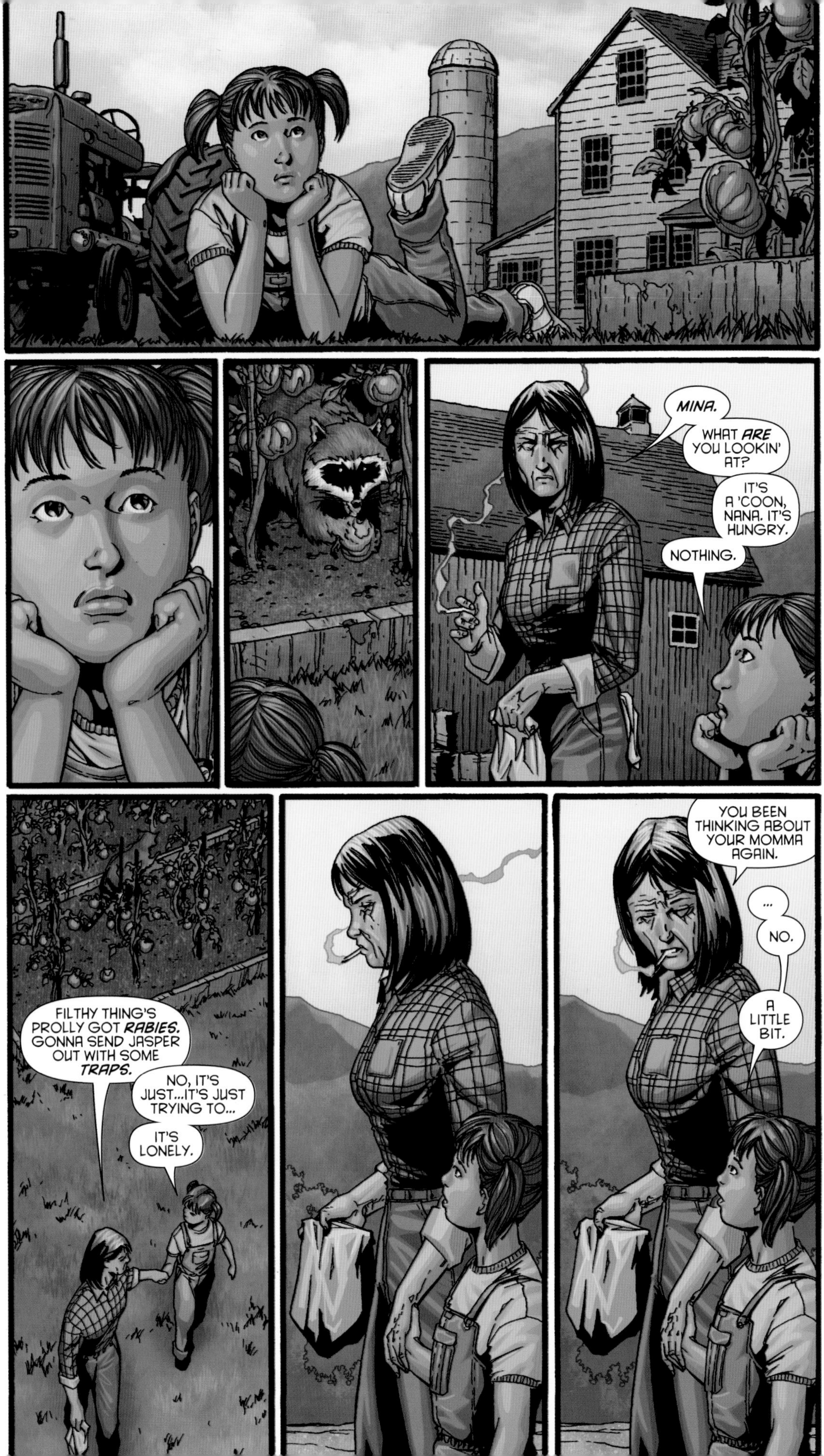
MINA.
WHAT ARE YOU LOOKIN' AT?
IT'S A 'COON, NANA. IT'S HUNGRY.
NOTHING.
FILTHY THING'S PROLLY GOT RABIES. GONNA SEND JASPER OUT WITH SOME TRAPS.
NO, IT'S JUST...IT'S JUST TRYING TO...
IT'S LONELY.
YOU BEEN THINKING ABOUT YOUR MOMMA AGAIN.
...
NO.
A LITTLE BIT.

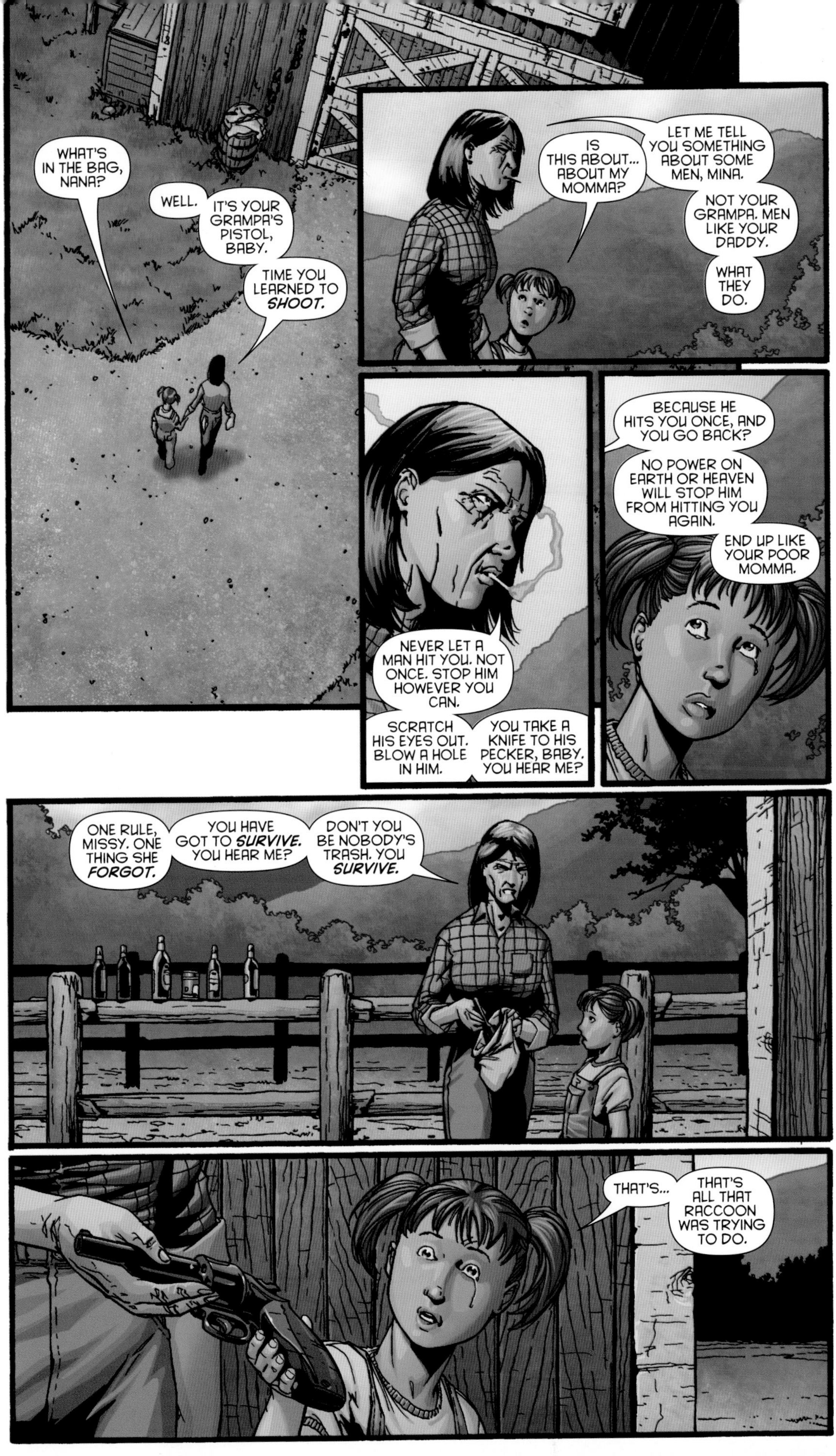
WHAT'S IN THE BAG, NANA?
WELL.
IT'S YOUR GRAMPA'S PISTOL, BABY.
TIME YOU LEARNED TO SHOOT.
LET ME TELL YOU SOMETHING ABOUT SOME MEN, MINA.
IS THIS ABOUT... ABOUT MY MOMMA?
NOT YOUR GRAMPA. MEN LIKE YOUR DADDY.
WHAT THEY DO.
NEVER LET A MAN HIT YOU. NOT ONCE. STOP HIM HOWEVER YOU CAN.
SCRATCH HIS EYES OUT. BLOW A HOLE IN HIM.
YOU TAKE A KNIFE TO HIS PECKER, BABY. YOU HEAR ME?
BECAUSE HE HITS YOU ONCE, AND YOU GO BACK?
NO POWER ON EARTH OR HEAVEN WILL STOP HIM FROM HITTING YOU AGAIN.
END UP LIKE YOUR POOR MOMMA.
ONE RULE, MISSY. ONE THING SHE FORGOT.
YOU HAVE GOT TO SURVIVE. YOU HEAR ME?
DON'T YOU BE NOBODY'S TRASH. YOU SURVIVE.
THAT'S...
THAT'S ALL THAT RACCOON WAS TRYING TO DO.

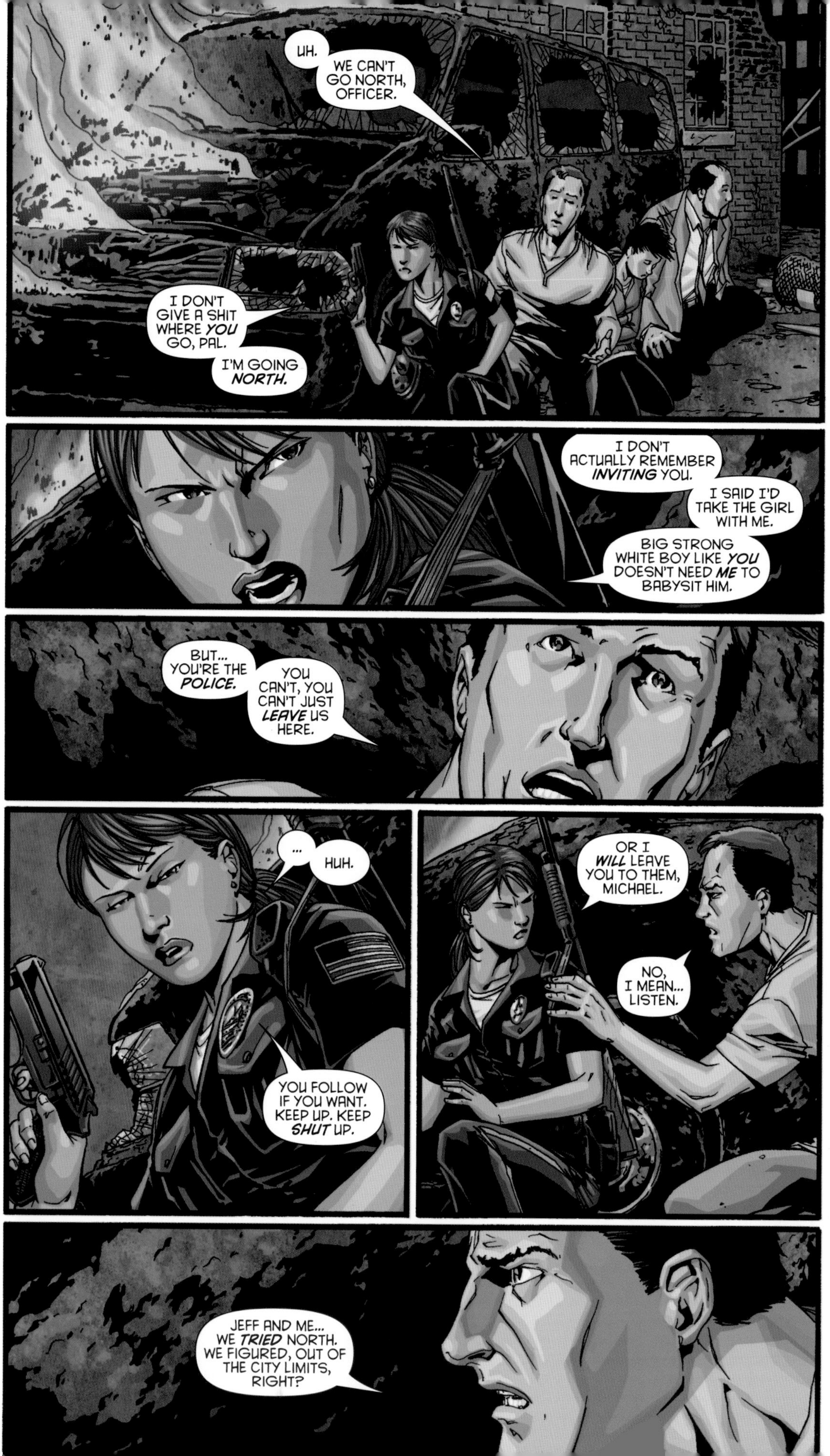
UH.
WE CAN'T GO NORTH, OFFICER.
I DON'T GIVE A SHIT WHERE *YOU* GO, PAL.
I'M GOING *NORTH.*
I DON'T ACTUALLY REMEMBER *INVITING* YOU.
I SAID I'D TAKE THE GIRL WITH ME.
BIG STRONG WHITE BOY LIKE *YOU* DOESN'T NEED *ME* TO BABYSIT HIM.
BUT... YOU'RE THE *POLICE.*
YOU CAN'T, YOU CAN'T JUST *LEAVE* US HERE.
...
HUH.
YOU FOLLOW IF YOU WANT. KEEP UP. KEEP *SHUT* UP.
OR I *WILL* LEAVE YOU TO THEM, MICHAEL.
NO, I MEAN... LISTEN.
JEFF AND ME... WE *TRIED* NORTH. WE FIGURED, OUT OF THE CITY LIMITS, RIGHT?

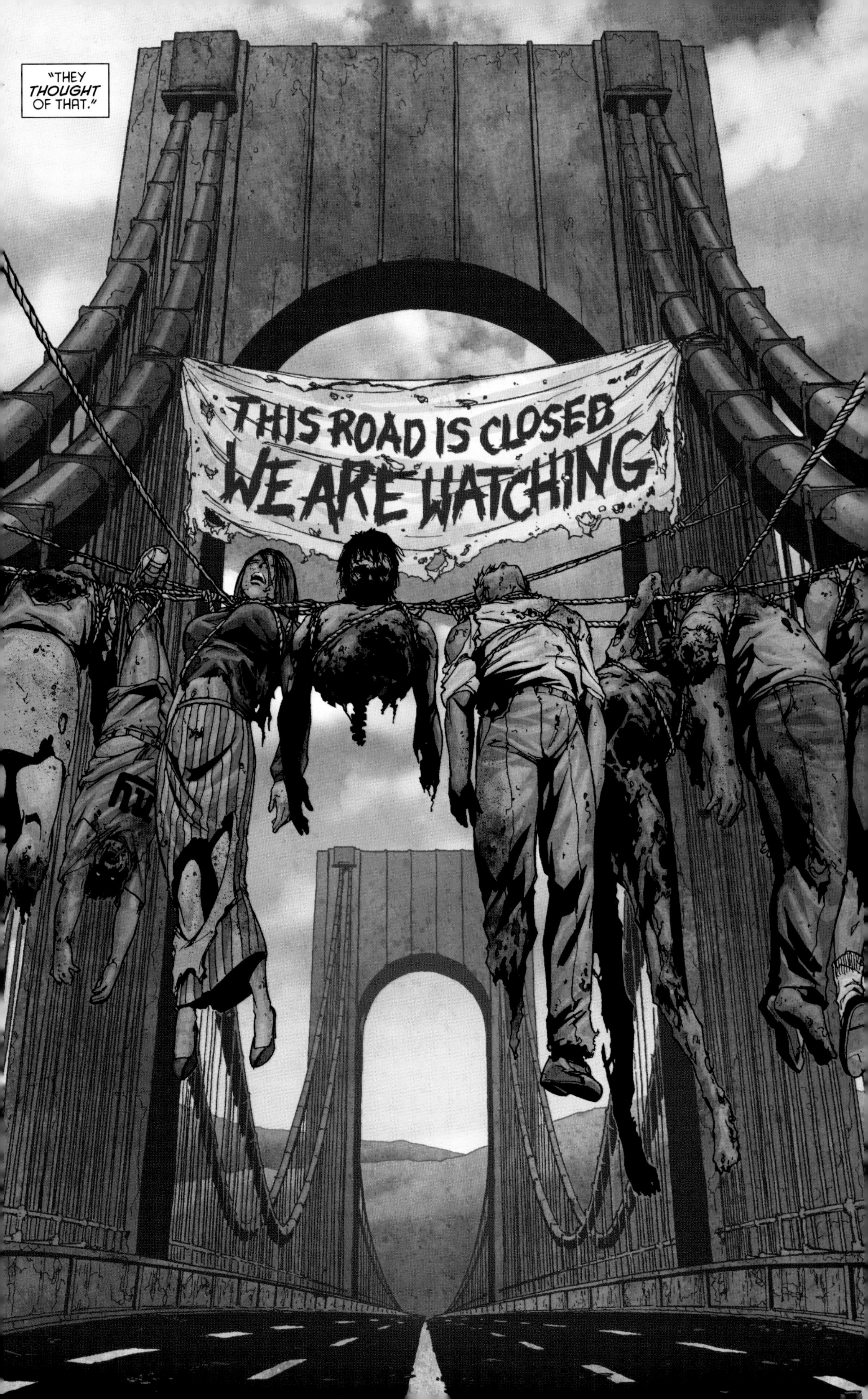
"THEY *THOUGHT* OF THAT."
THIS ROAD IS CLOSED
WE ARE WATCHING

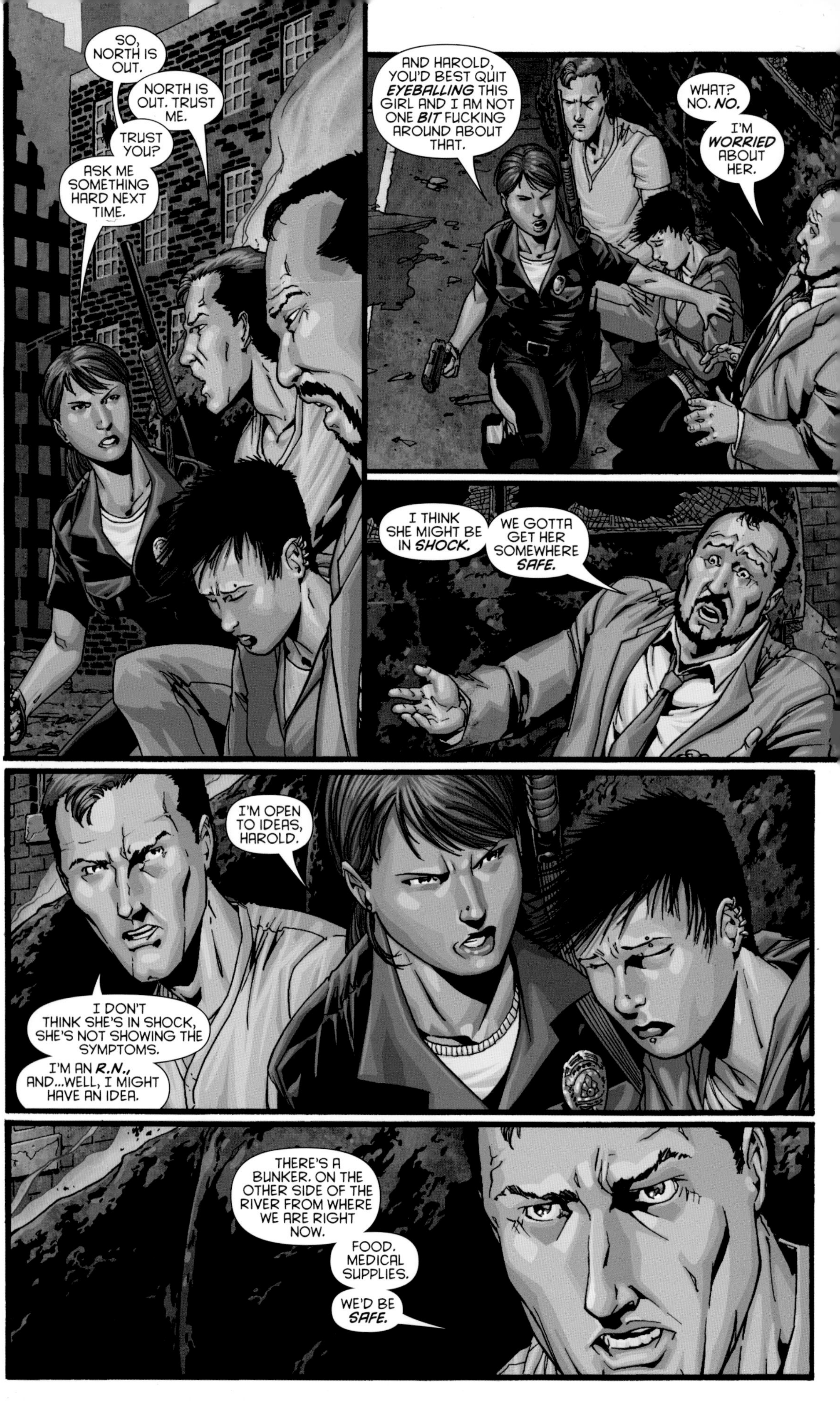
SO, NORTH IS OUT.
NORTH IS OUT. TRUST ME.
TRUST YOU?
ASK ME SOMETHING HARD NEXT TIME.
AND HAROLD, YOU'D BEST QUIT EYEBALLING THIS GIRL AND I AM NOT ONE BIT FUCKING AROUND ABOUT THAT.
WHAT? NO. NO.
I'M WORRIED ABOUT HER.
I THINK SHE MIGHT BE IN SHOCK.
WE GOTTA GET HER SOMEWHERE SAFE.
I'M OPEN TO IDEAS, HAROLD.
I DON'T THINK SHE'S IN SHOCK, SHE'S NOT SHOWING THE SYMPTOMS.
I'M AN R.N., AND...WELL, I MIGHT HAVE AN IDEA.
THERE'S A BUNKER. ON THE OTHER SIDE OF THE RIVER FROM WHERE WE ARE RIGHT NOW.
FOOD. MEDICAL SUPPLIES.
WE'D BE SAFE.

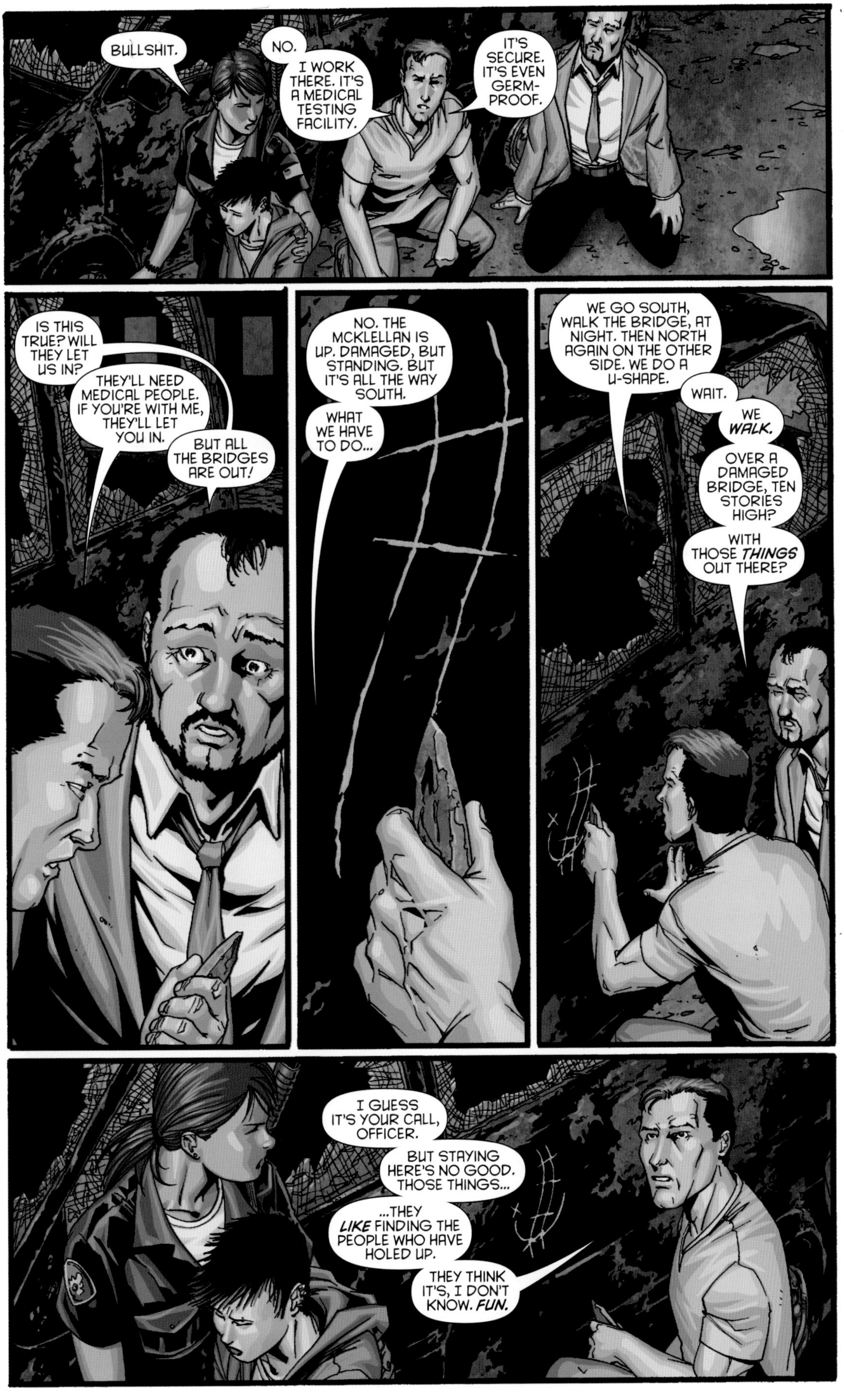
BULLSHIT.
NO.
I WORK THERE. IT'S A MEDICAL TESTING FACILITY.
IT'S SECURE. IT'S EVEN GERM-PROOF.
IS THIS TRUE? WILL THEY LET US IN?
THEY'LL NEED MEDICAL PEOPLE. IF YOU'RE WITH ME, THEY'LL LET YOU IN.
BUT ALL THE BRIDGES ARE OUT!
NO. THE MCKLELLAN IS UP. DAMAGED, BUT STANDING. BUT IT'S ALL THE WAY SOUTH.
WHAT WE HAVE TO DO...
WE GO SOUTH, WALK THE BRIDGE, AT NIGHT. THEN NORTH AGAIN ON THE OTHER SIDE. WE DO A U-SHAPE.
WAIT.
WE *WALK.*
OVER A DAMAGED BRIDGE, TEN STORIES HIGH?
WITH THOSE *THINGS* OUT THERE?
I GUESS IT'S YOUR CALL, OFFICER.
BUT STAYING HERE'S NO GOOD. THOSE THINGS...
...THEY *LIKE* FINDING THE PEOPLE WHO HAVE HOLED UP.
THEY THINK IT'S, I DON'T KNOW. *FUN.*

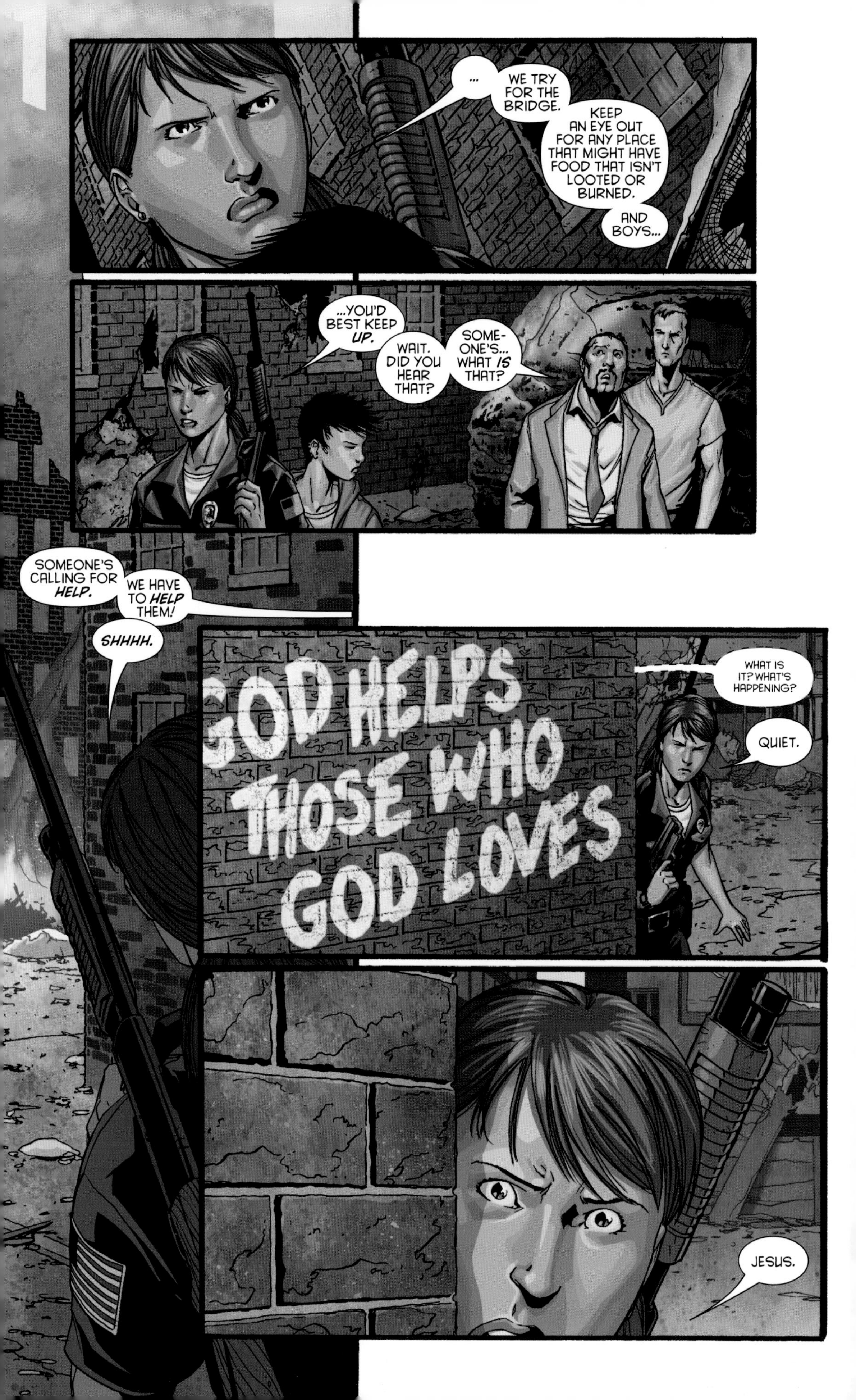
...
WE TRY FOR THE BRIDGE.
KEEP AN EYE OUT FOR ANY PLACE THAT MIGHT HAVE FOOD THAT ISN'T LOOTED OR BURNED.
AND BOYS...
...YOU'D BEST KEEP UP.
WAIT. DID YOU HEAR THAT?
SOME-ONE'S... WHAT IS THAT?
SOMEONE'S CALLING FOR HELP.
WE HAVE TO HELP THEM!
SHHHH.
GOD HELPS THOSE WHO GOD LOVES
WHAT IS IT? WHAT'S HAPPENING?
QUIET.
JESUS.

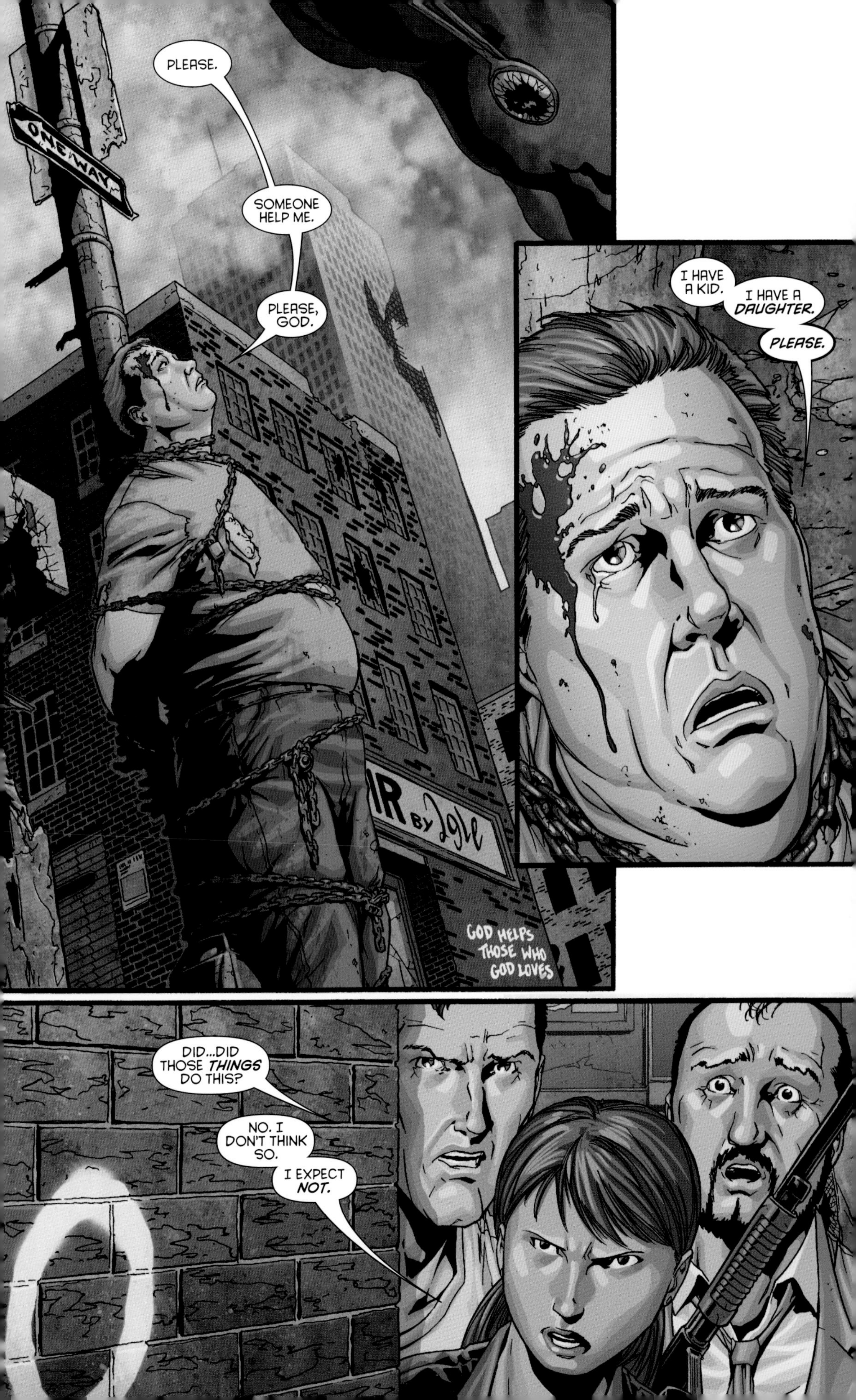
ONE WAY
PLEASE.
SOMEONE HELP ME.
PLEASE, GOD.
GOD HELPS THOSE WHO GOD LOVES
I HAVE A KID.
I HAVE A *DAUGHTER.*
PLEASE.
DID...DID THOSE *THINGS* DO THIS?
NO. I DON'T THINK SO.
I EXPECT *NOT.*

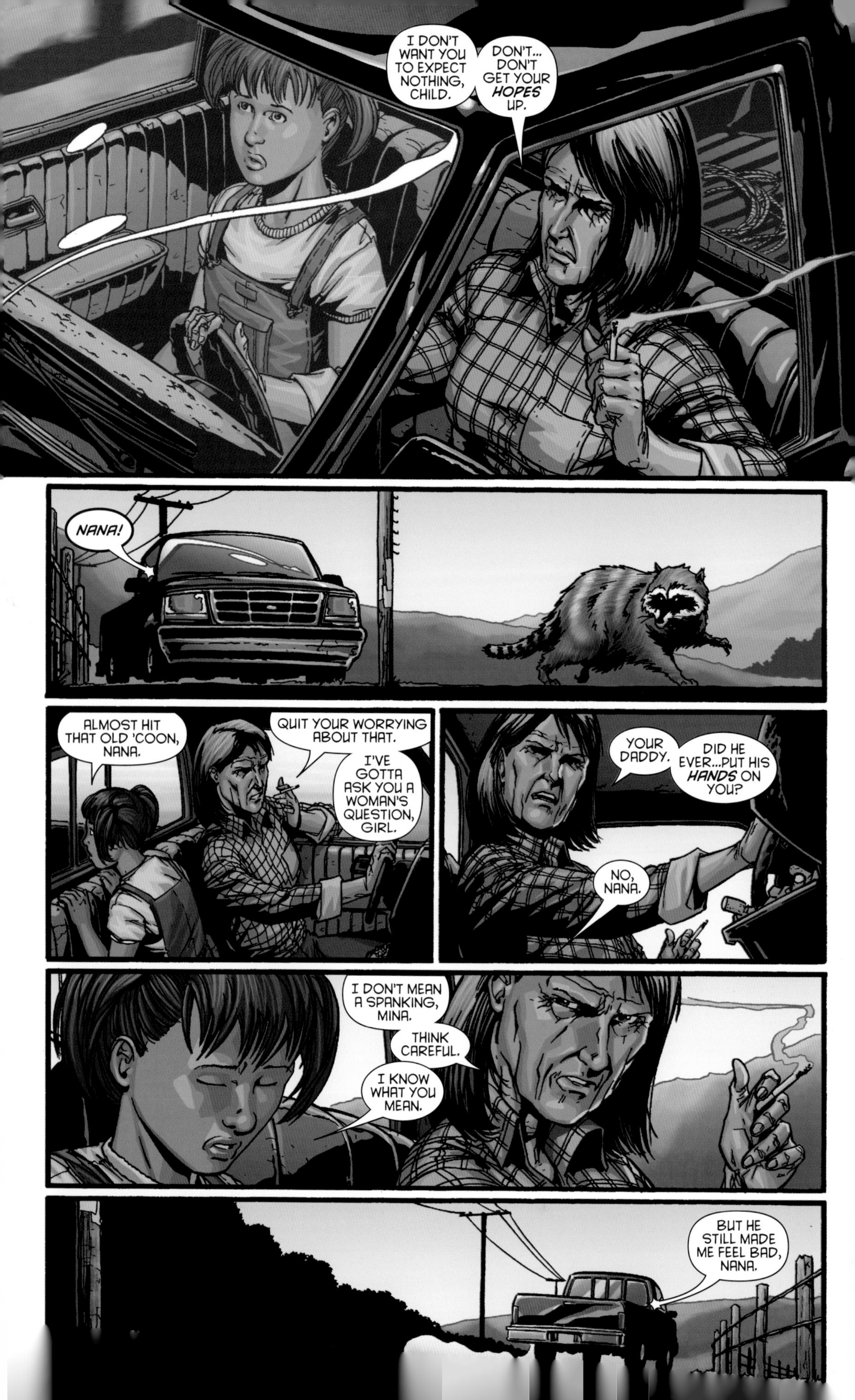

I DON'T WANT YOU TO EXPECT NOTHING, CHILD.
DON'T... DON'T GET YOUR *HOPES* UP.
NANA!
ALMOST HIT THAT OLD 'COON, NANA.
QUIT YOUR WORRYING ABOUT THAT.
I'VE GOTTA ASK YOU A WOMAN'S QUESTION, GIRL.
YOUR DADDY.
DID HE EVER...PUT HIS *HANDS* ON YOU?
NO, NANA.
I DON'T MEAN A SPANKING, MINA.
THINK CAREFUL.
I KNOW WHAT YOU MEAN.
BUT HE STILL MADE ME FEEL BAD, NANA.

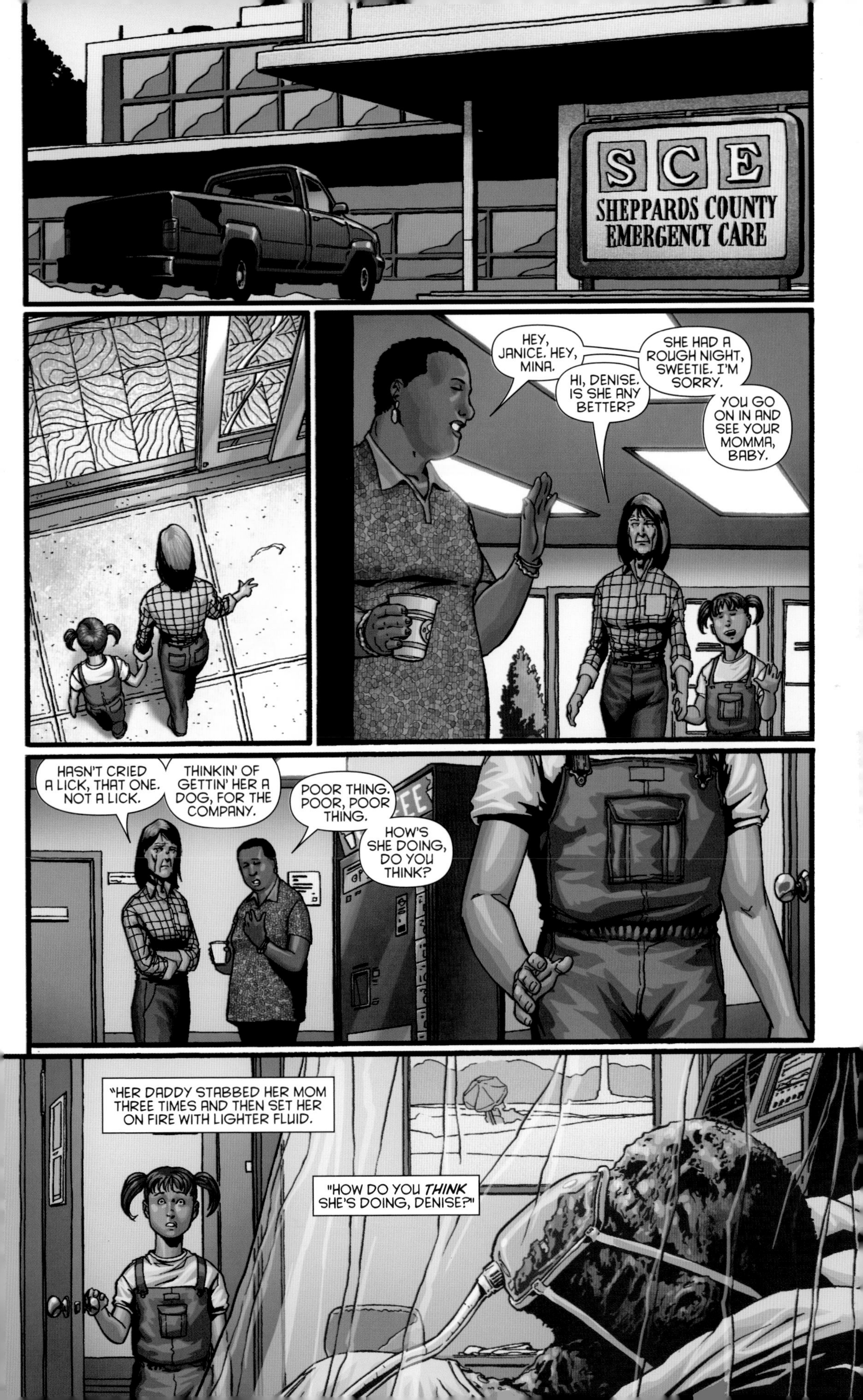
SCE
SHEPPARDS COUNTY EMERGENCY CARE
HEY, JANICE. HEY, MINA.
SHE HAD A ROUGH NIGHT, SWEETIE. I'M SORRY.
HI, DENISE. IS SHE ANY BETTER?
YOU GO ON IN AND SEE YOUR MOMMA, BABY.
HASN'T CRIED A LICK, THAT ONE. NOT A LICK.
THINKIN' OF GETTIN' HER A DOG, FOR THE COMPANY.
POOR THING. POOR, POOR THING.
HOW'S SHE DOING, DO YOU THINK?
"HER DADDY STABBED HER MOM THREE TIMES AND THEN SET HER ON FIRE WITH LIGHTER FLUID.
"HOW DO YOU *THINK* SHE'S DOING, DENISE?"

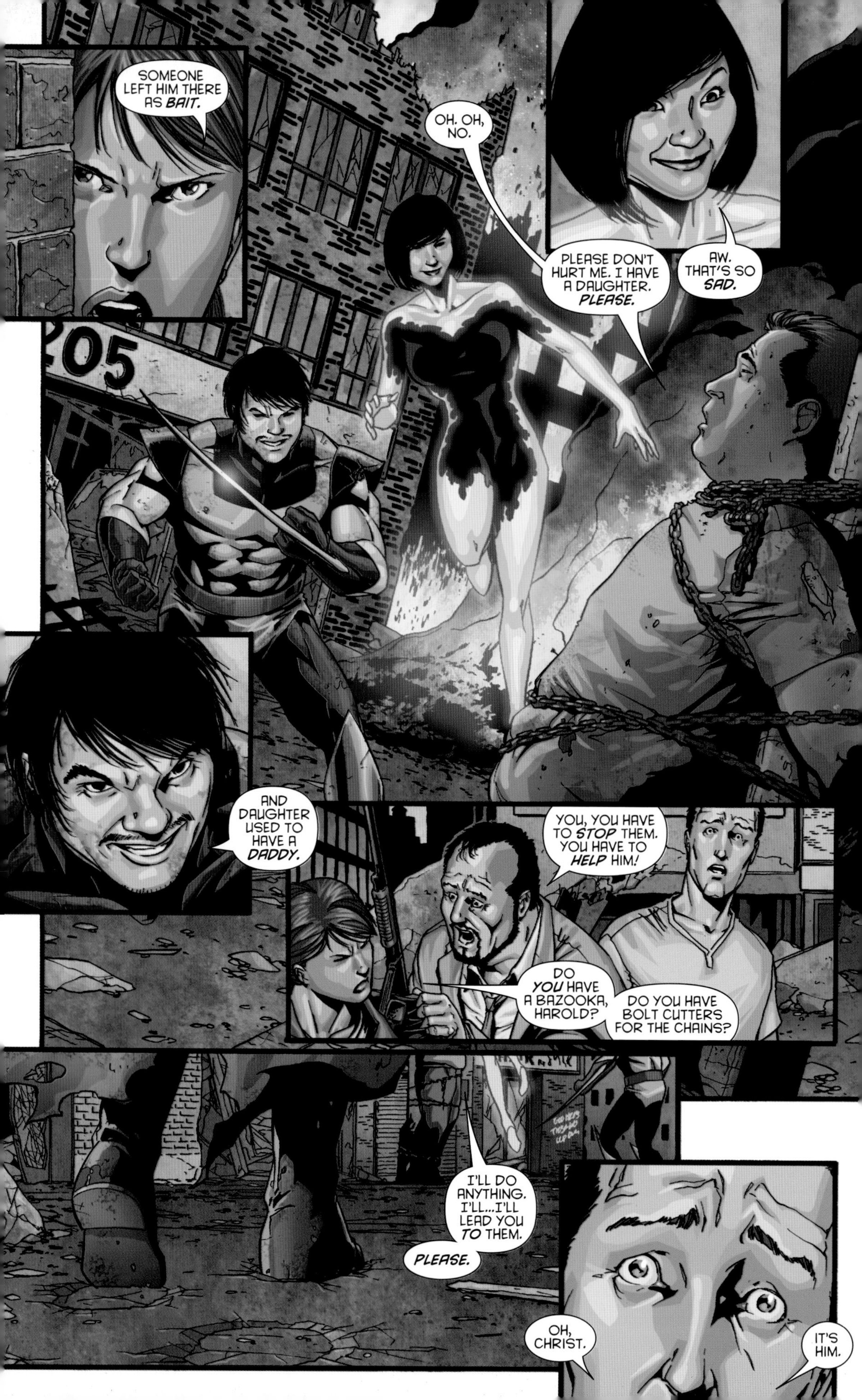
SOMEONE LEFT HIM THERE AS BAIT.
OH. OH, NO.
PLEASE DON'T HURT ME. I HAVE A DAUGHTER. PLEASE.
AW. THAT'S SO SAD.
205
AND DAUGHTER USED TO HAVE A DADDY.
YOU, YOU HAVE TO STOP THEM. YOU HAVE TO HELP HIM!
DO YOU HAVE A BAZOOKA, HAROLD?
DO YOU HAVE BOLT CUTTERS FOR THE CHAINS?
I'LL DO ANYTHING. I'LL...I'LL LEAD YOU TO THEM.
PLEASE.
OH, CHRIST.
IT'S HIM.

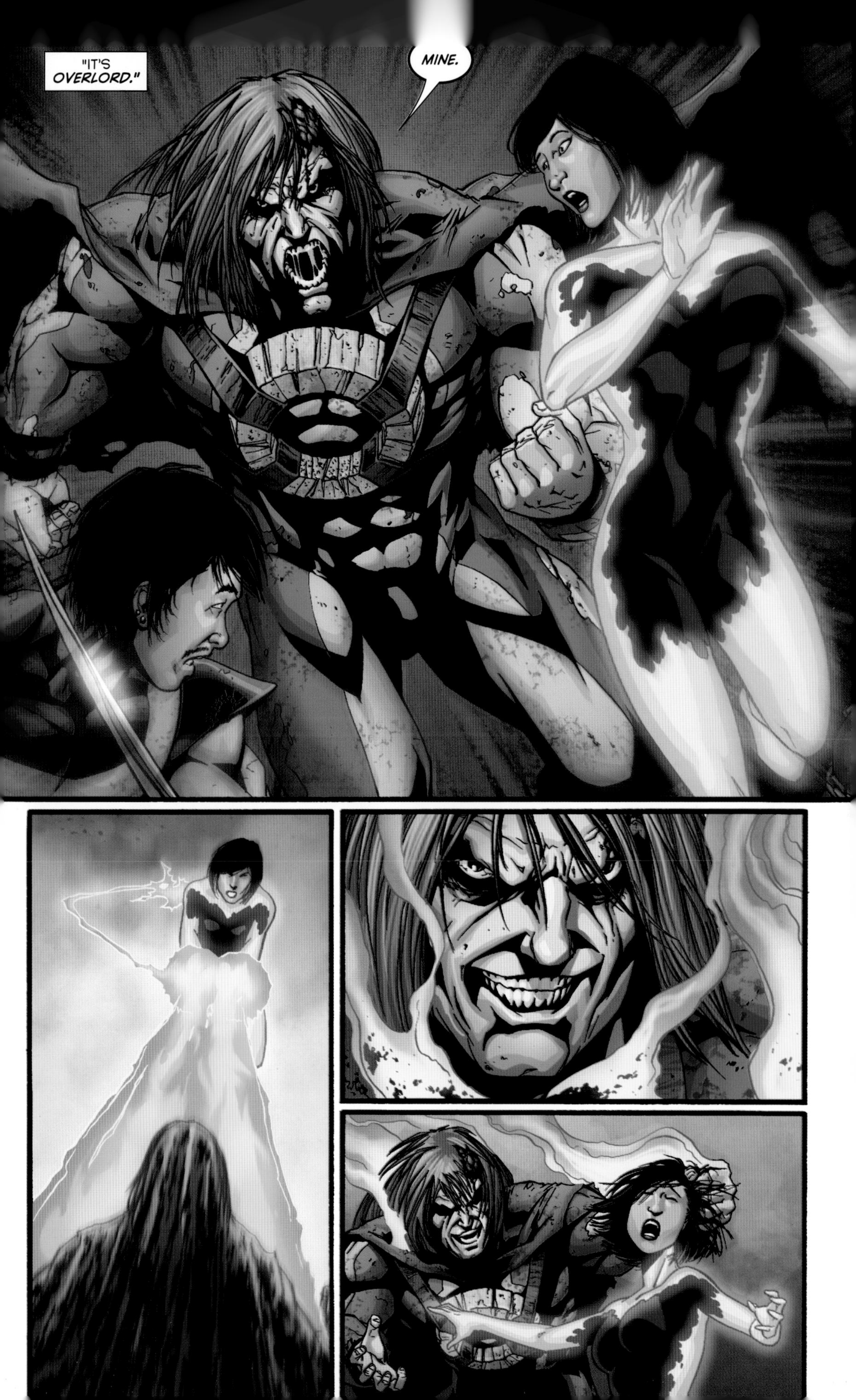
"IT'S OVERLORD."
MINE.

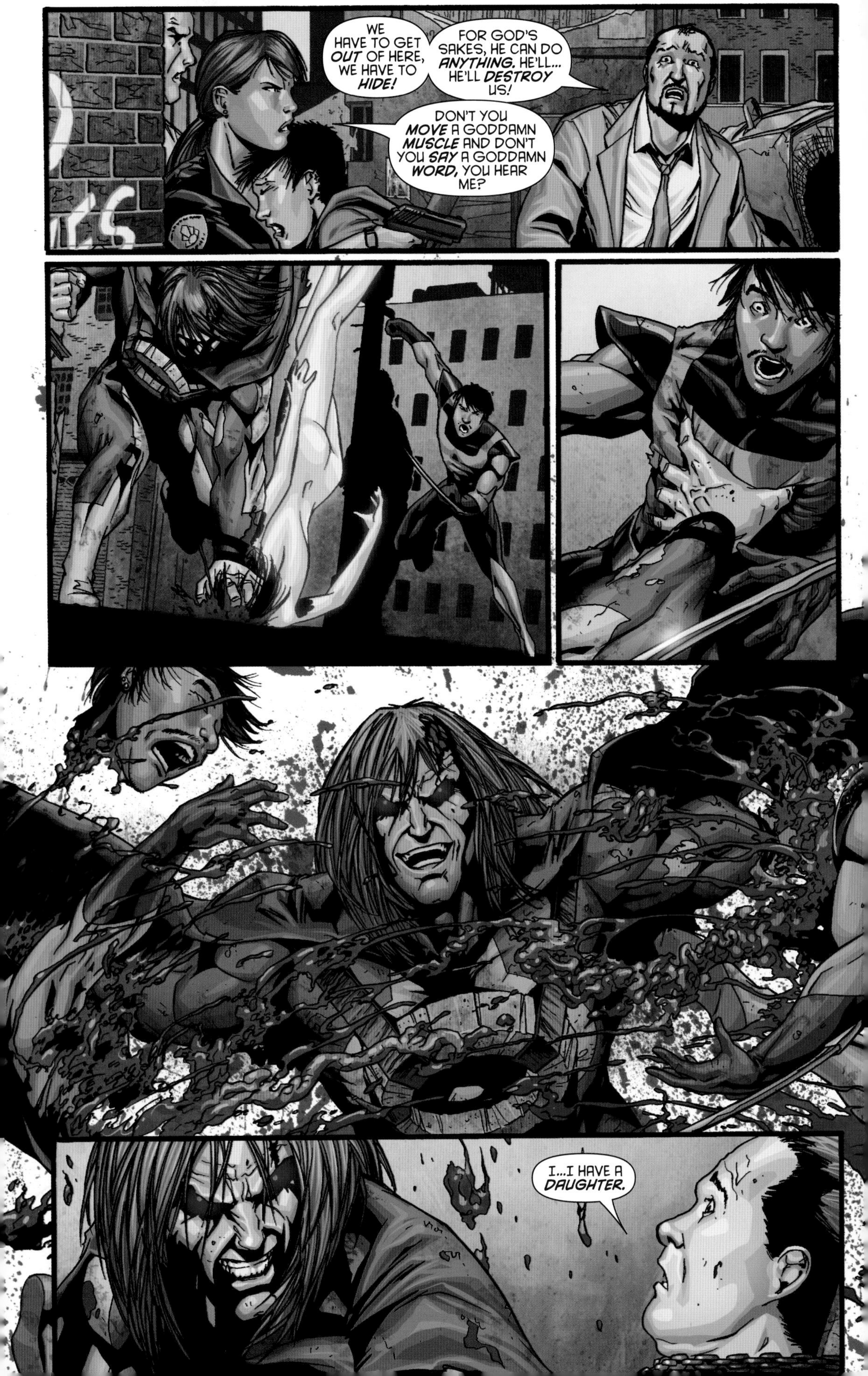
WE HAVE TO GET OUT OF HERE, WE HAVE TO HIDE!
FOR GOD'S SAKES, HE CAN DO ANYTHING. HE'LL... HE'LL DESTROY US!
DON'T YOU MOVE A GODDAMN MUSCLE AND DON'T YOU SAY A GODDAMN WORD, YOU HEAR ME?
I...I HAVE A DAUGHTER.

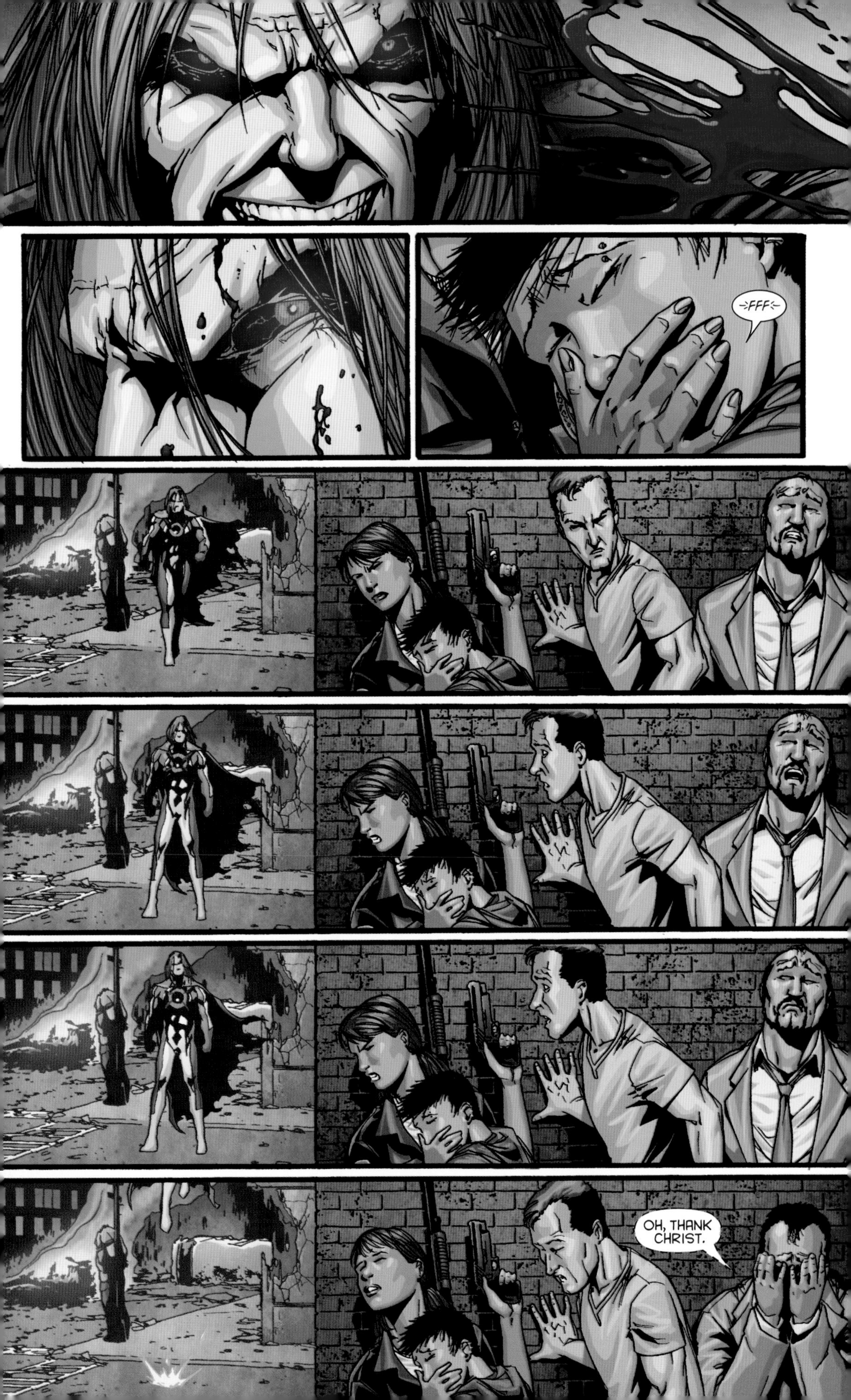
FFF
OH, THANK CHRIST.

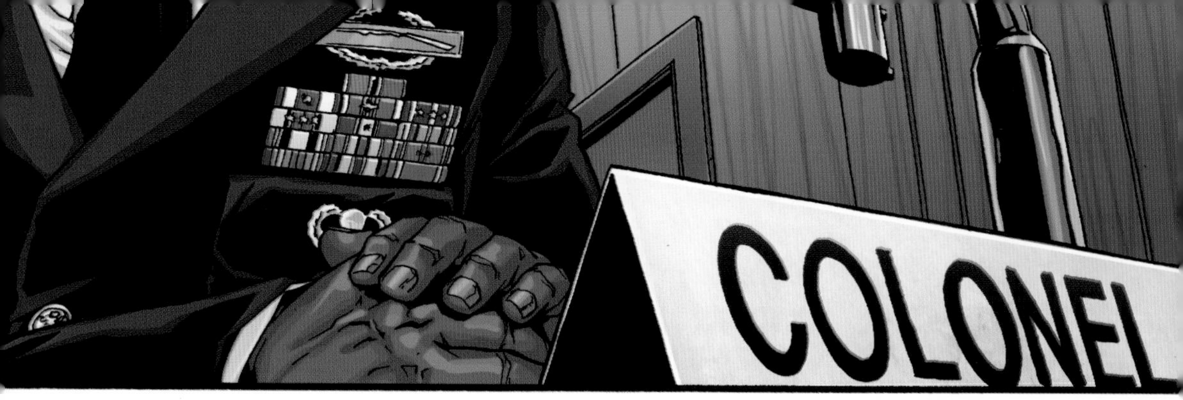
COLONEL

SENATOR BELL: Now, Colonel Culver, how long have you been in the National Guard?

CULVER: A little over ten years, Senator. It's been my honor to serve my country.

SENATOR BELL: And you're...do they still say "full bird," Colonel?

CULVER: They do.

SENATOR BELL: Colonel Culver, I want to know what your thinking was when you blockaded the Shenqua Bridge, preventing citizens from leaving the city.

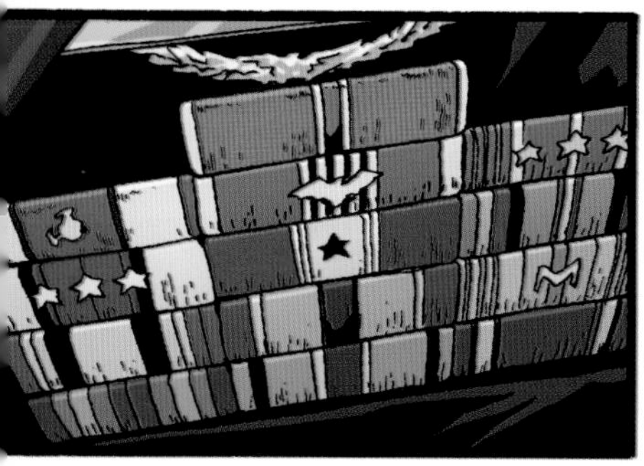

CULVER: My thoughts, Ma'am?

SENATOR BELL: Yes, please.

CULVER: I didn't have any thoughts. I had orders.

SENATOR BELL: Colonel Culver, I have to remind you that there is absolutely no record of an order given to deter evacuees.

CULVER: We were told there was a biochemical incident.

SENATOR BELL: That's not the question at hand, Colonel.

CULVER: We were, as we usually are domestically, the first military responders. We could have been quarantining a PLAGUE. My KIDS were within the city limits, Senator. Do you think I did this on my own authority?

SENATOR BELL: And that's when the evacuees stormed the bridge, is that right, Colonel?

CULVER: ...

SENATOR BELL: And you ordered your men to open fire on the civilian mass, is that right?

CULVER: ...

SENATOR BELL: Is that RIGHT, Colonel?

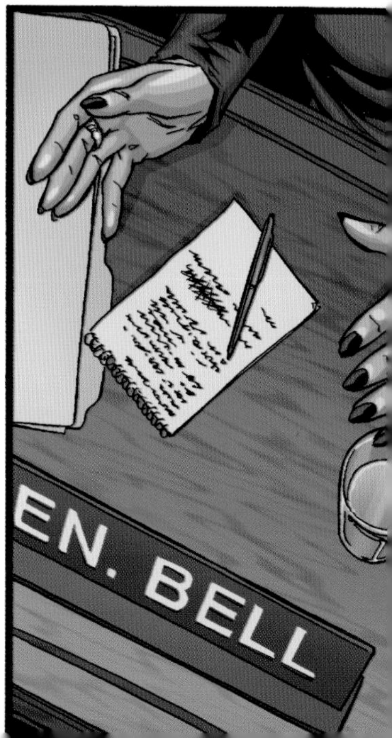
EN. BELL

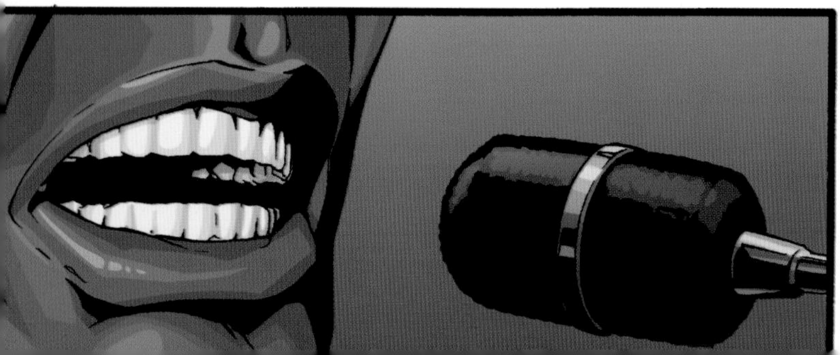

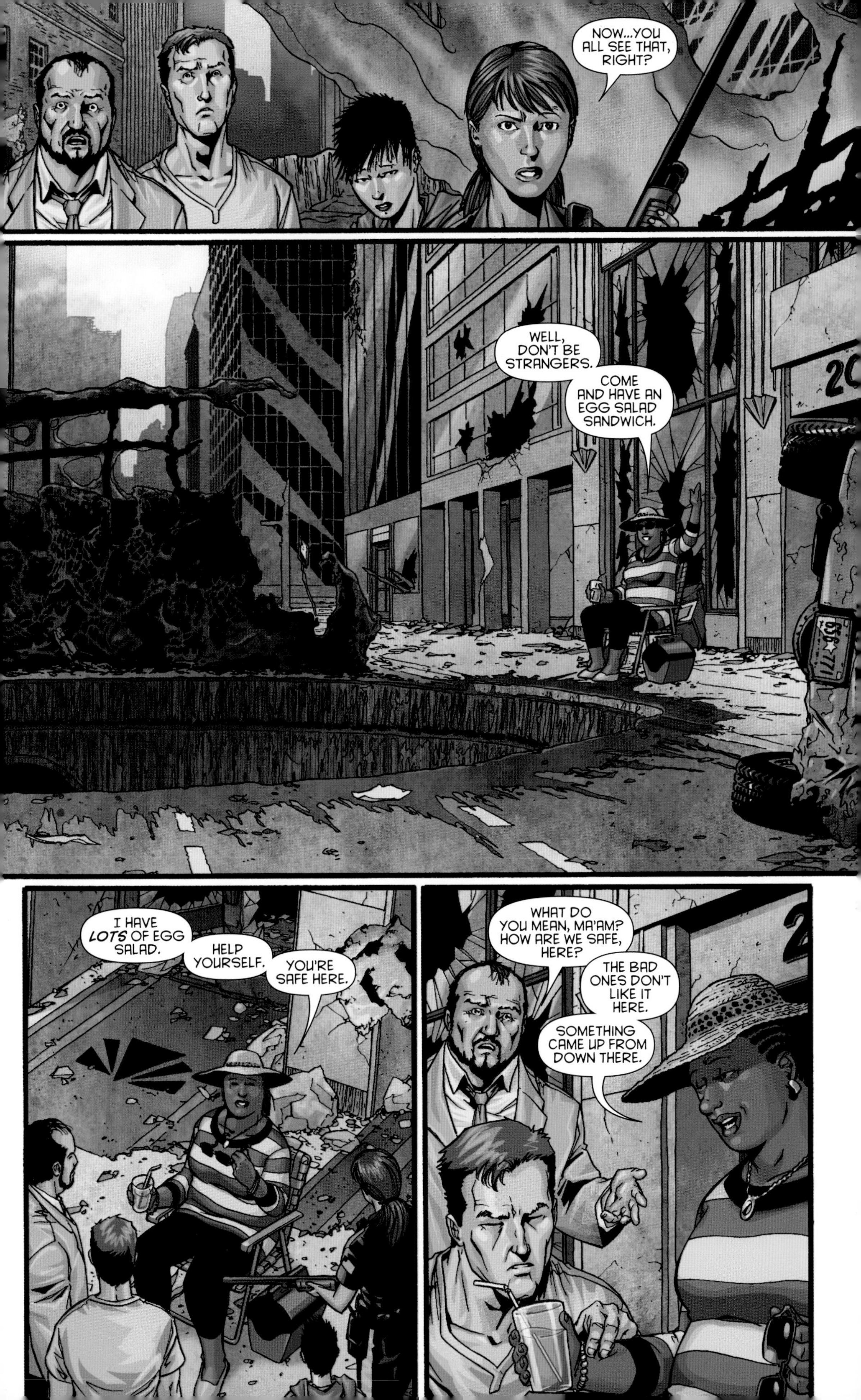
NOW...YOU ALL SEE THAT, RIGHT?
WELL, DON'T BE STRANGERS.
COME AND HAVE AN EGG SALAD SANDWICH.
I HAVE *LOTS* OF EGG SALAD.
HELP YOURSELF.
YOU'RE SAFE HERE.
WHAT DO YOU MEAN, MA'AM? HOW ARE WE SAFE, HERE?
THE BAD ONES DON'T LIKE IT HERE.
SOMETHING CAME UP FROM DOWN THERE.

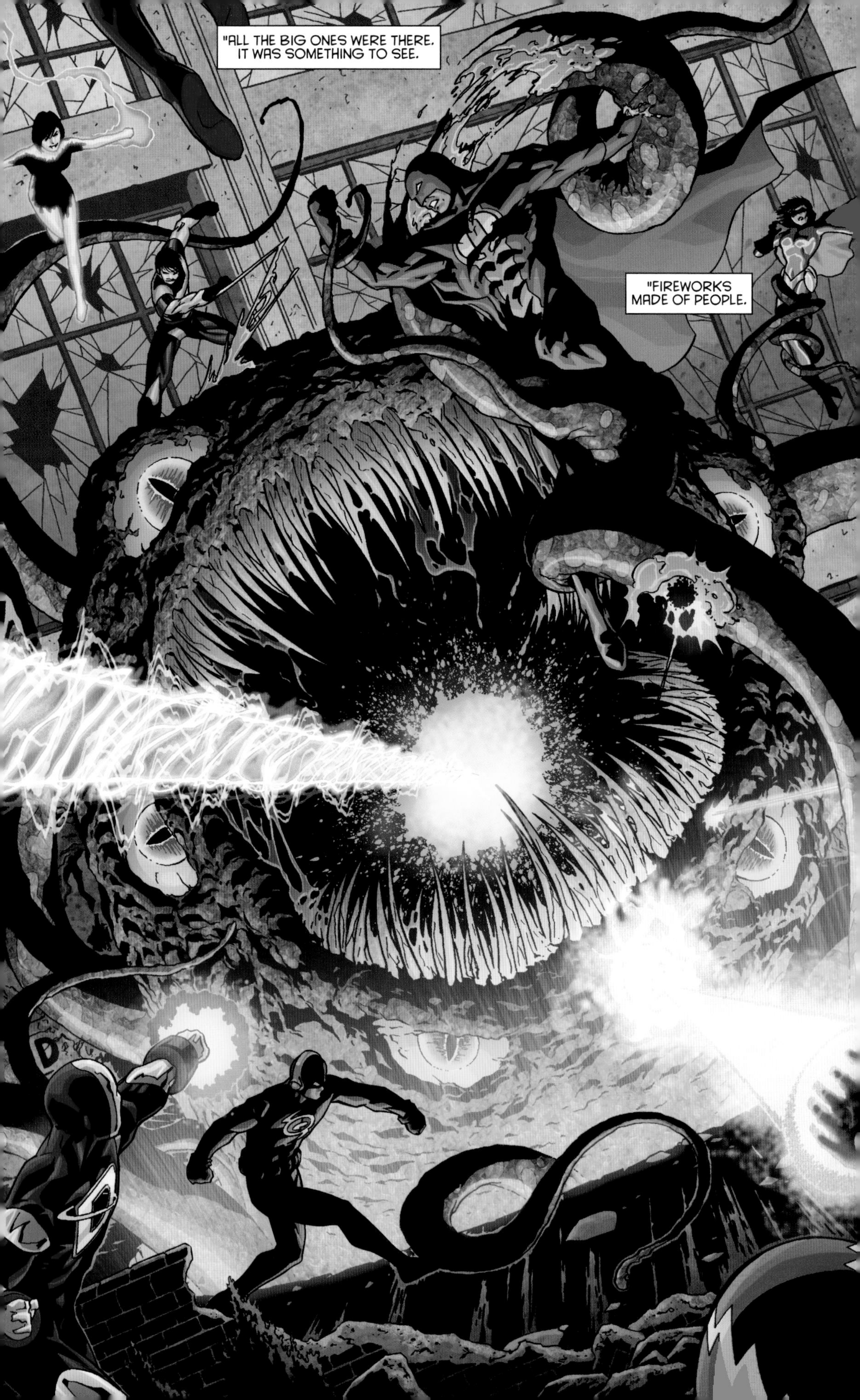
"ALL THE BIG ONES WERE THERE. IT WAS SOMETHING TO SEE.
"FIREWORKS MADE OF PEOPLE.

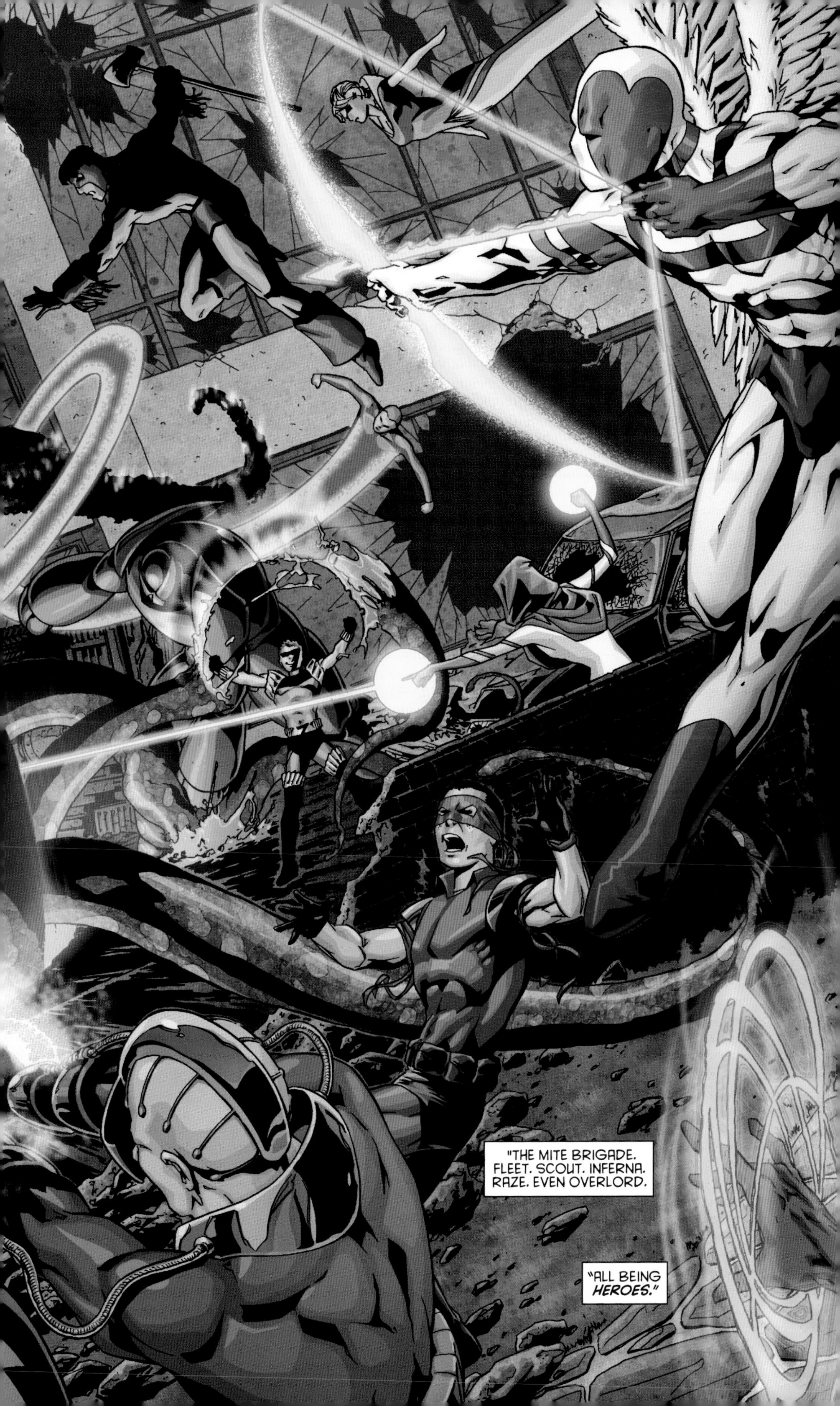
"THE MITE BRIGADE. FLEET. SCOUT. INFERNA. RAZE. EVEN OVERLORD.
"ALL BEING *HEROES.*"

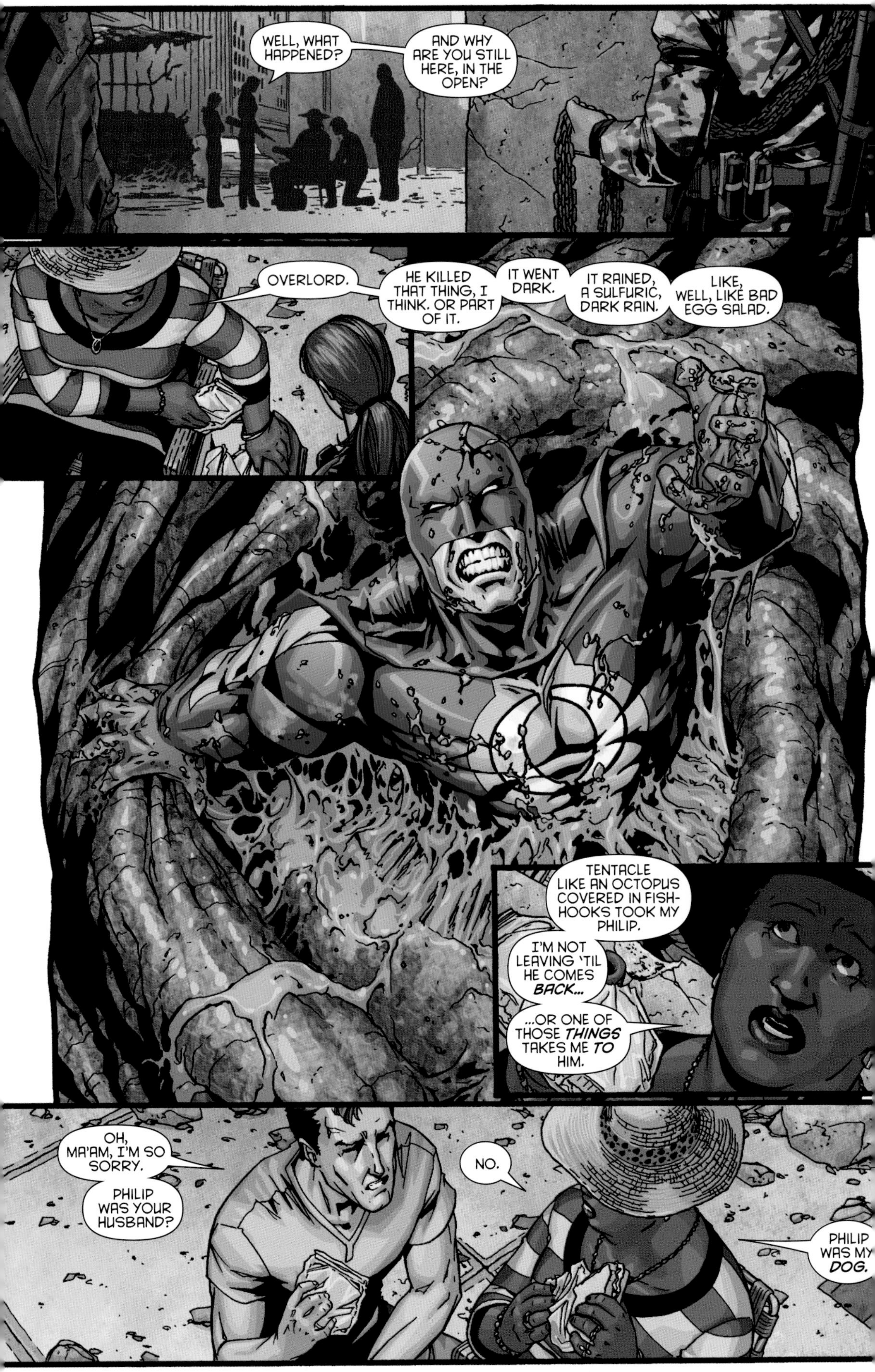
WELL, WHAT HAPPENED?
AND WHY ARE YOU STILL HERE, IN THE OPEN?
OVERLORD.
HE KILLED THAT THING, I THINK. OR PART OF IT.
IT WENT DARK.
IT RAINED, A SULFURIC, DARK RAIN.
LIKE, WELL, LIKE BAD EGG SALAD.
TENTACLE LIKE AN OCTOPUS COVERED IN FISH-HOOKS TOOK MY PHILIP.
I'M NOT LEAVING 'TIL HE COMES BACK...
...OR ONE OF THOSE THINGS TAKES ME TO HIM.
OH, MA'AM, I'M SO SORRY.
PHILIP WAS YOUR HUSBAND?
NO.
PHILIP WAS MY DOG.

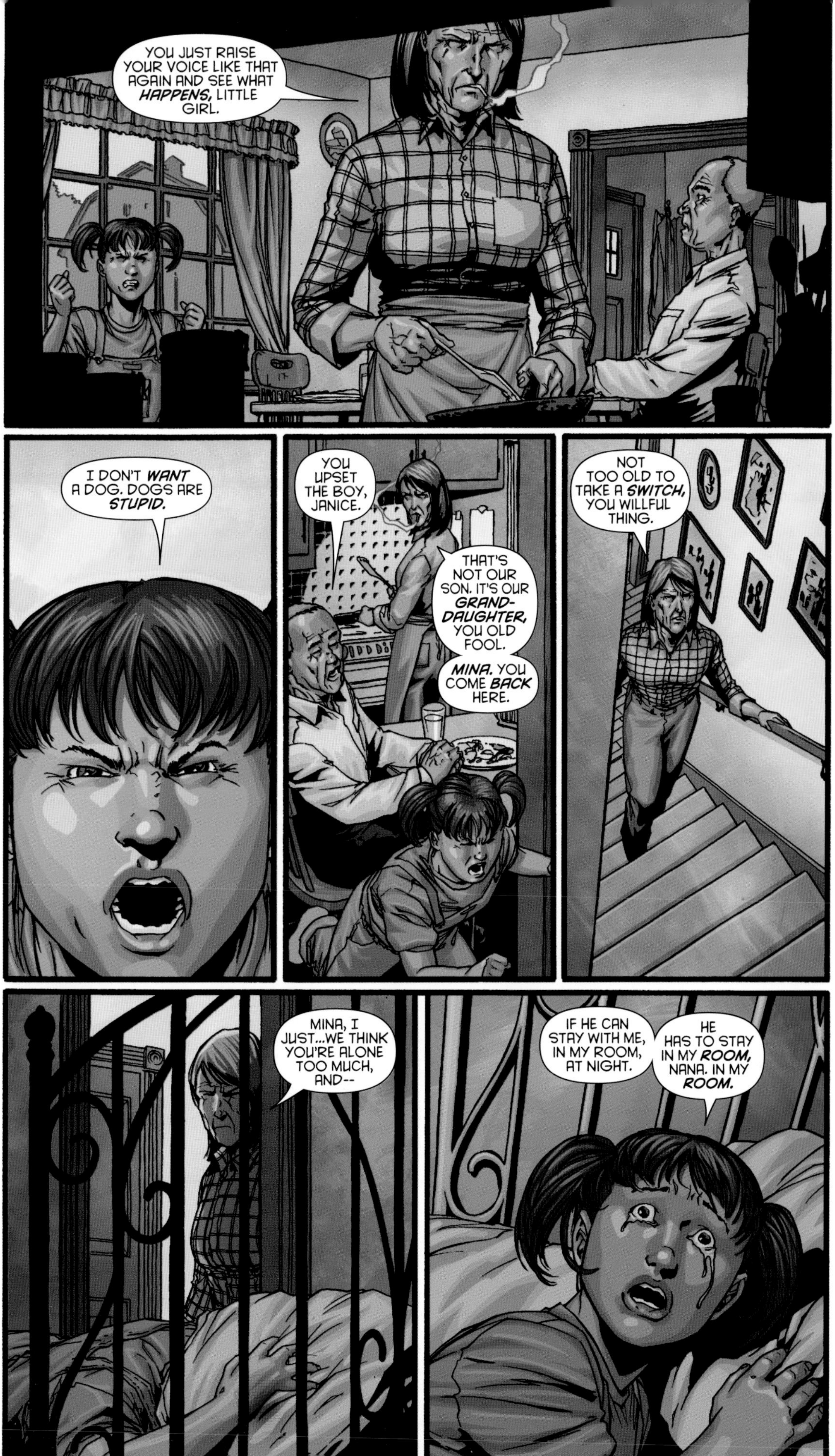

YOU JUST RAISE YOUR VOICE LIKE THAT AGAIN AND SEE WHAT HAPPENS, LITTLE GIRL.
I DON'T WANT A DOG. DOGS ARE STUPID.
YOU UPSET THE BOY, JANICE.
THAT'S NOT OUR SON. IT'S OUR GRAND-DAUGHTER, YOU OLD FOOL.
MINA. YOU COME BACK HERE.
NOT TOO OLD TO TAKE A SWITCH, YOU WILLFUL THING.
MINA, I JUST...WE THINK YOU'RE ALONE TOO MUCH, AND--
IF HE CAN STAY WITH ME, IN MY ROOM, AT NIGHT.
HE HAS TO STAY IN MY ROOM, NANA. IN MY ROOM.

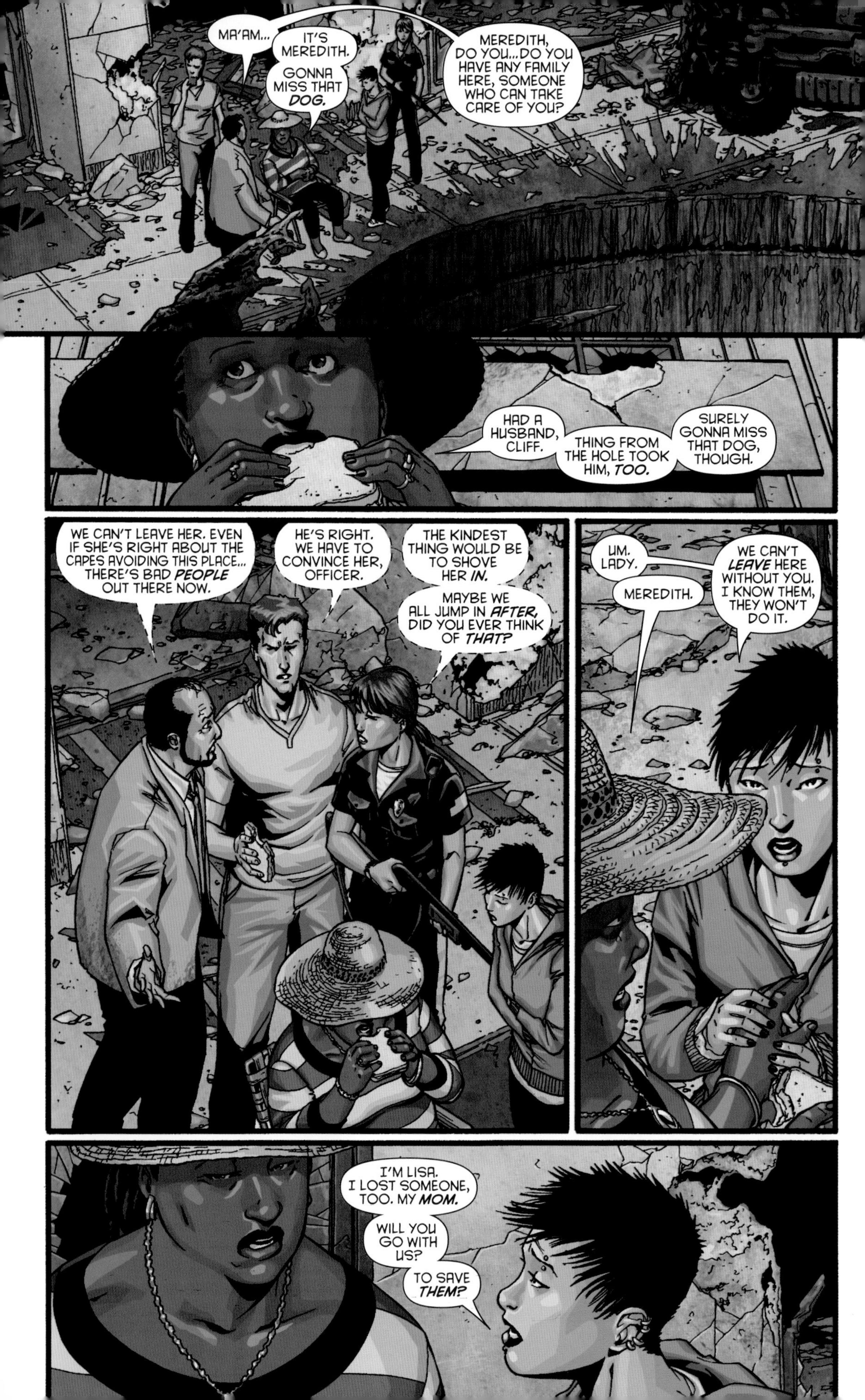

MA'AM...
IT'S MEREDITH.
GONNA MISS THAT DOG.
MEREDITH, DO YOU...DO YOU HAVE ANY FAMILY HERE, SOMEONE WHO CAN TAKE CARE OF YOU?
HAD A HUSBAND, CLIFF.
THING FROM THE HOLE TOOK HIM, TOO.
SURELY GONNA MISS THAT DOG, THOUGH.
WE CAN'T LEAVE HER. EVEN IF SHE'S RIGHT ABOUT THE CAPES AVOIDING THIS PLACE... THERE'S BAD PEOPLE OUT THERE NOW.
HE'S RIGHT. WE HAVE TO CONVINCE HER, OFFICER.
THE KINDEST THING WOULD BE TO SHOVE HER IN.
MAYBE WE ALL JUMP IN AFTER, DID YOU EVER THINK OF THAT?
UM. LADY.
MEREDITH.
WE CAN'T LEAVE HERE WITHOUT YOU. I KNOW THEM, THEY WON'T DO IT.
I'M LISA. I LOST SOMEONE, TOO. MY MOM.
WILL YOU GO WITH US?
TO SAVE THEM?

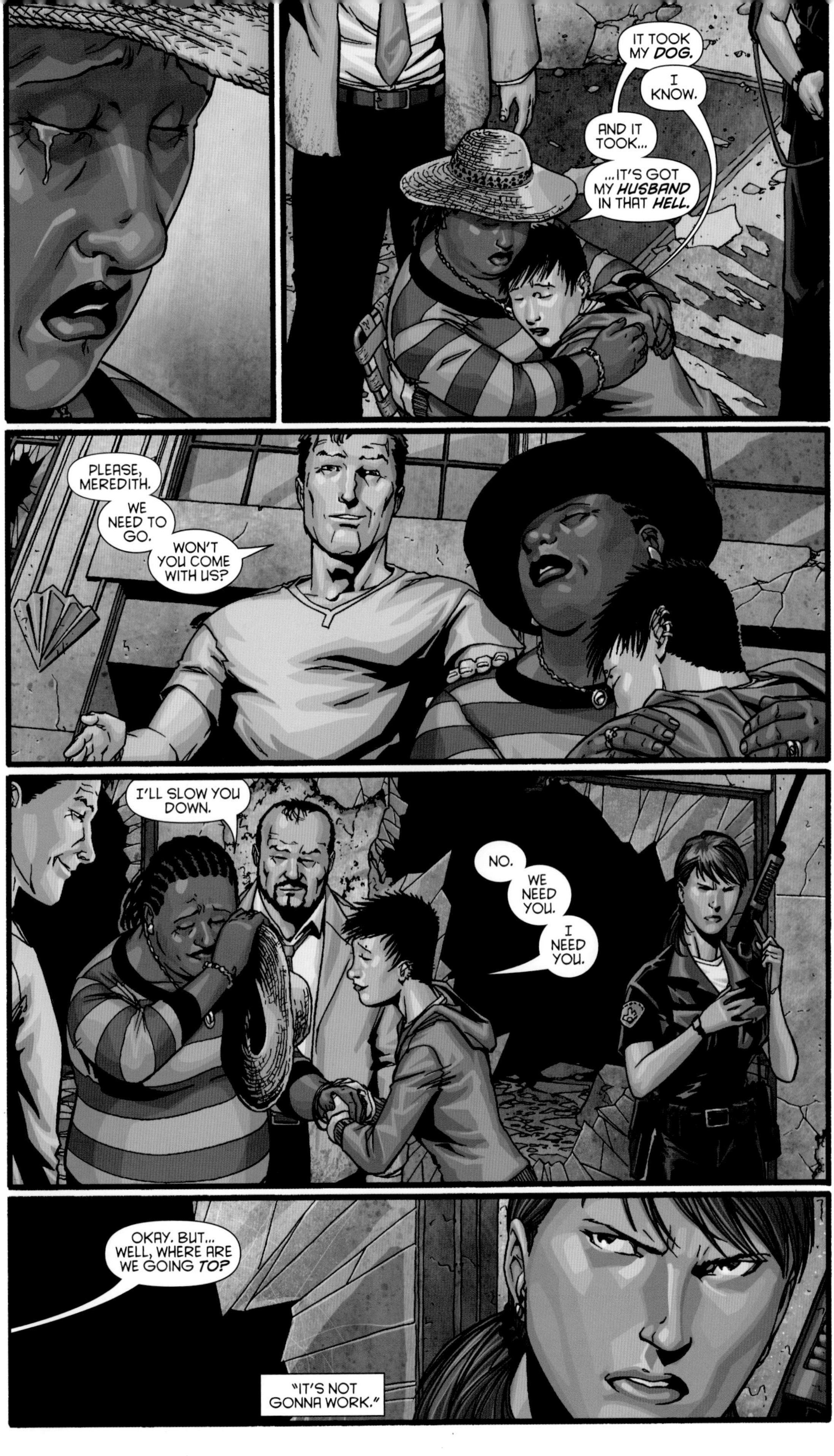
IT TOOK MY DOG.
I KNOW.
AND IT TOOK...
...IT'S GOT MY HUSBAND IN THAT HELL.
PLEASE, MEREDITH.
WE NEED TO GO.
WON'T YOU COME WITH US?
I'LL SLOW YOU DOWN.
NO.
WE NEED YOU.
I NEED YOU.
OKAY. BUT... WELL, WHERE ARE WE GOING TO?
"IT'S NOT GONNA WORK."

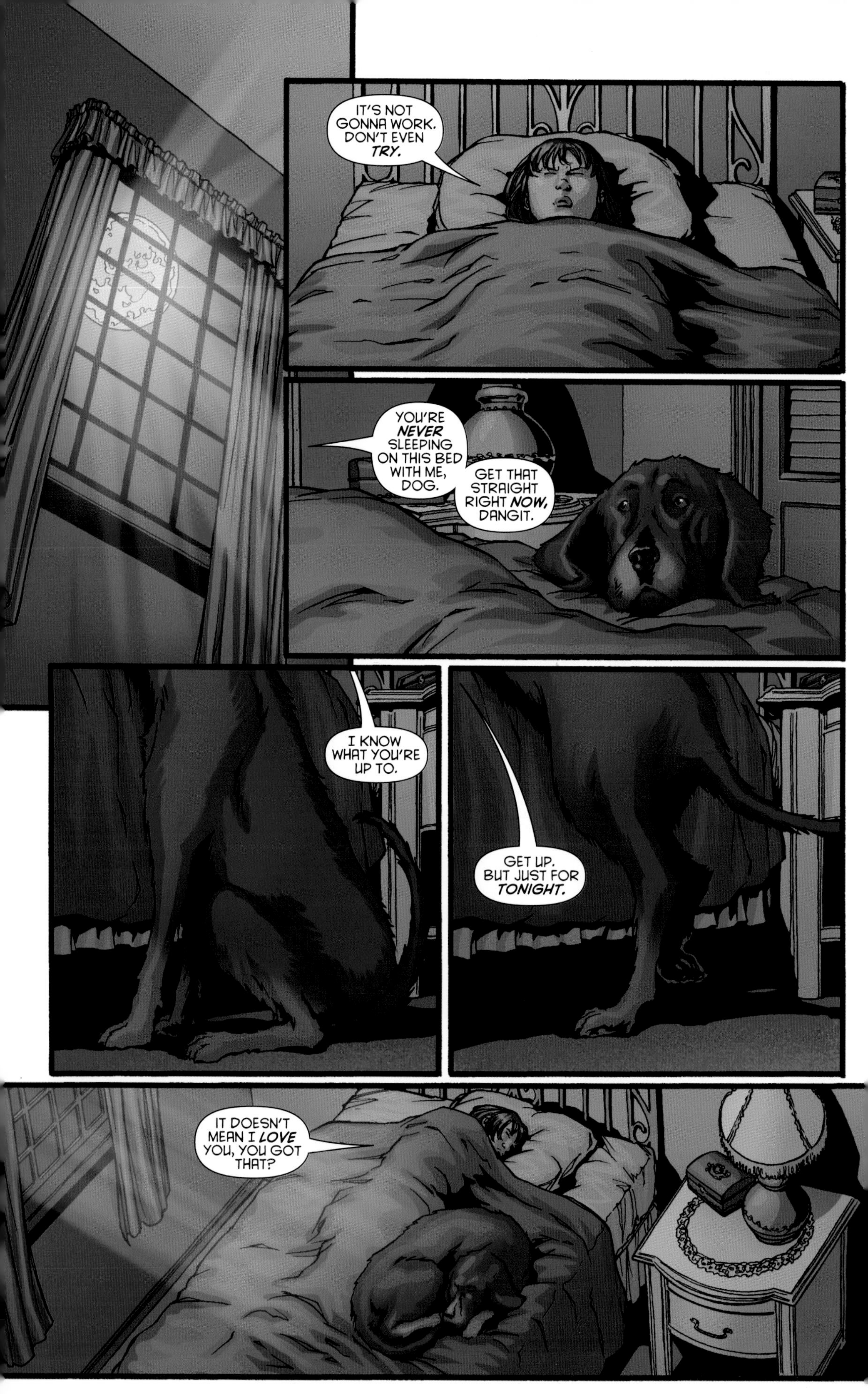
IT'S NOT GONNA WORK. DON'T EVEN TRY.
YOU'RE NEVER SLEEPING ON THIS BED WITH ME, DOG.
GET THAT STRAIGHT RIGHT NOW, DANGIT.
I KNOW WHAT YOU'RE UP TO.
GET UP. BUT JUST FOR TONIGHT.
IT DOESN'T MEAN I LOVE YOU, YOU GOT THAT?

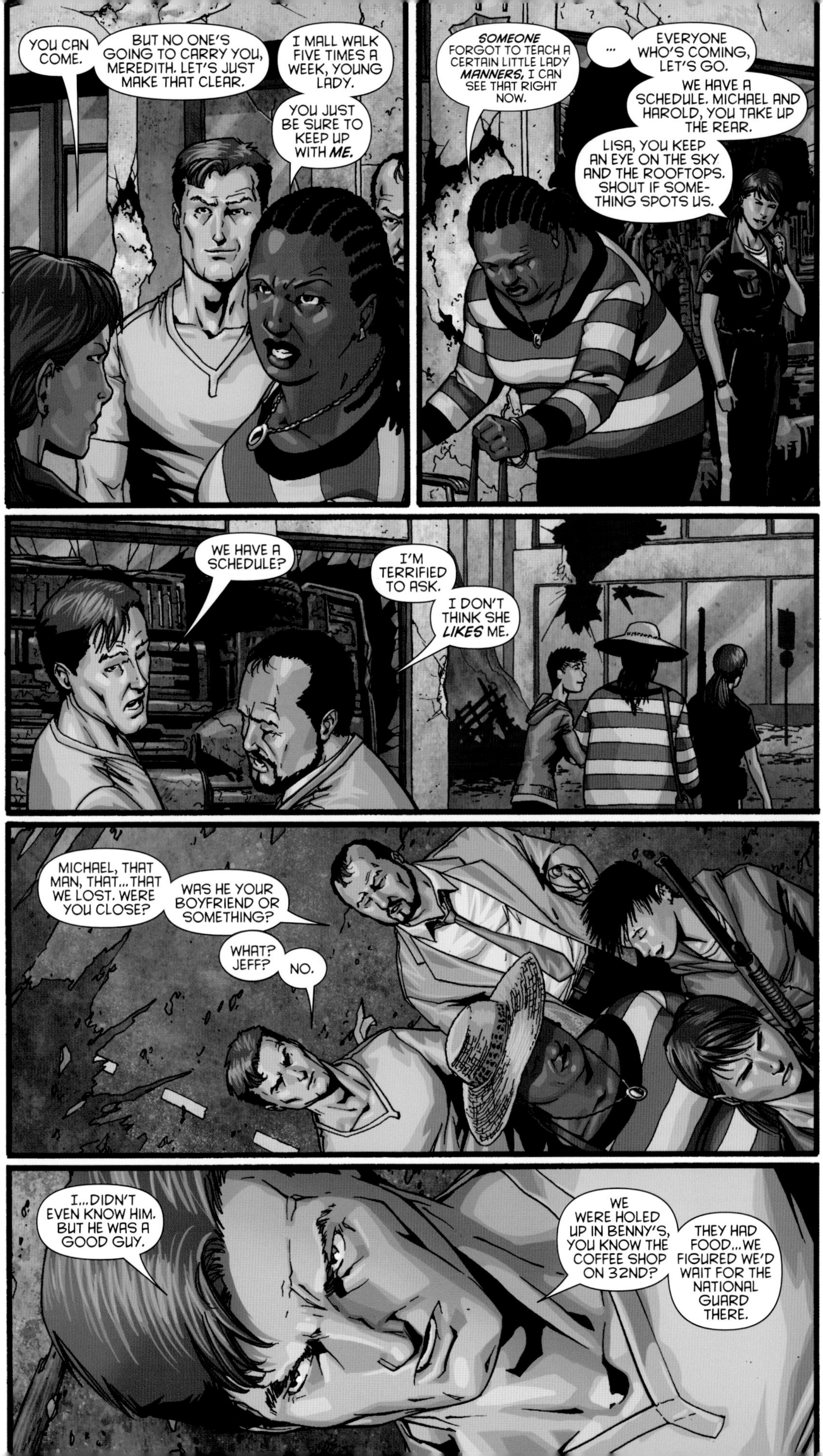
YOU CAN COME.
BUT NO ONE'S GOING TO CARRY YOU, MEREDITH. LET'S JUST MAKE THAT CLEAR.
I MALL WALK FIVE TIMES A WEEK, YOUNG LADY.
YOU JUST BE SURE TO KEEP UP WITH ME.
SOMEONE FORGOT TO TEACH A CERTAIN LITTLE LADY MANNERS, I CAN SEE THAT RIGHT NOW.
...
EVERYONE WHO'S COMING, LET'S GO.
WE HAVE A SCHEDULE. MICHAEL AND HAROLD, YOU TAKE UP THE REAR.
LISA, YOU KEEP AN EYE ON THE SKY AND THE ROOFTOPS. SHOUT IF SOMETHING SPOTS US.
WE HAVE A SCHEDULE?
I'M TERRIFIED TO ASK.
I DON'T THINK SHE LIKES ME.
MICHAEL, THAT MAN, THAT...THAT WE LOST. WERE YOU CLOSE?
WAS HE YOUR BOYFRIEND OR SOMETHING?
WHAT? JEFF?
NO.
I...DIDN'T EVEN KNOW HIM. BUT HE WAS A GOOD GUY.
WE WERE HOLED UP IN BENNY'S, YOU KNOW THE COFFEE SHOP ON 32ND?
THEY HAD FOOD...WE FIGURED WE'D WAIT FOR THE NATIONAL GUARD THERE.

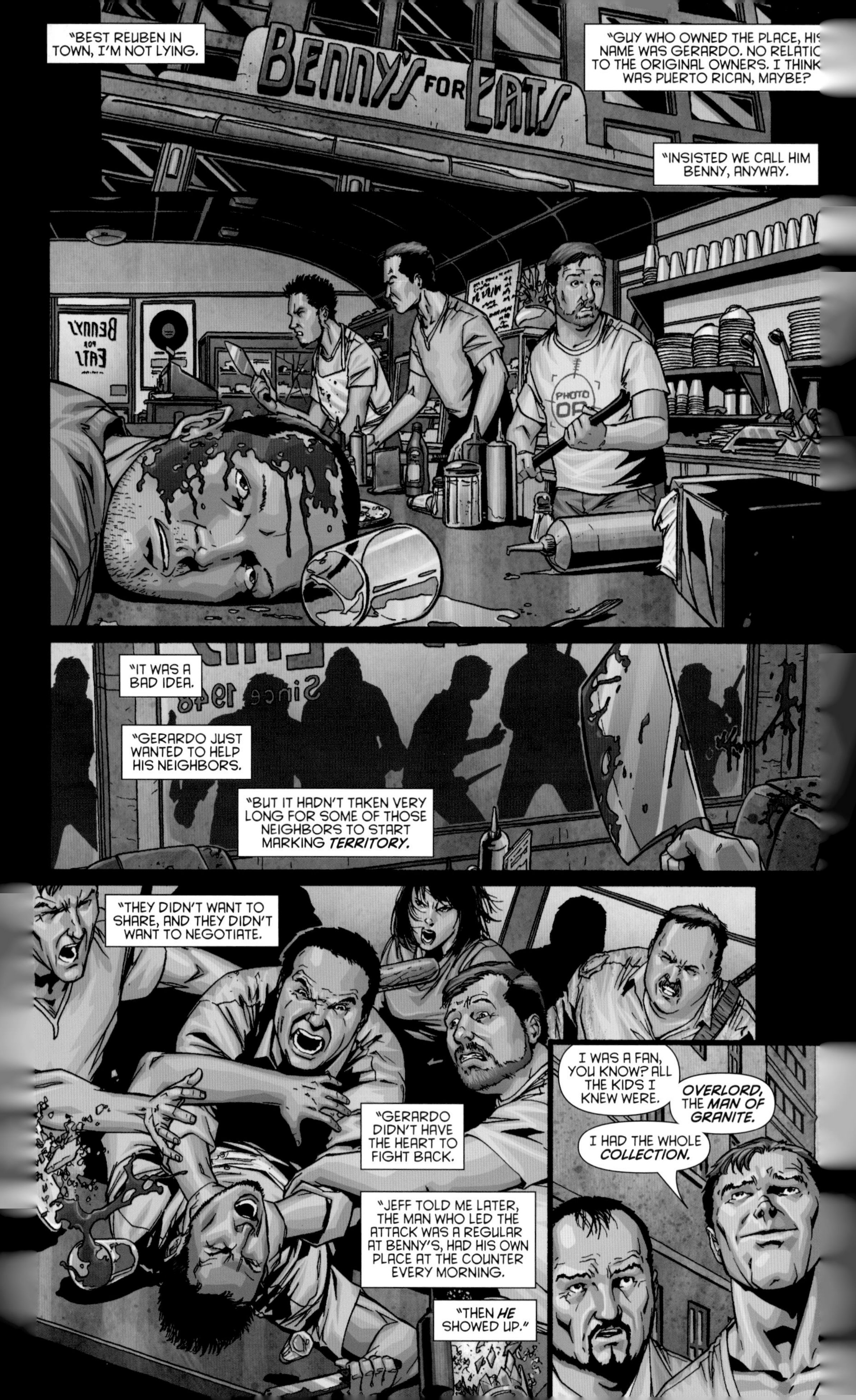

"BEST REUBEN IN TOWN, I'M NOT LYING.
BENNY'S FOR EATS
"GUY WHO OWNED THE PLACE, HIS NAME WAS GERARDO. NO RELATIO TO THE ORIGINAL OWNERS. I THINK WAS PUERTO RICAN, MAYBE?
"INSISTED WE CALL HIM BENNY, ANYWAY.
PHOTO OP
"IT WAS A BAD IDEA.
"GERARDO JUST WANTED TO HELP HIS NEIGHBORS.
"BUT IT HADN'T TAKEN VERY LONG FOR SOME OF THOSE NEIGHBORS TO START MARKING *TERRITORY.*
"THEY DIDN'T WANT TO SHARE, AND THEY DIDN'T WANT TO NEGOTIATE.
"GERARDO DIDN'T HAVE THE HEART TO FIGHT BACK.
"JEFF TOLD ME LATER, THE MAN WHO LED THE ATTACK WAS A REGULAR AT BENNY'S, HAD HIS OWN PLACE AT THE COUNTER EVERY MORNING.
"THEN *HE* SHOWED UP."
I WAS A FAN, YOU KNOW? ALL THE KIDS I KNEW WERE.
OVERLORD, THE *MAN OF GRANITE.*
I HAD THE WHOLE *COLLECTION.*

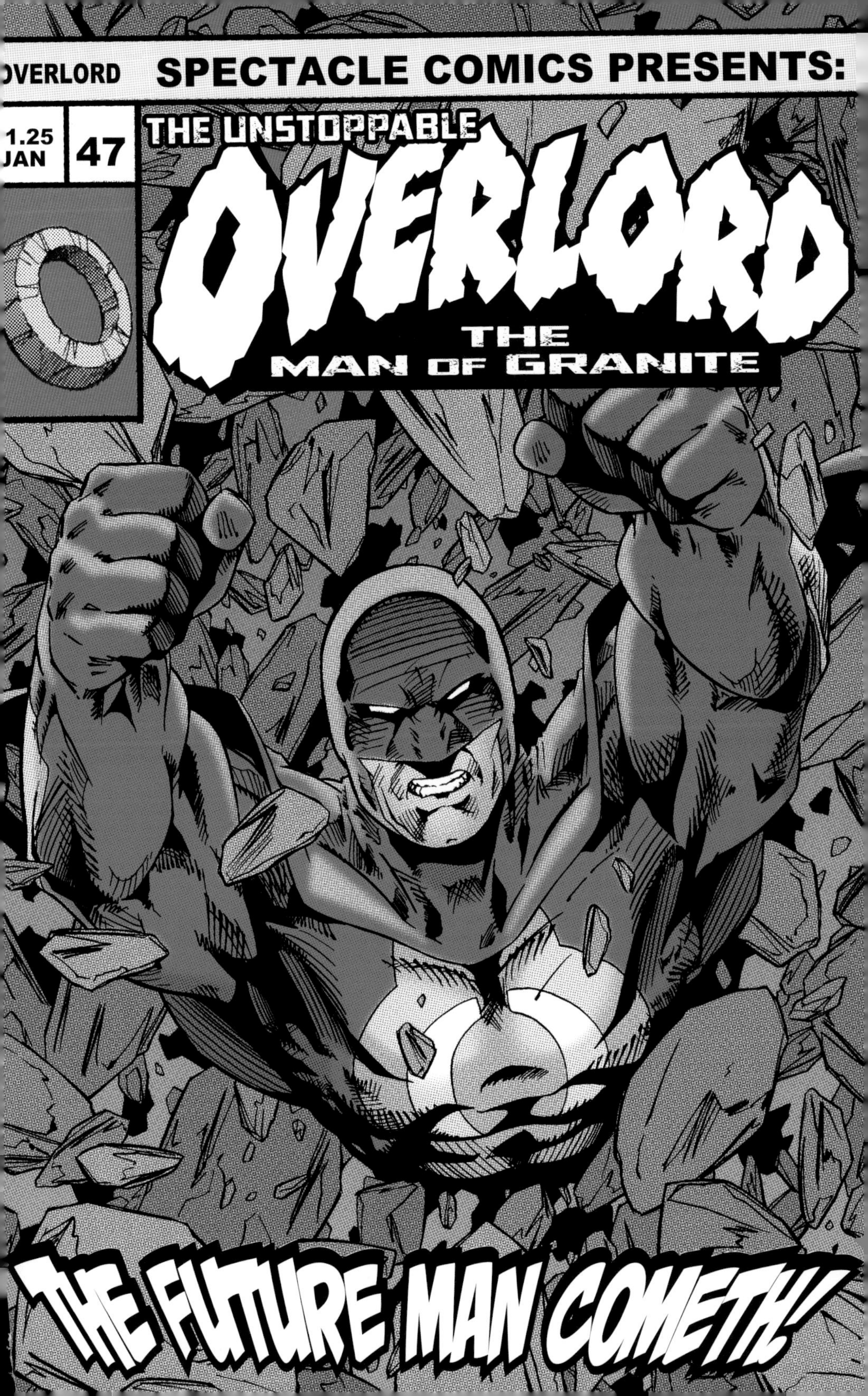
OVERLORD
SPECTACLE COMICS PRESENTS:
1.25
JAN
47
THE UNSTOPPABLE
OVERLORD
THE
MAN OF GRANITE
THE FUTURE MAN COMETH!

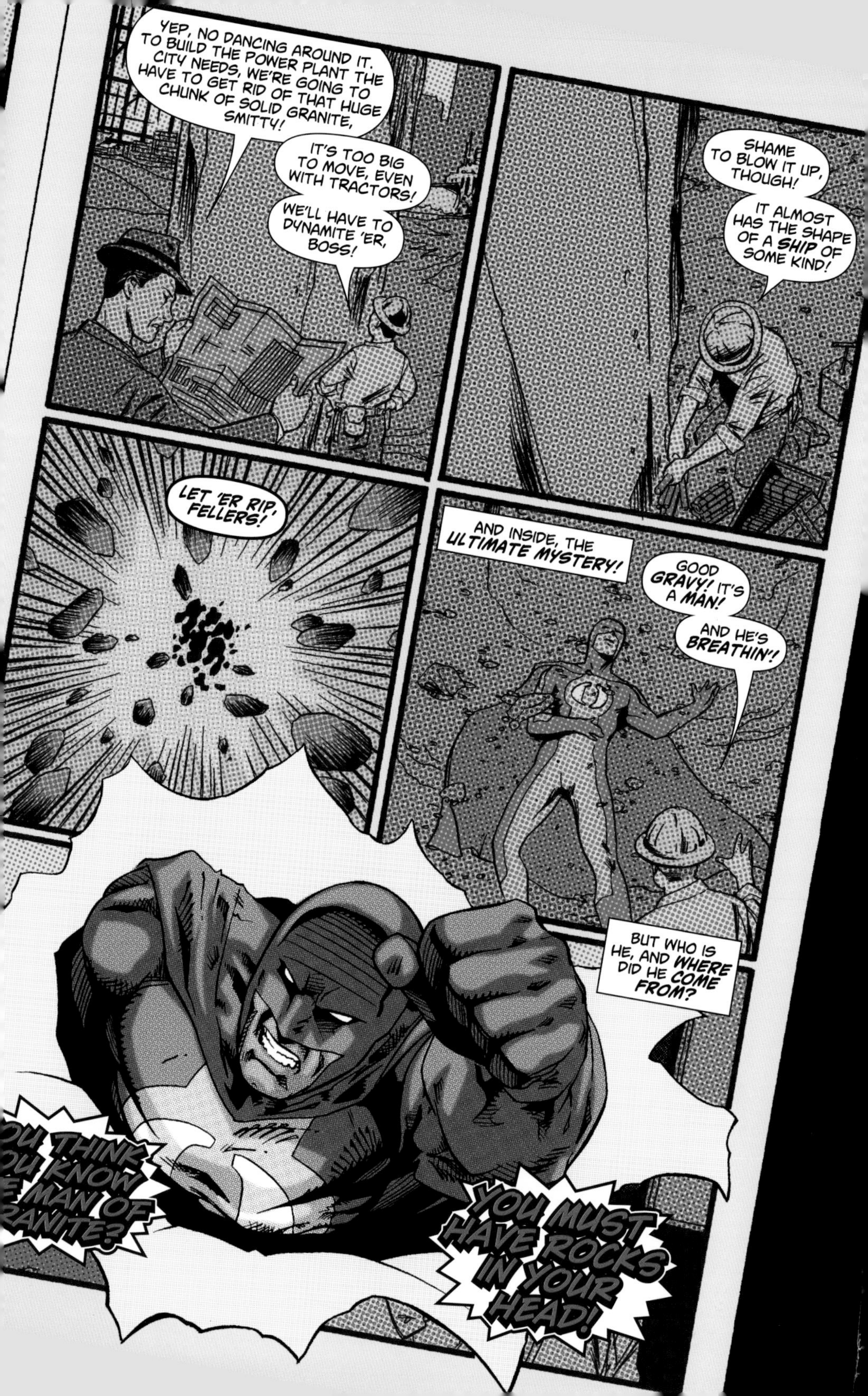
YEP, NO DANCING AROUND IT. TO BUILD THE POWER PLANT THE CITY NEEDS, WE'RE GOING TO HAVE TO GET RID OF THAT HUGE CHUNK OF SOLID GRANITE, SMITTY!
IT'S TOO BIG TO MOVE, EVEN WITH TRACTORS!
WE'LL HAVE TO DYNAMITE 'ER, BOSS!
SHAME TO BLOW IT UP, THOUGH!
IT ALMOST HAS THE SHAPE OF A SHIP OF SOME KIND!
LET 'ER RIP, FELLERS!
AND INSIDE, THE ULTIMATE MYSTERY!
GOOD GRAVY! IT'S A MAN!
AND HE'S BREATHIN'!
BUT WHO IS HE, AND WHERE DID HE COME FROM?
OU THINK OU KNOW E MAN OF RANITE?
YOU MUST HAVE ROCKS IN YOUR HEAD!

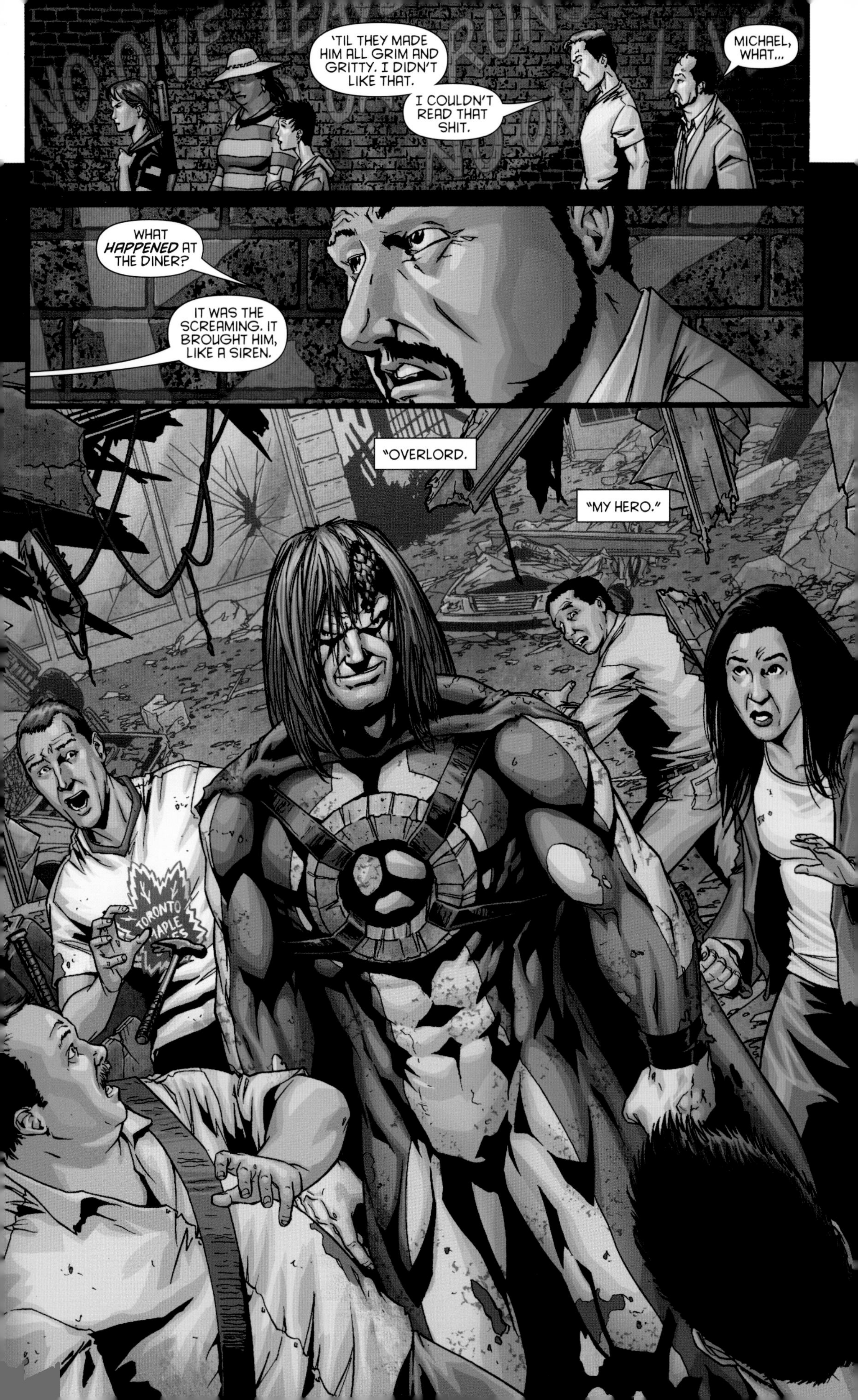

'TIL THEY MADE HIM ALL GRIM AND GRITTY. I DIDN'T LIKE THAT.
I COULDN'T READ THAT SHIT.
MICHAEL, WHAT...
WHAT *HAPPENED* AT THE DINER?
IT WAS THE SCREAMING. IT BROUGHT HIM, LIKE A SIREN.
"OVERLORD.
"MY HERO."
TORONTO MAPLE LEAFS

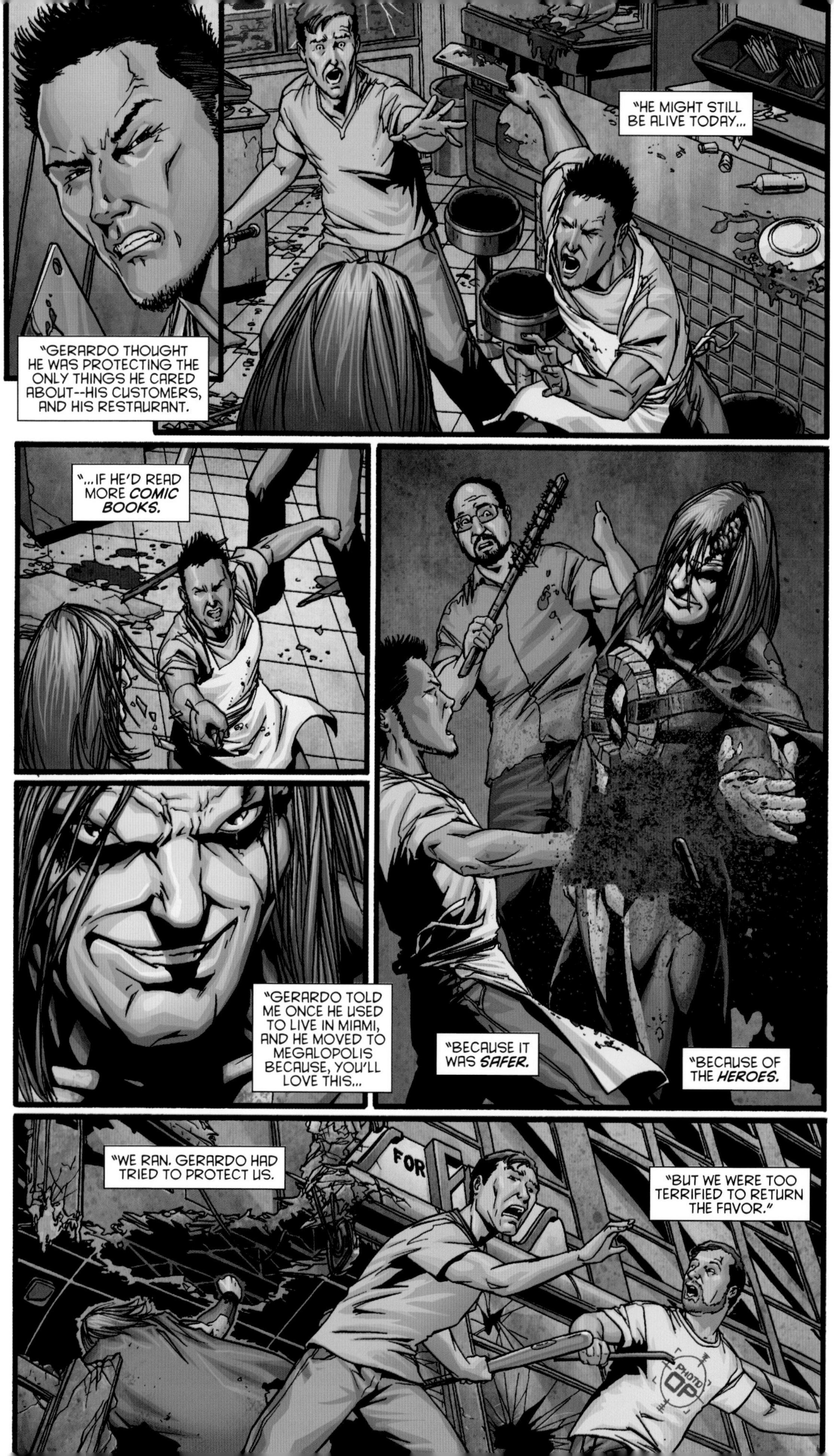
"GERARDO THOUGHT HE WAS PROTECTING THE ONLY THINGS HE CARED ABOUT--HIS CUSTOMERS, AND HIS RESTAURANT.
"HE MIGHT STILL BE ALIVE TODAY...
"...IF HE'D READ MORE *COMIC BOOKS.*
"GERARDO TOLD ME ONCE HE USED TO LIVE IN MIAMI, AND HE MOVED TO MEGALOPOLIS BECAUSE, YOU'LL LOVE THIS...
"BECAUSE IT WAS *SAFER.*
"BECAUSE OF THE *HEROES.*
"WE RAN. GERARDO HAD TRIED TO PROTECT US.
"BUT WE WERE TOO TERRIFIED TO RETURN THE FAVOR."
FOR
PHOTO OP

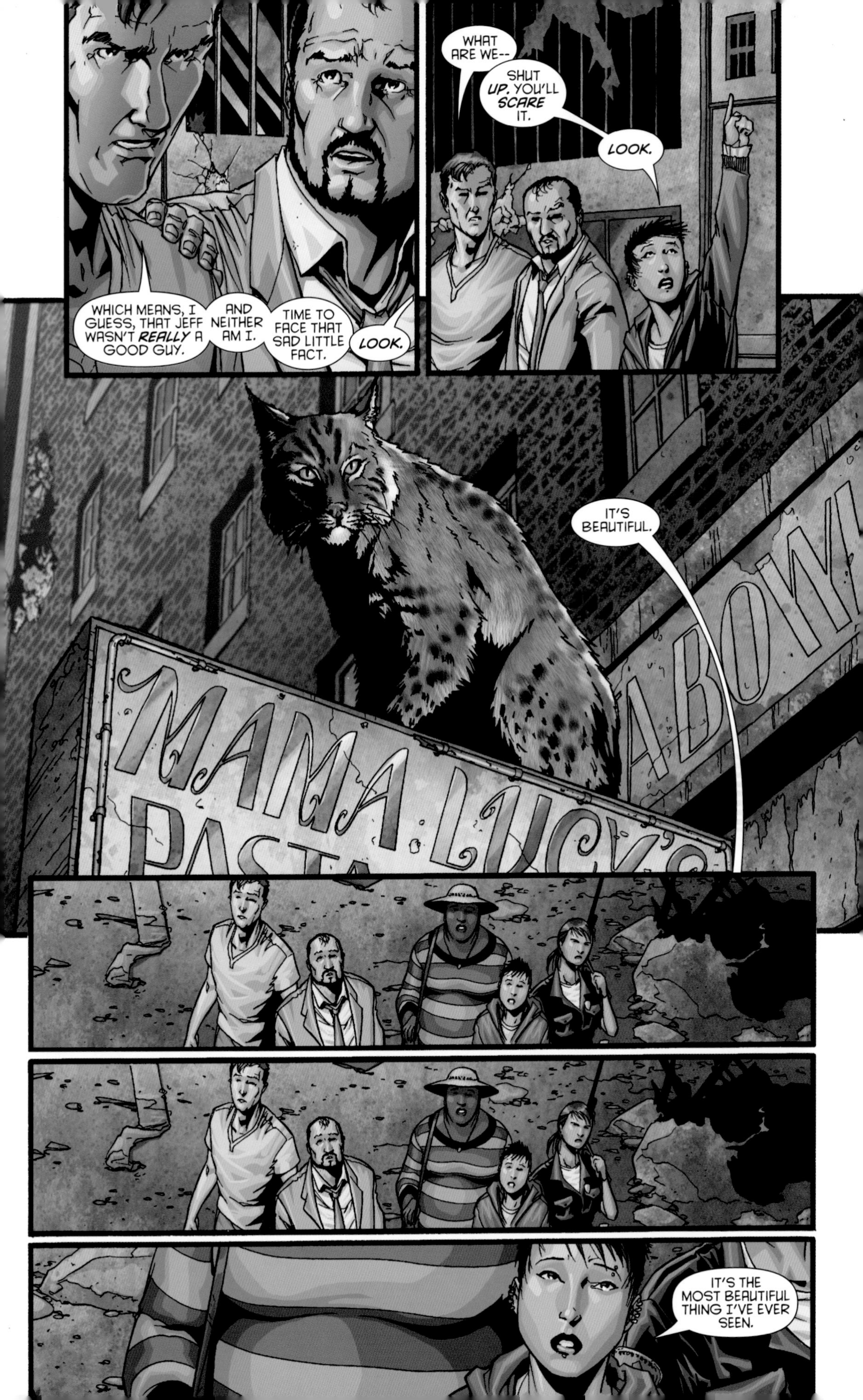
WHICH MEANS, I GUESS, THAT JEFF WASN'T *REALLY* A GOOD GUY.
AND NEITHER AM I.
TIME TO FACE THAT SAD LITTLE FACT.
LOOK.
WHAT ARE WE--
SHUT *UP.* YOU'LL *SCARE* IT.
LOOK.
IT'S BEAUTIFUL.
MAMA LUCY'S PASTA
ABOW
IT'S THE MOST BEAUTIFUL THING I'VE EVER SEEN.

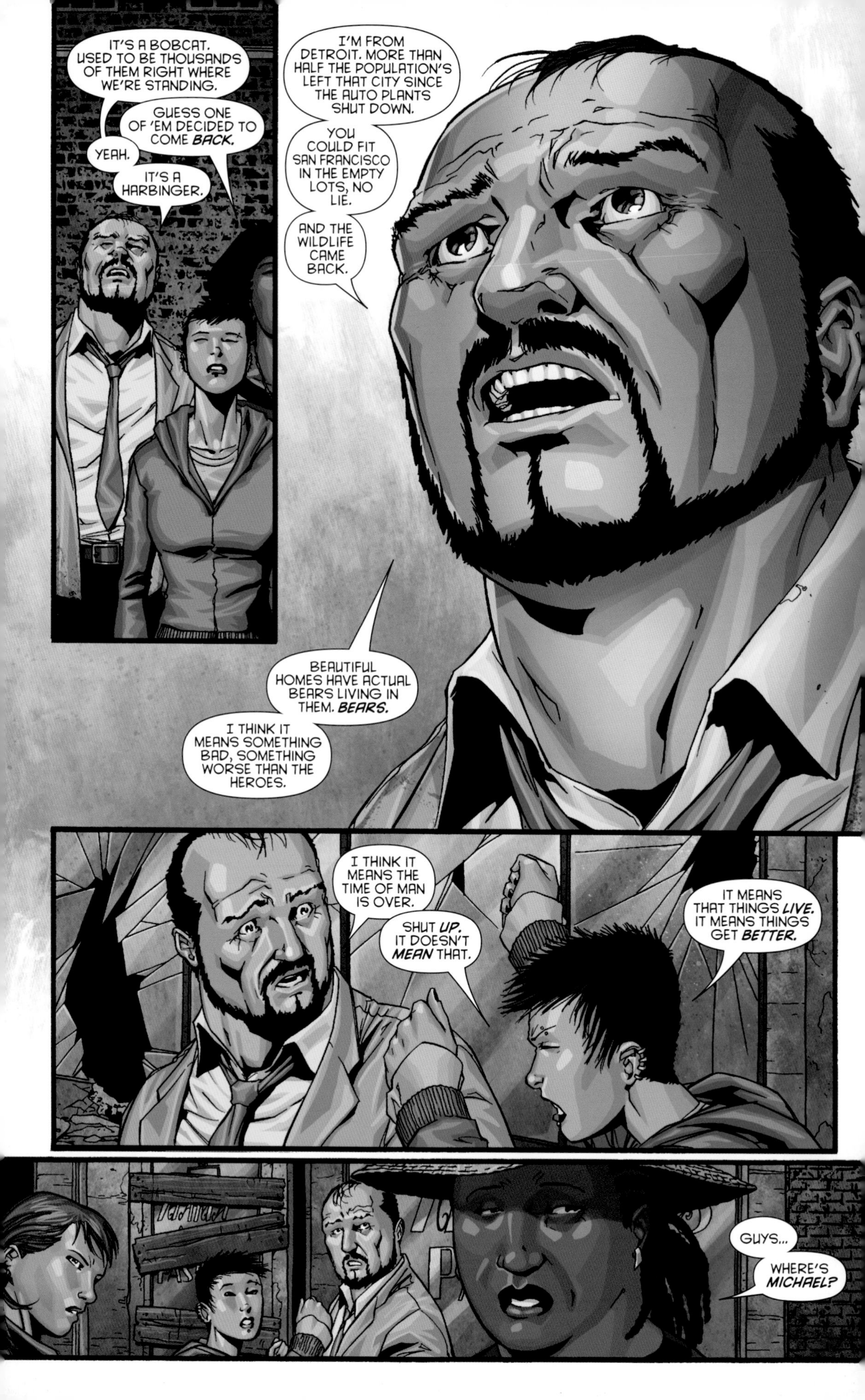

IT'S A BOBCAT. USED TO BE THOUSANDS OF THEM RIGHT WHERE WE'RE STANDING.
GUESS ONE OF 'EM DECIDED TO COME BACK.
YEAH.
IT'S A HARBINGER.
I'M FROM DETROIT. MORE THAN HALF THE POPULATION'S LEFT THAT CITY SINCE THE AUTO PLANTS SHUT DOWN.
YOU COULD FIT SAN FRANCISCO IN THE EMPTY LOTS, NO LIE.
AND THE WILDLIFE CAME BACK.
BEAUTIFUL HOMES HAVE ACTUAL BEARS LIVING IN THEM. BEARS.
I THINK IT MEANS SOMETHING BAD, SOMETHING WORSE THAN THE HEROES.
I THINK IT MEANS THE TIME OF MAN IS OVER.
SHUT UP. IT DOESN'T MEAN THAT.
IT MEANS THAT THINGS LIVE. IT MEANS THINGS GET BETTER.
GUYS...
WHERE'S MICHAEL?

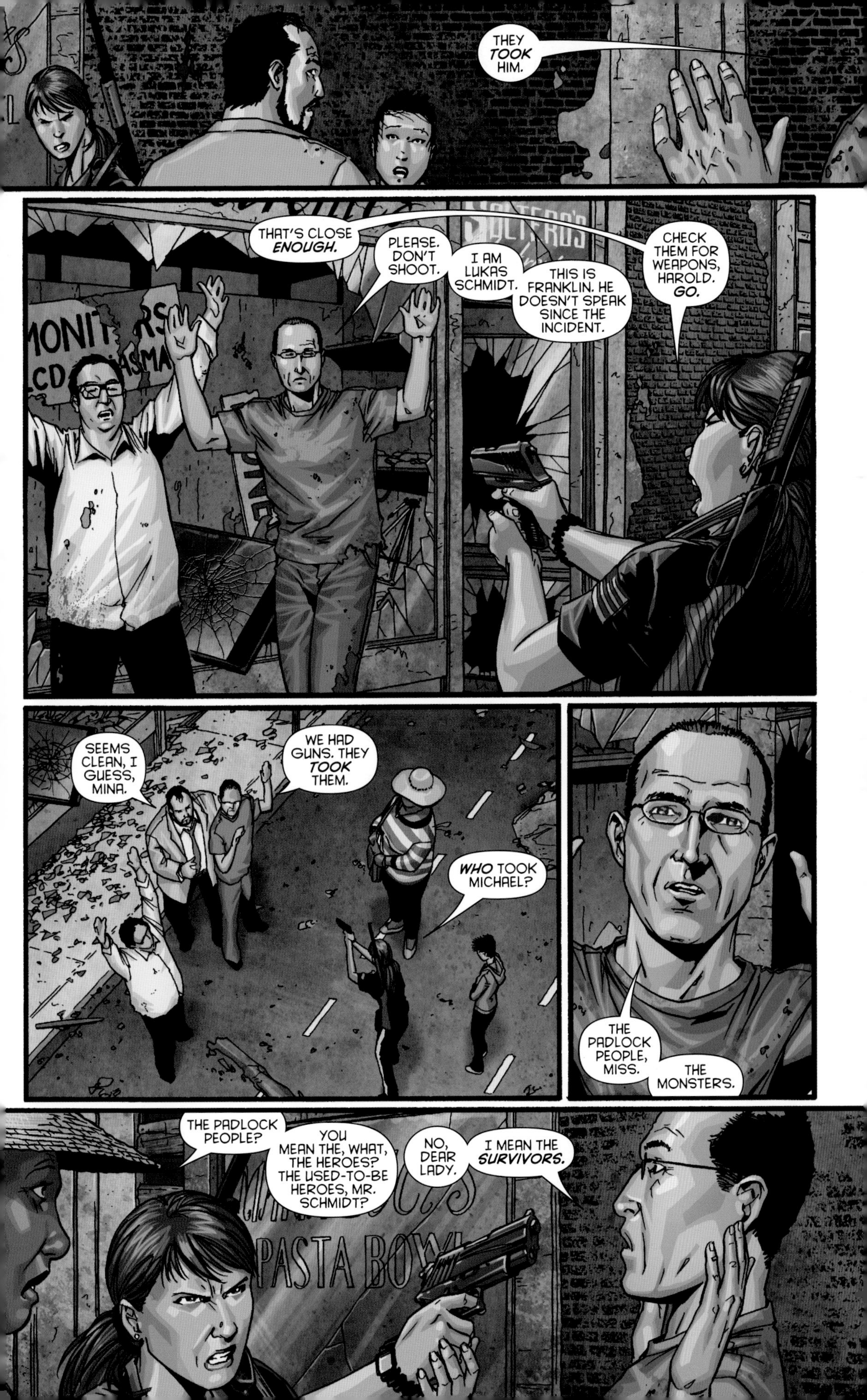
THEY *TOOK* HIM.
THAT'S CLOSE ***ENOUGH.***
PLEASE. DON'T SHOOT.
I AM LUKAS SCHMIDT.
THIS IS FRANKLIN. HE DOESN'T SPEAK SINCE THE INCIDENT.
CHECK THEM FOR WEAPONS, HAROLD. ***GO.***
MONITORS
LCD PLASMA
SEEMS CLEAN, I GUESS, MINA.
WE HAD GUNS. THEY *TOOK* THEM.
WHO TOOK MICHAEL?
THE PADLOCK PEOPLE, MISS.
THE MONSTERS.
THE PADLOCK PEOPLE?
YOU MEAN THE, WHAT, THE HEROES? THE USED-TO-BE HEROES, MR. SCHMIDT?
NO, DEAR LADY.
I MEAN THE ***SURVIVORS.***
PASTA BOWL

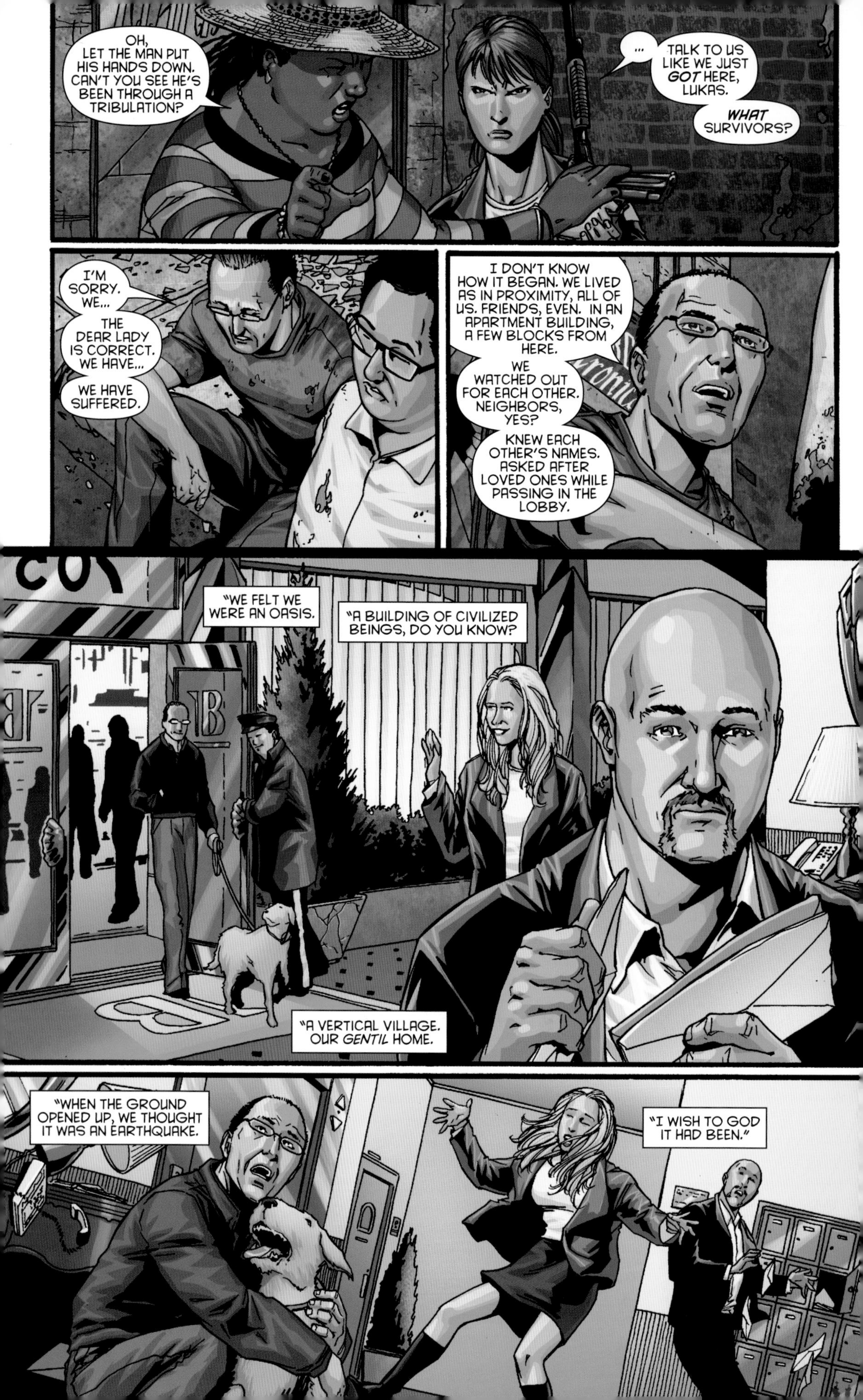
OH, LET THE MAN PUT HIS HANDS DOWN. CAN'T YOU SEE HE'S BEEN THROUGH A TRIBULATION?
... TALK TO US LIKE WE JUST *GOT* HERE, LUKAS.
WHAT SURVIVORS?
I'M SORRY. WE...
THE DEAR LADY IS CORRECT. WE HAVE...
WE HAVE SUFFERED.
I DON'T KNOW HOW IT BEGAN. WE LIVED AS IN PROXIMITY, ALL OF US. FRIENDS, EVEN. IN AN APARTMENT BUILDING, A FEW BLOCKS FROM HERE.
WE WATCHED OUT FOR EACH OTHER. NEIGHBORS, YES?
KNEW EACH OTHER'S NAMES. ASKED AFTER LOVED ONES WHILE PASSING IN THE LOBBY.
"WE FELT WE WERE AN OASIS.
"A BUILDING OF CIVILIZED BEINGS, DO YOU KNOW?
"A VERTICAL VILLAGE. OUR *GENTIL* HOME.
"WHEN THE GROUND OPENED UP, WE THOUGHT IT WAS AN EARTHQUAKE.
"I WISH TO GOD IT HAD BEEN."

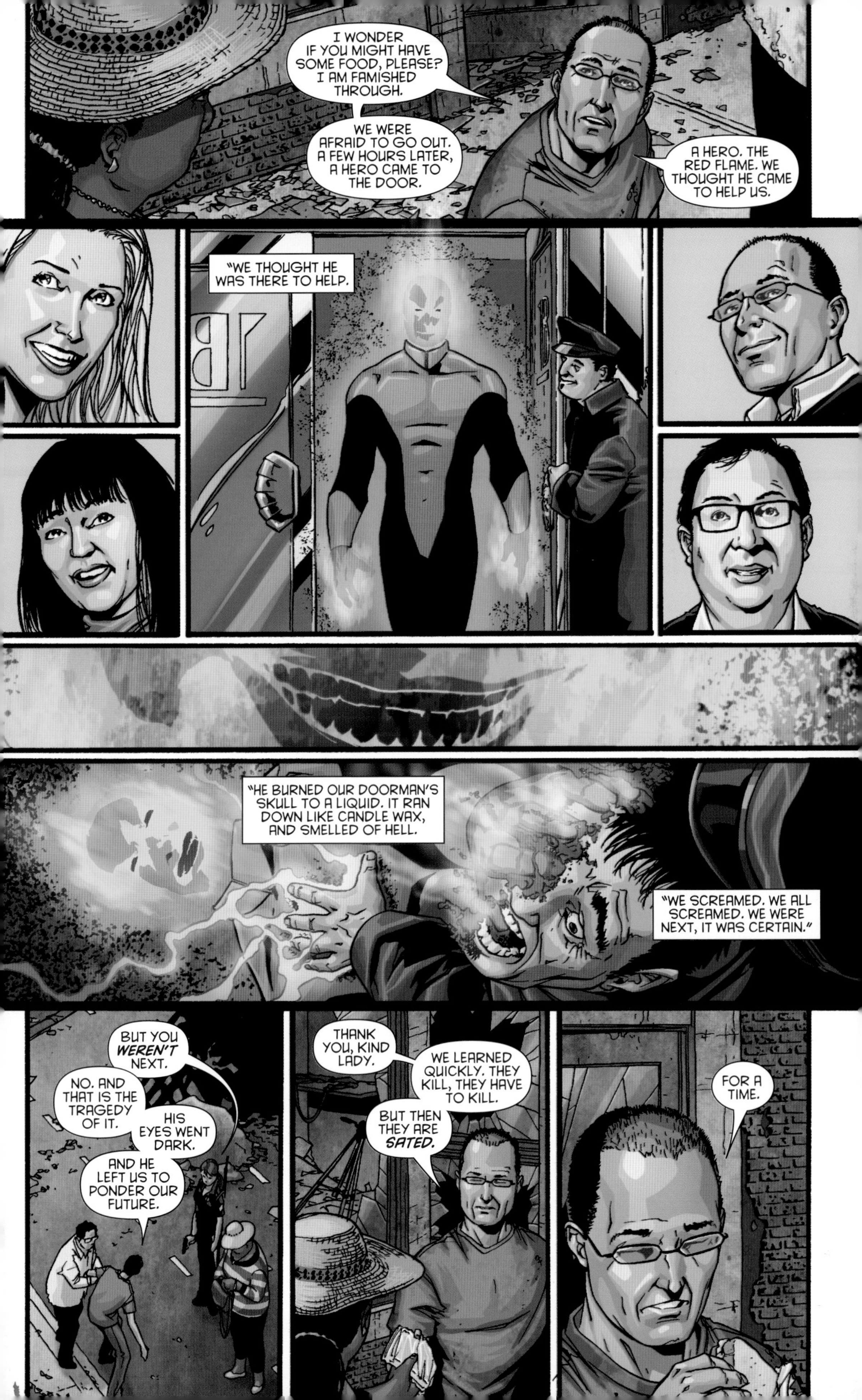
I WONDER IF YOU MIGHT HAVE SOME FOOD, PLEASE? I AM FAMISHED THROUGH.
WE WERE AFRAID TO GO OUT. A FEW HOURS LATER, A HERO CAME TO THE DOOR.
A HERO. THE RED FLAME. WE THOUGHT HE CAME TO HELP US.
"WE THOUGHT HE WAS THERE TO HELP.
"HE BURNED OUR DOORMAN'S SKULL TO A LIQUID. IT RAN DOWN LIKE CANDLE WAX, AND SMELLED OF HELL.
"WE SCREAMED. WE ALL SCREAMED. WE WERE NEXT, IT WAS CERTAIN."
BUT YOU *WEREN'T* NEXT.
NO. AND THAT IS THE TRAGEDY OF IT.
HIS EYES WENT DARK.
AND HE LEFT US TO PONDER OUR FUTURE.
THANK YOU, KIND LADY.
WE LEARNED QUICKLY. THEY KILL, THEY HAVE TO KILL.
BUT THEN THEY ARE *SATED.*
FOR A TIME.

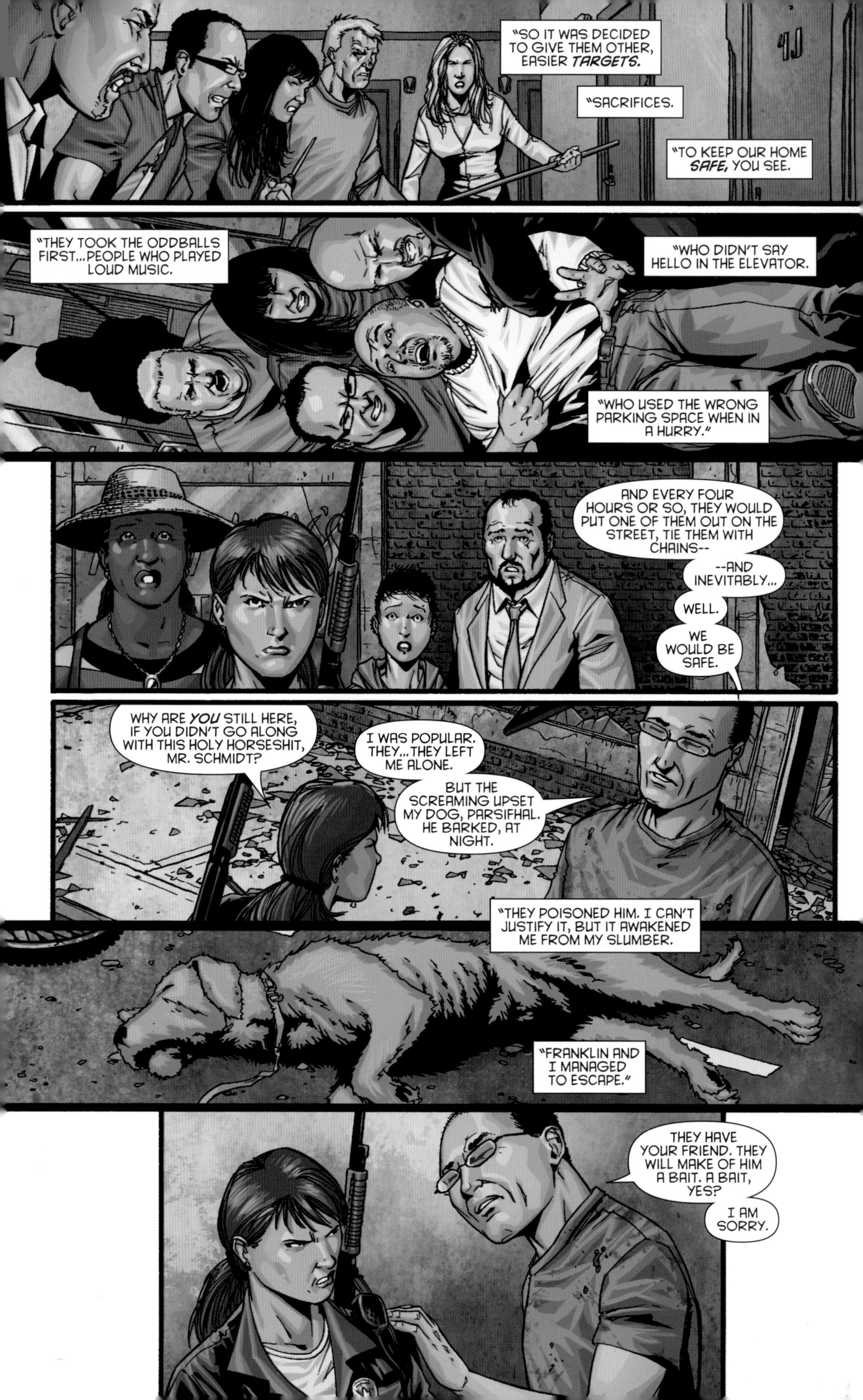
"SO IT WAS DECIDED TO GIVE THEM OTHER, EASIER *TARGETS.*
"SACRIFICES.
"TO KEEP OUR HOME *SAFE,* YOU SEE.
"THEY TOOK THE ODDBALLS FIRST...PEOPLE WHO PLAYED LOUD MUSIC.
"WHO DIDN'T SAY HELLO IN THE ELEVATOR.
"WHO USED THE WRONG PARKING SPACE WHEN IN A HURRY."
AND EVERY FOUR HOURS OR SO, THEY WOULD PUT ONE OF THEM OUT ON THE STREET, TIE THEM WITH CHAINS--
--AND INEVITABLY...
WELL.
WE WOULD BE SAFE.
WHY ARE *YOU* STILL HERE, IF YOU DIDN'T GO ALONG WITH THIS HOLY HORSESHIT, MR. SCHMIDT?
I WAS POPULAR. THEY...THEY LEFT ME ALONE.
BUT THE SCREAMING UPSET MY DOG, PARSIFHAL. HE BARKED, AT NIGHT.
"THEY POISONED HIM. I CAN'T JUSTIFY IT, BUT IT AWAKENED ME FROM MY SLUMBER.
"FRANKLIN AND I MANAGED TO ESCAPE."
THEY HAVE YOUR FRIEND. THEY WILL MAKE OF HIM A BAIT. A BAIT, YES?
I AM SORRY.

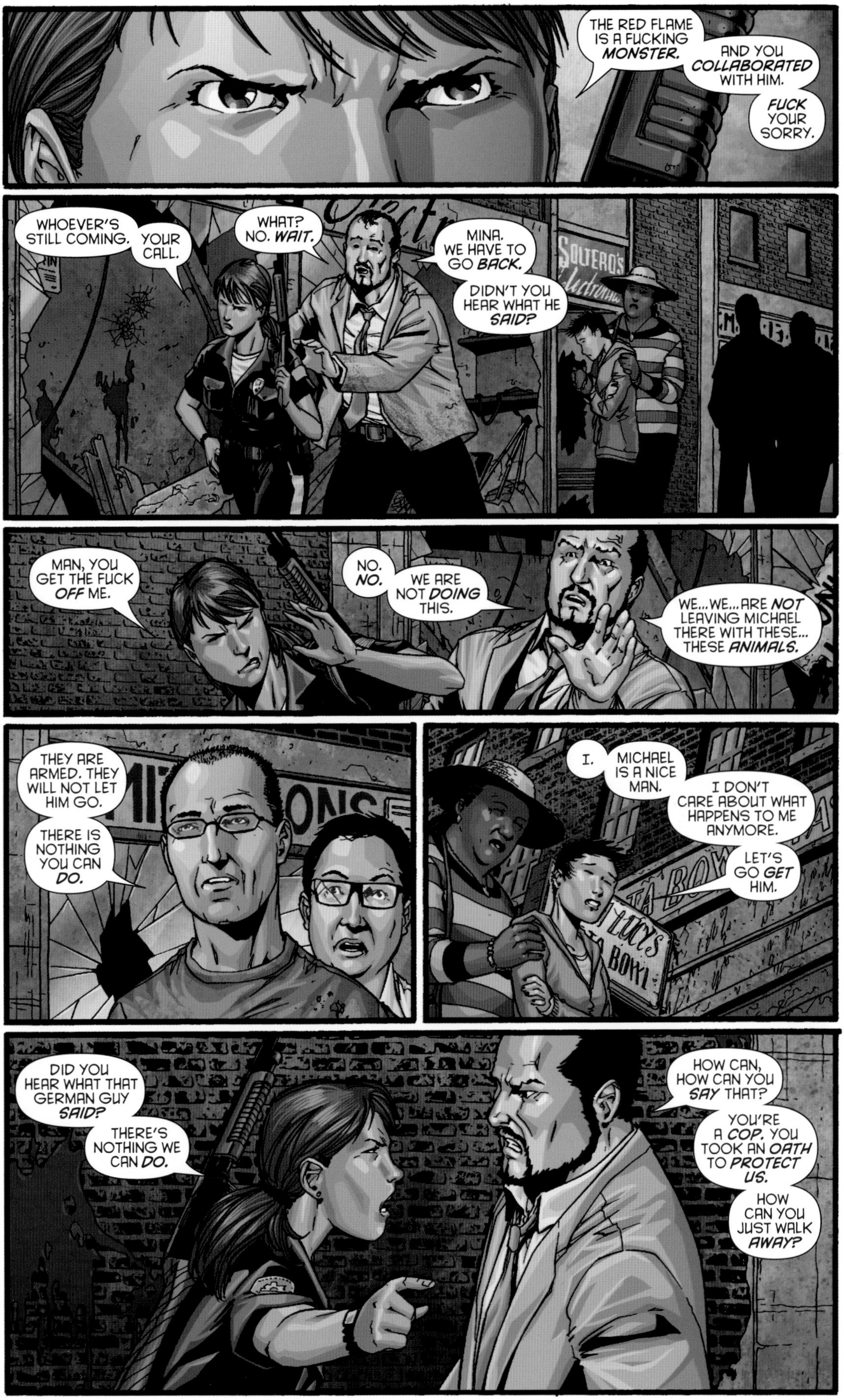
THE RED FLAME IS A FUCKING MONSTER.
AND YOU COLLABORATED WITH HIM.
FUCK YOUR SORRY.
WHOEVER'S STILL COMING.
YOUR CALL.
WHAT? NO. WAIT.
MINA. WE HAVE TO GO BACK.
DIDN'T YOU HEAR WHAT HE SAID?
MAN, YOU GET THE FUCK OFF ME.
NO. NO.
WE ARE NOT DOING THIS.
WE...WE...ARE NOT LEAVING MICHAEL THERE WITH THESE... THESE ANIMALS.
THEY ARE ARMED. THEY WILL NOT LET HIM GO.
THERE IS NOTHING YOU CAN DO.
I.
MICHAEL IS A NICE MAN.
I DON'T CARE ABOUT WHAT HAPPENS TO ME ANYMORE.
LET'S GO GET HIM.
DID YOU HEAR WHAT THAT GERMAN GUY SAID?
THERE'S NOTHING WE CAN DO.
HOW CAN, HOW CAN YOU SAY THAT?
YOU'RE A COP. YOU TOOK AN OATH TO PROTECT US.
HOW CAN YOU JUST WALK AWAY?

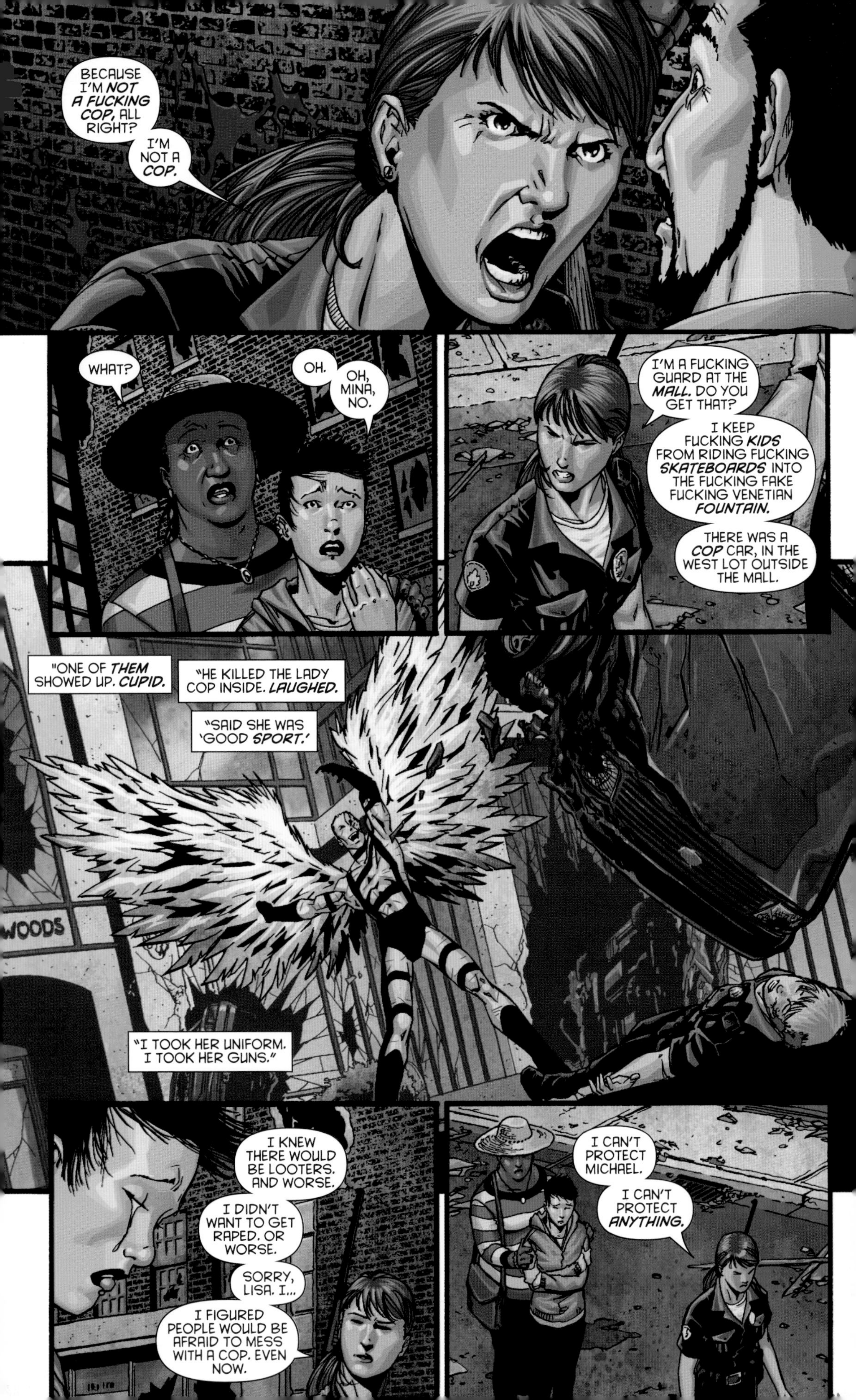

BECAUSE I'M NOT A FUCKING COP, ALL RIGHT?
I'M NOT A COP.
WHAT?
OH.
OH, MINA, NO.
I'M A FUCKING GUARD AT THE MALL. DO YOU GET THAT?
I KEEP FUCKING KIDS FROM RIDING FUCKING SKATEBOARDS INTO THE FUCKING FAKE FUCKING VENETIAN FOUNTAIN.
THERE WAS A COP CAR, IN THE WEST LOT OUTSIDE THE MALL.
"ONE OF THEM SHOWED UP. CUPID.
"HE KILLED THE LADY COP INSIDE. LAUGHED.
"SAID SHE WAS 'GOOD SPORT.'
WOODS
"I TOOK HER UNIFORM. I TOOK HER GUNS."
I KNEW THERE WOULD BE LOOTERS. AND WORSE.
I DIDN'T WANT TO GET RAPED. OR WORSE.
SORRY, LISA. I...
I FIGURED PEOPLE WOULD BE AFRAID TO MESS WITH A COP. EVEN NOW.
I CAN'T PROTECT MICHAEL.
I CAN'T PROTECT ANYTHING.

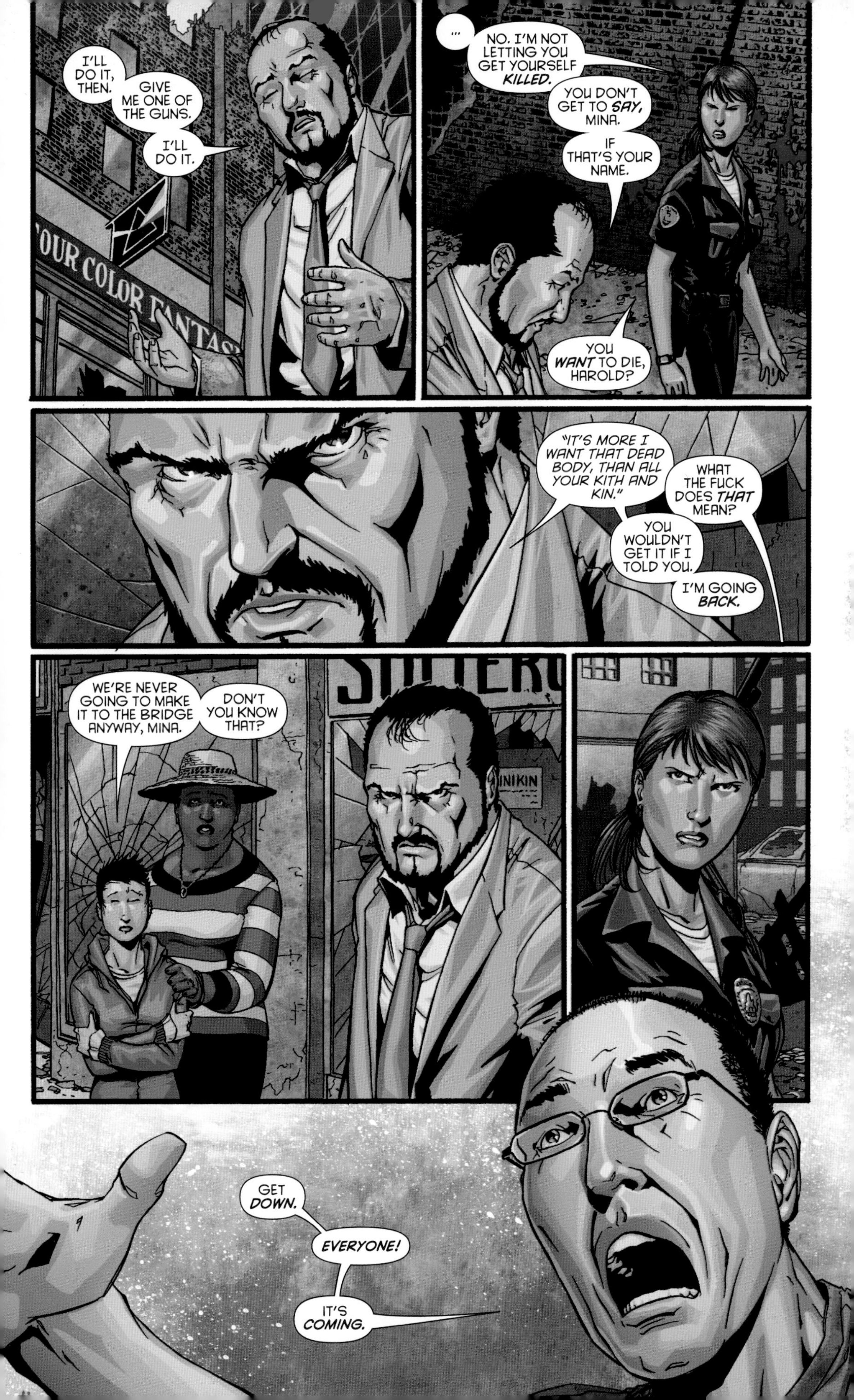
I'LL DO IT, THEN.
GIVE ME ONE OF THE GUNS.
I'LL DO IT.
FOUR COLOR FANTAS
...
NO. I'M NOT LETTING YOU GET YOURSELF KILLED.
YOU DON'T GET TO SAY, MINA.
IF THAT'S YOUR NAME.
YOU WANT TO DIE, HAROLD?
"IT'S MORE I WANT THAT DEAD BODY, THAN ALL YOUR KITH AND KIN."
WHAT THE FUCK DOES THAT MEAN?
YOU WOULDN'T GET IT IF I TOLD YOU.
I'M GOING BACK.
WE'RE NEVER GOING TO MAKE IT TO THE BRIDGE ANYWAY, MINA.
DON'T YOU KNOW THAT?
GET DOWN.
EVERYONE!
IT'S COMING.

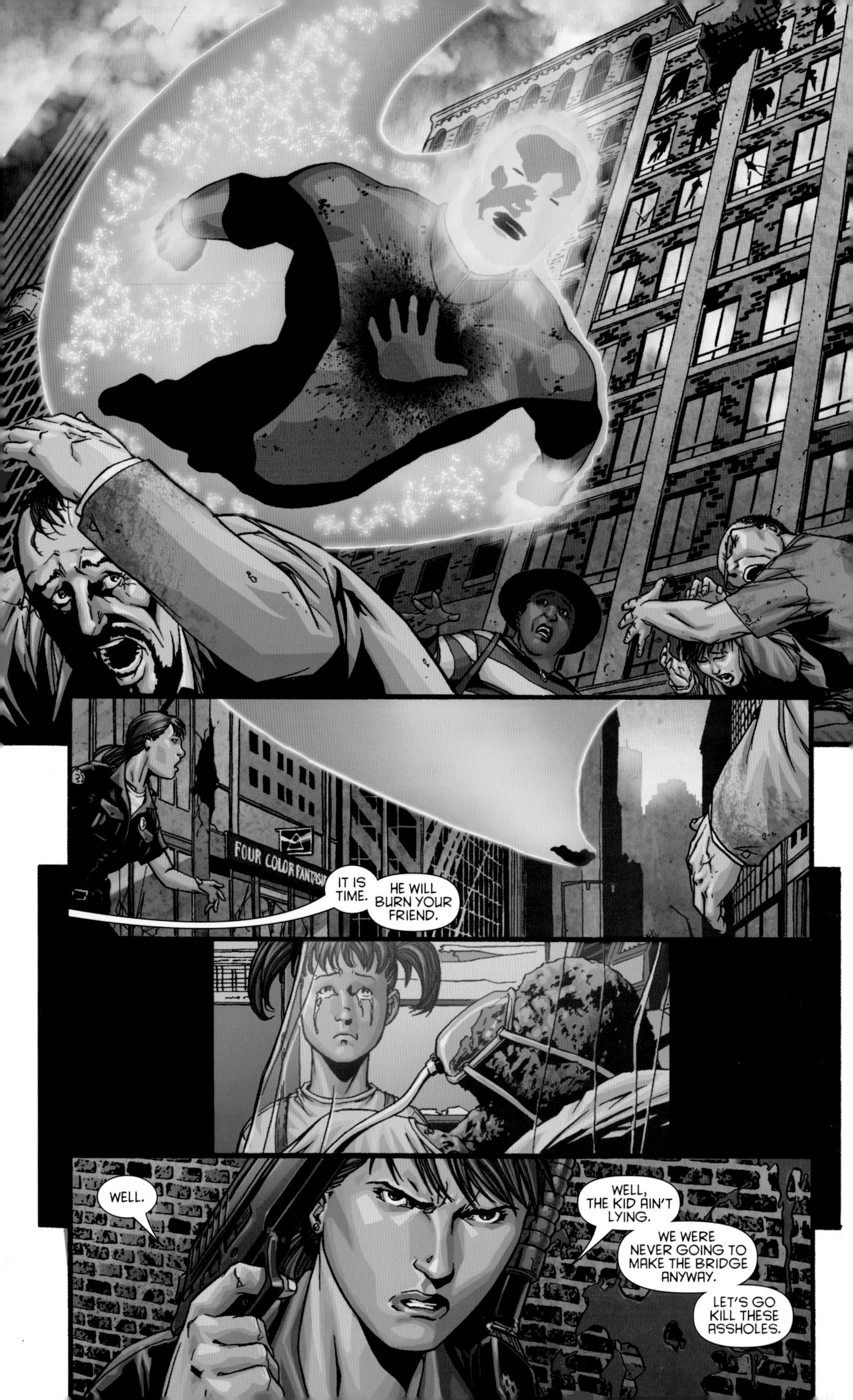
FOUR COLOR FANTASI
IT IS TIME.
HE WILL BURN YOUR FRIEND.
WELL.
WELL, THE KID AIN'T LYING.
WE WERE NEVER GOING TO MAKE THE BRIDGE ANYWAY.
LET'S GO KILL THESE ASSHOLES.

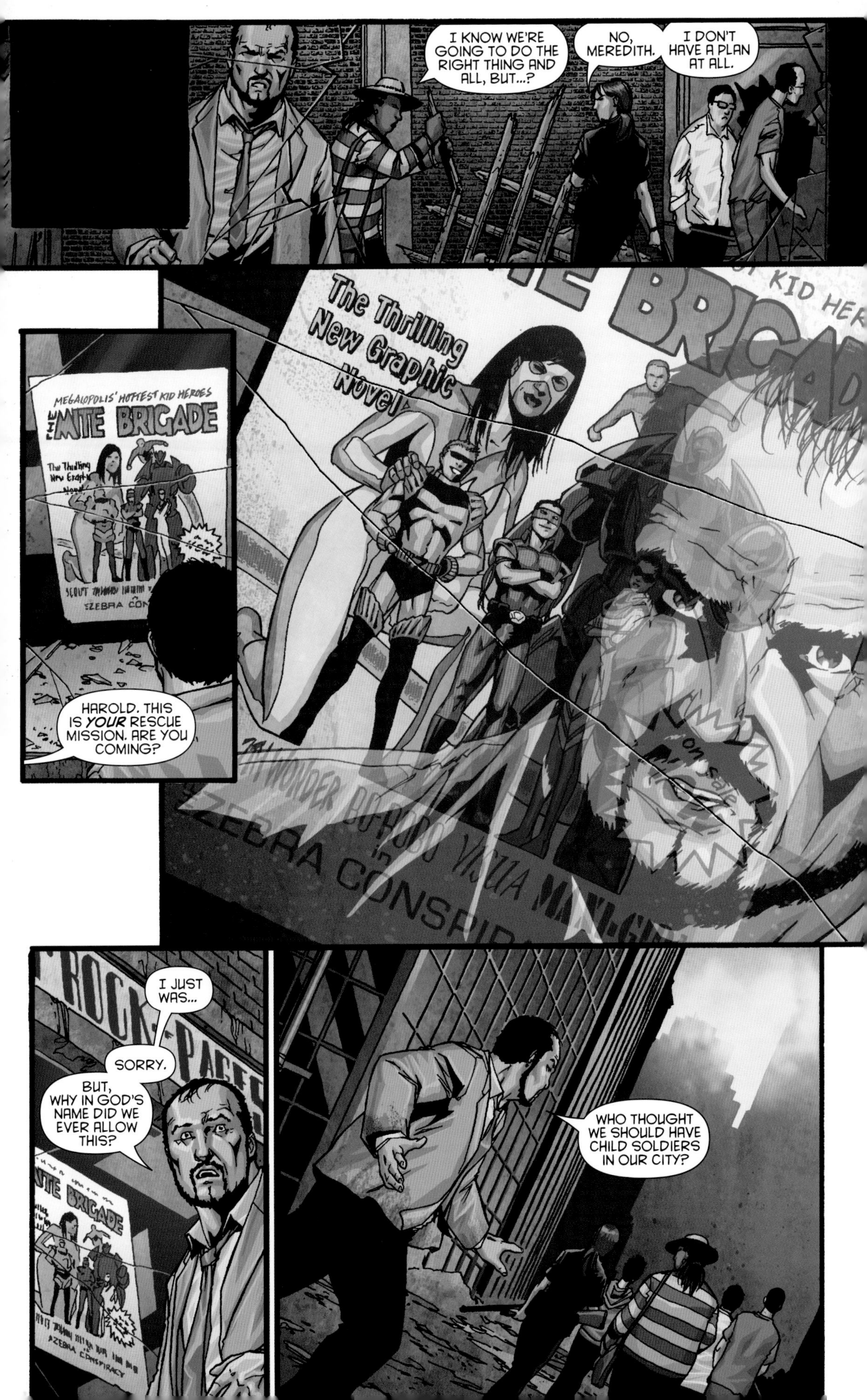

I KNOW WE'RE GOING TO DO THE RIGHT THING AND ALL, BUT...?
NO, MEREDITH.
I DON'T HAVE A PLAN AT ALL.
The Thrilling New Graphic Novel
MEGALOPOLIS' HOTTEST KID HEROES
THE MITE BRIGADE
ZEBRA CON
HAROLD. THIS IS *YOUR* RESCUE MISSION. ARE YOU COMING?
on sale
ZEBRA CONSPIRA
I JUST WAS...
SORRY.
BUT, WHY IN GOD'S NAME DID WE EVER ALLOW THIS?
WHO THOUGHT WE SHOULD HAVE CHILD SOLDIERS IN OUR CITY?

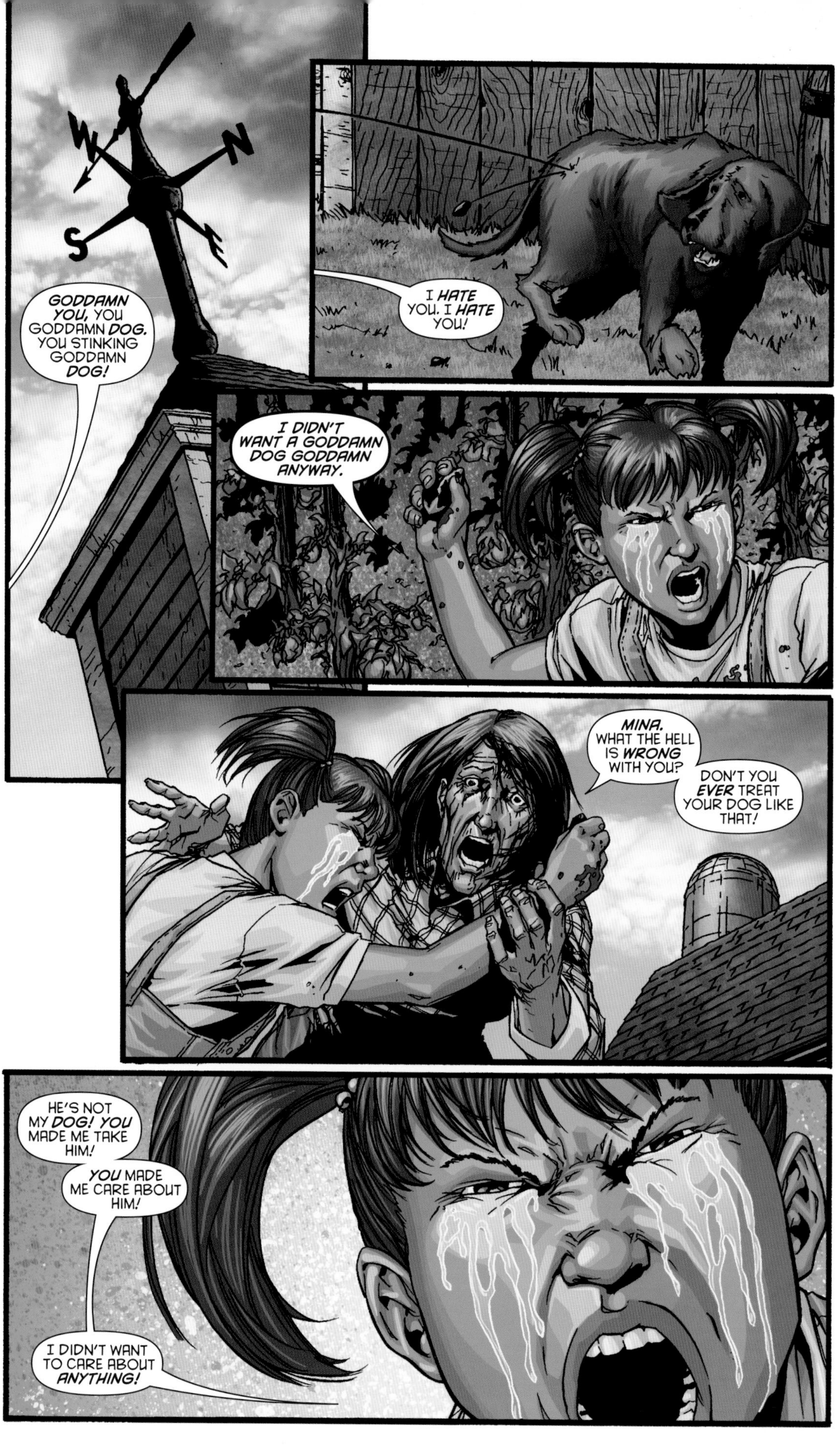
GODDAMN YOU, YOU GODDAMN DOG. YOU STINKING GODDAMN DOG!
W
N
S
E
I HATE YOU. I HATE YOU!
I DIDN'T WANT A GODDAMN DOG GODDAMN ANYWAY.
MINA. WHAT THE HELL IS WRONG WITH YOU?
DON'T YOU EVER TREAT YOUR DOG LIKE THAT!
HE'S NOT MY DOG! YOU MADE ME TAKE HIM!
YOU MADE ME CARE ABOUT HIM!
I DIDN'T WANT TO CARE ABOUT ANYTHING!

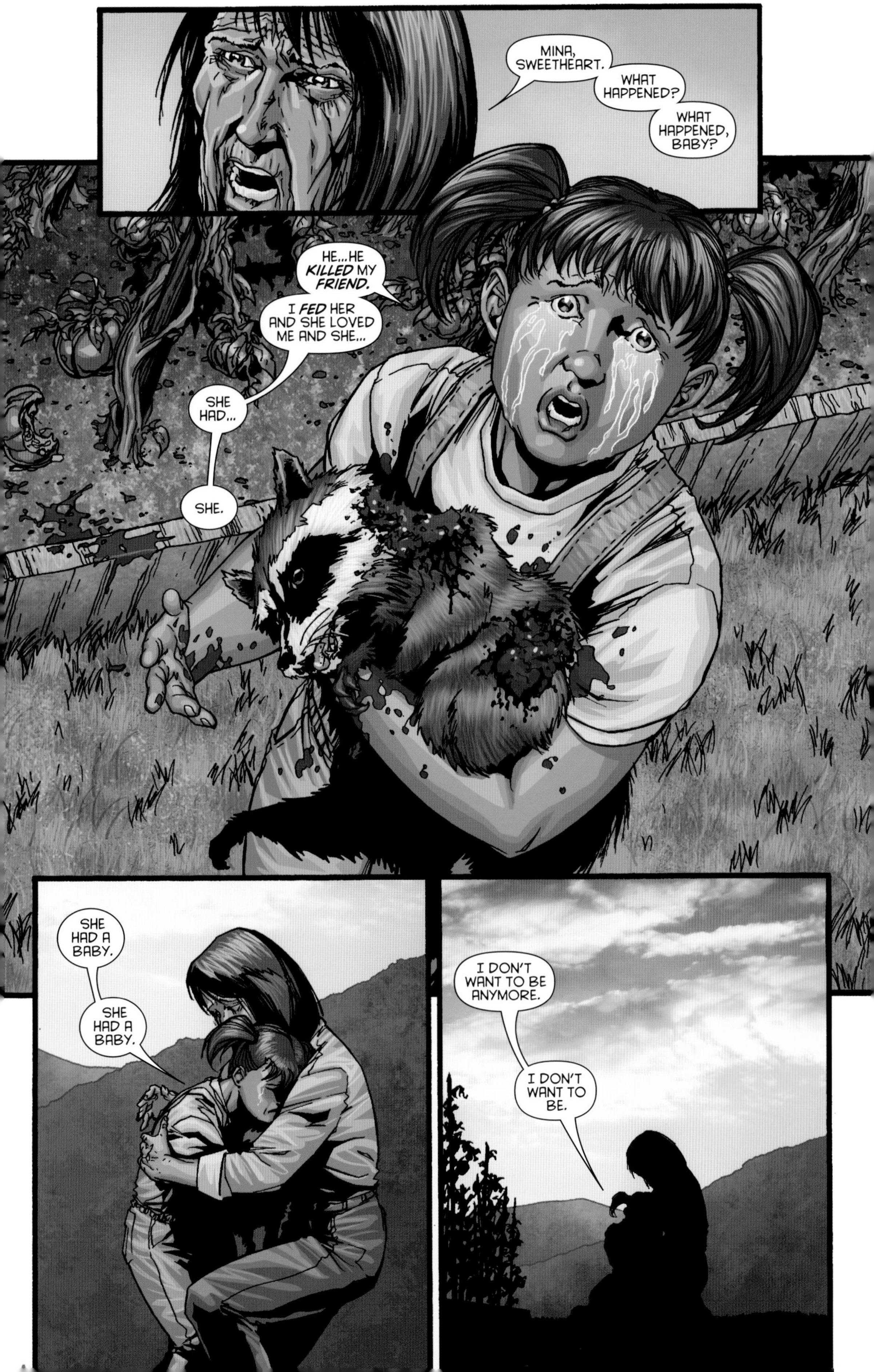

MINA, SWEETHEART.
WHAT HAPPENED?
WHAT HAPPENED, BABY?
HE...HE **KILLED** MY **FRIEND.**
I **FED** HER AND SHE LOVED ME AND SHE...
SHE HAD...
SHE.
SHE HAD A BABY.
SHE HAD A BABY.
I DON'T WANT TO BE ANYMORE.
I DON'T WANT TO BE.

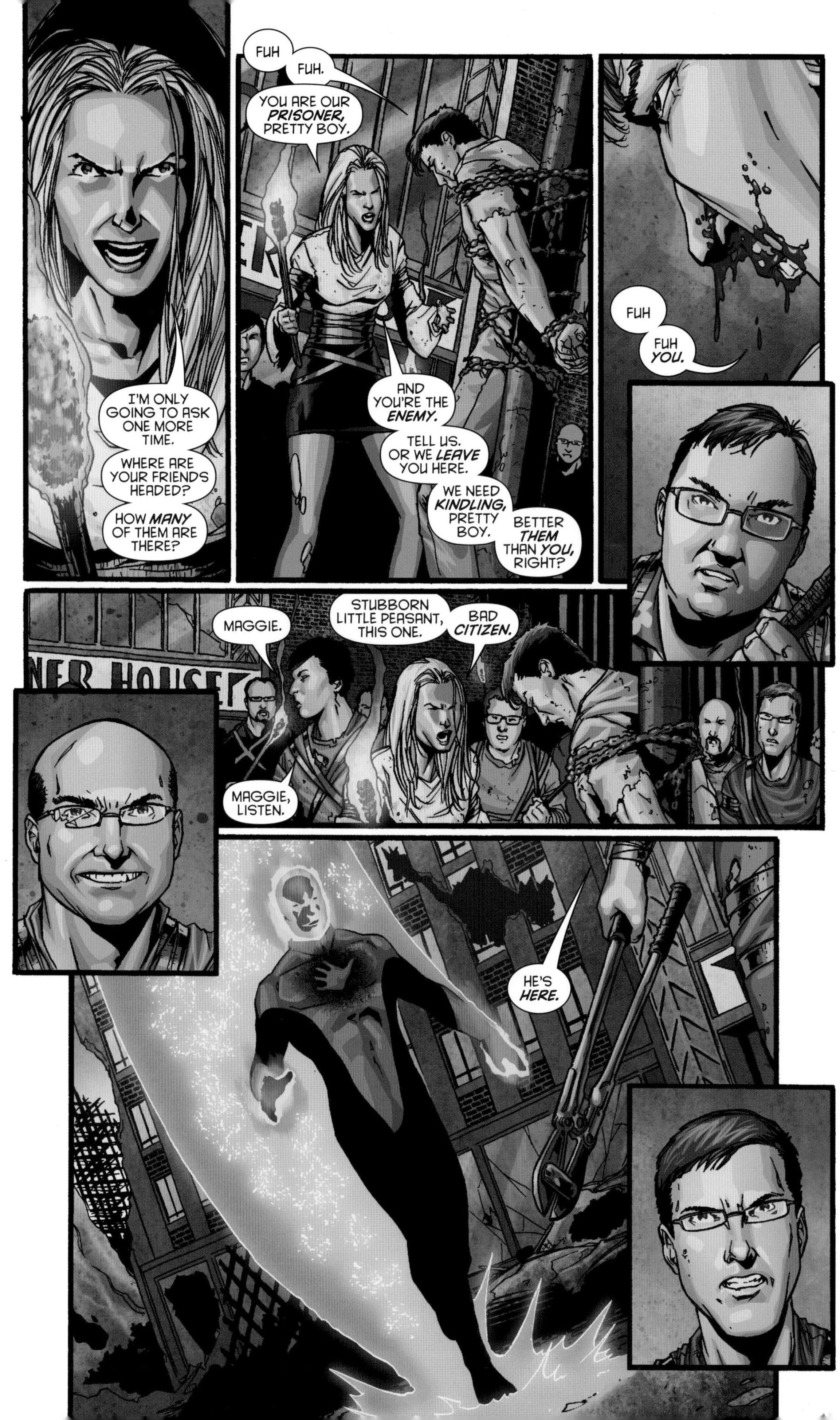
I'M ONLY GOING TO ASK ONE MORE TIME.
WHERE ARE YOUR FRIENDS HEADED?
HOW MANY OF THEM ARE THERE?
FUH
FUH.
YOU ARE OUR PRISONER, PRETTY BOY.
AND YOU'RE THE ENEMY.
TELL US. OR WE LEAVE YOU HERE.
WE NEED KINDLING, PRETTY BOY.
BETTER THEM THAN YOU, RIGHT?
FUH
FUH YOU.
MAGGIE.
STUBBORN LITTLE PEASANT, THIS ONE.
BAD CITIZEN.
MAGGIE, LISTEN.
HE'S HERE.

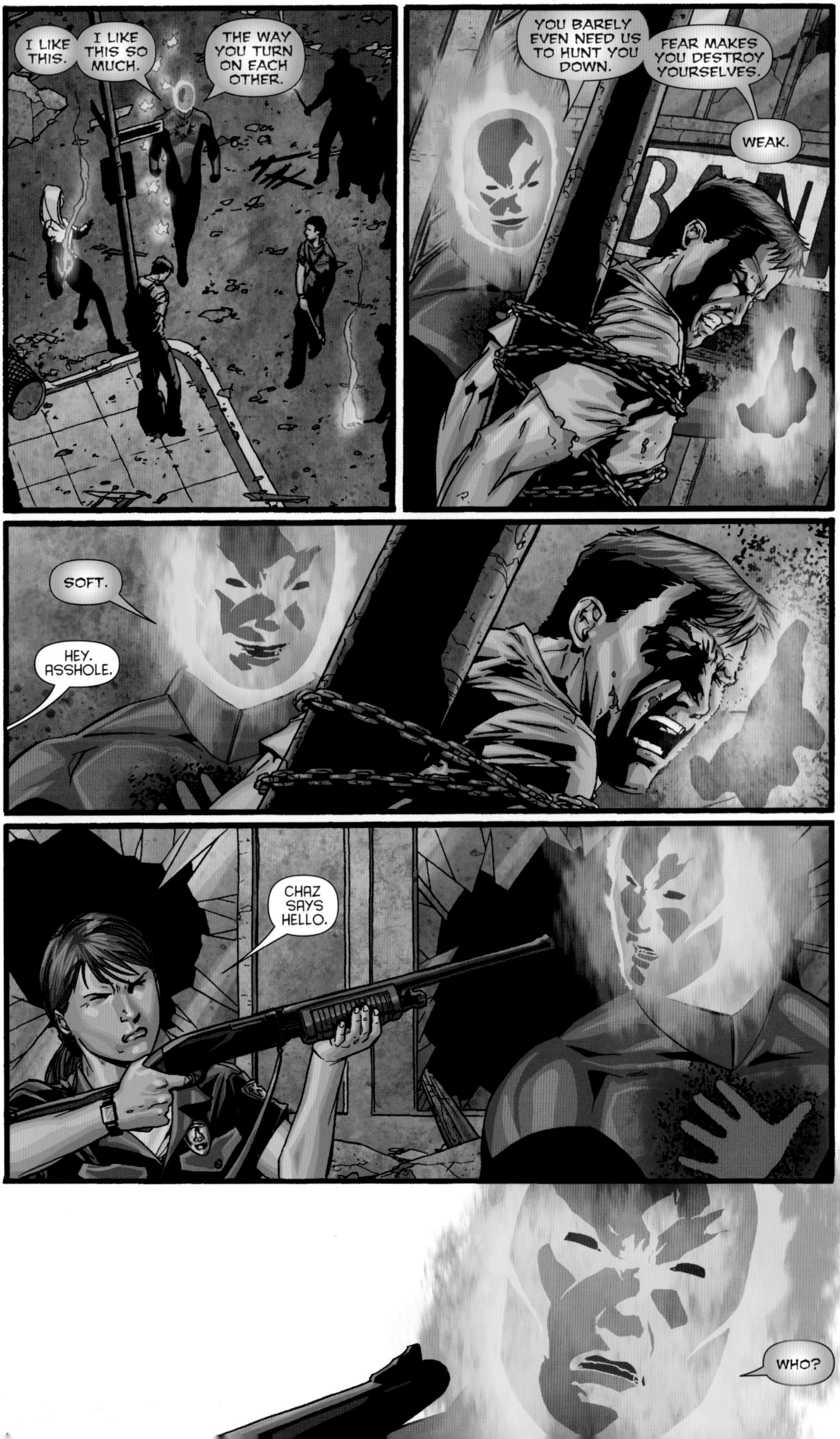
I LIKE THIS.
I LIKE THIS SO MUCH.
THE WAY YOU TURN ON EACH OTHER.
YOU BARELY EVEN NEED US TO HUNT YOU DOWN.
FEAR MAKES YOU DESTROY YOURSELVES.
WEAK.
SOFT.
HEY. ASSHOLE.
CHAZ SAYS HELLO.
WHO?

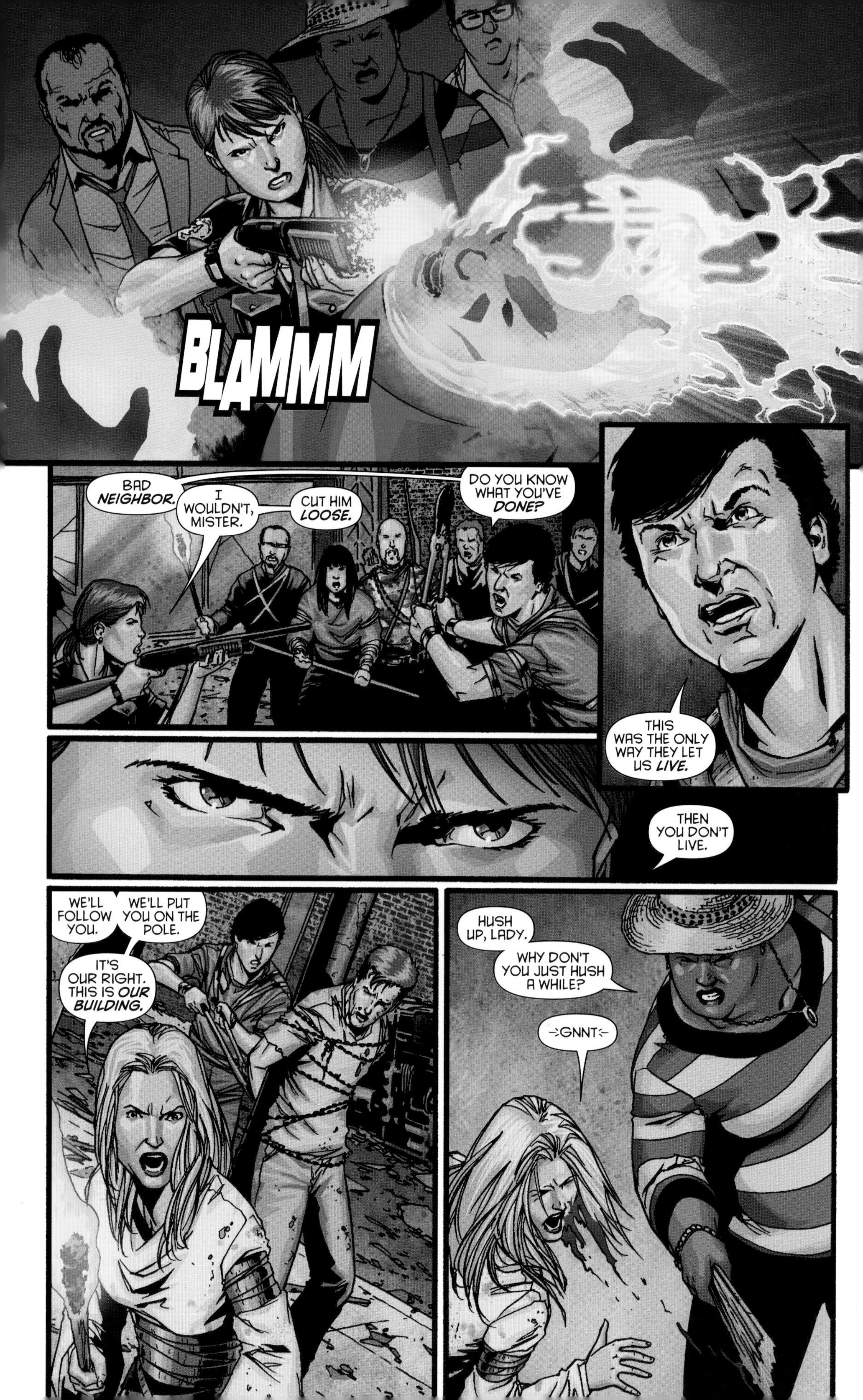
BLAMMM
BAD NEIGHBOR.
I WOULDN'T, MISTER.
CUT HIM LOOSE.
DO YOU KNOW WHAT YOU'VE DONE?
THIS WAS THE ONLY WAY THEY LET US LIVE.
THEN YOU DON'T LIVE.
WE'LL FOLLOW YOU.
WE'LL PUT YOU ON THE POLE.
IT'S OUR RIGHT. THIS IS OUR BUILDING.
HUSH UP, LADY.
WHY DON'T YOU JUST HUSH A WHILE?
GNNT

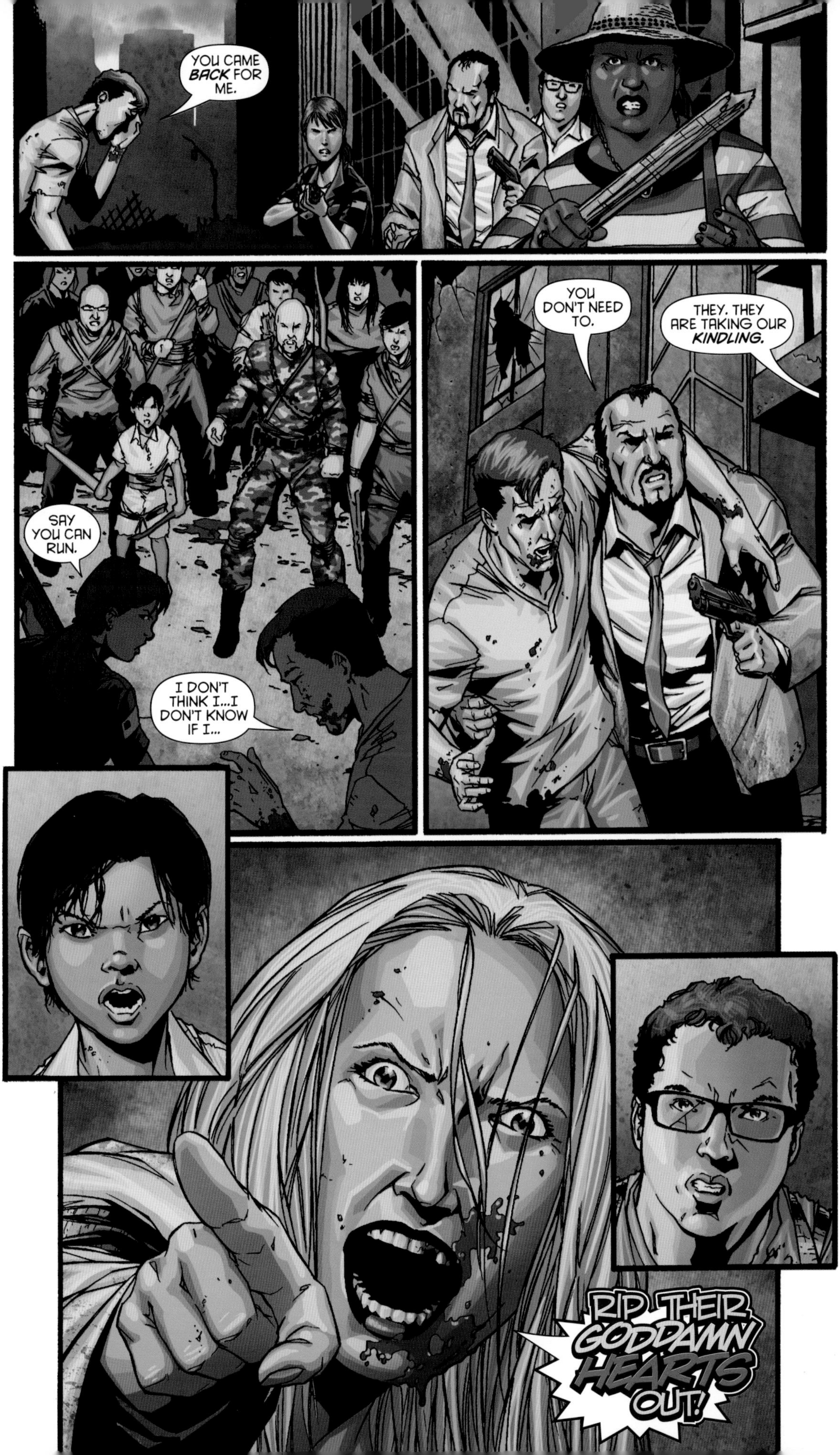
YOU CAME BACK FOR ME.
SAY YOU CAN RUN.
I DON'T THINK I...I DON'T KNOW IF I...
YOU DON'T NEED TO.
THEY. THEY ARE TAKING OUR KINDLING.
RIP THEIR GODDAMN HEARTS OUT!

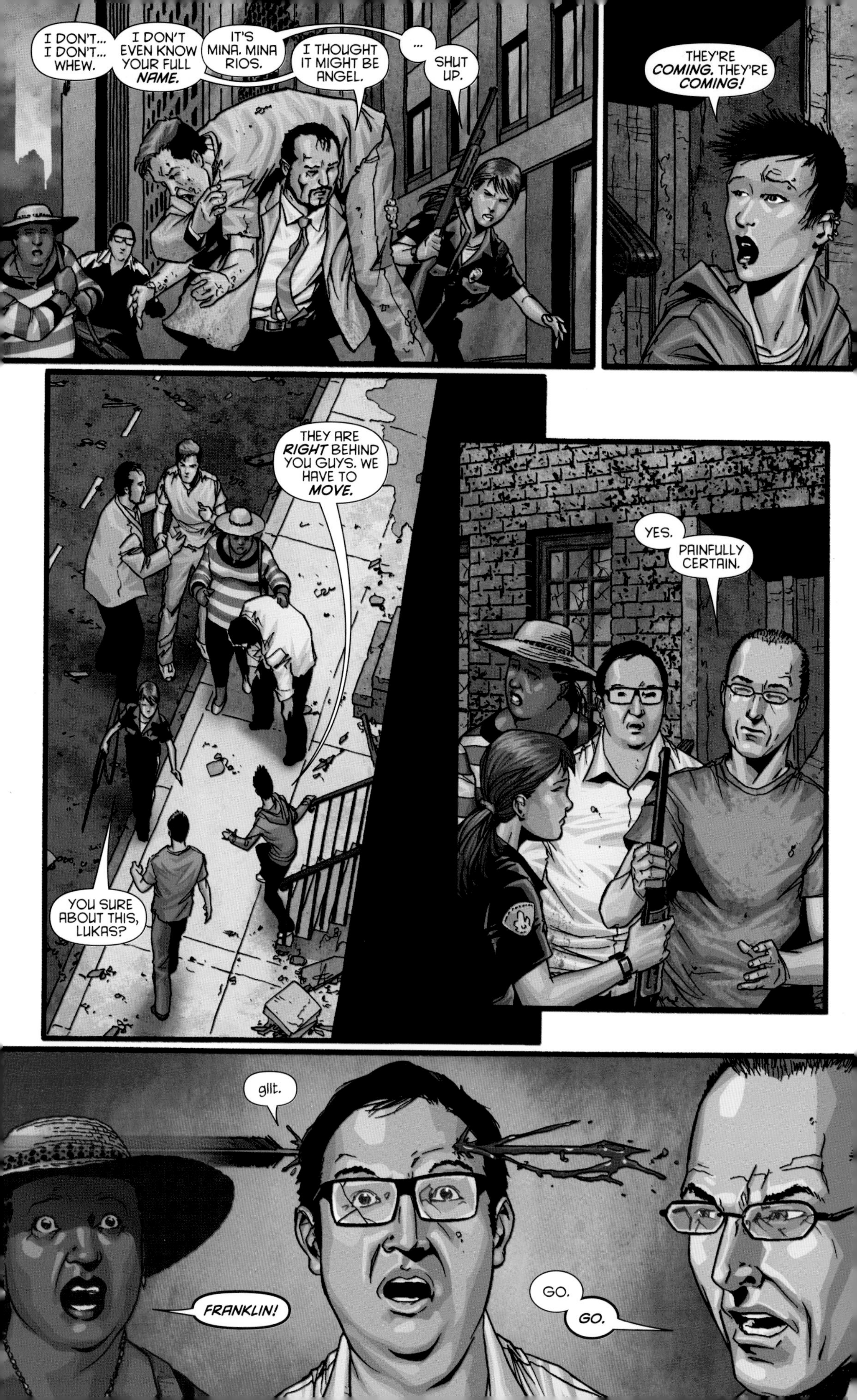
I DON'T... I DON'T... WHEW.
I DON'T EVEN KNOW YOUR FULL NAME.
IT'S MINA. MINA RIOS.
I THOUGHT IT MIGHT BE ANGEL.
...
SHUT UP.
THEY'RE COMING. THEY'RE COMING!
THEY ARE RIGHT BEHIND YOU GUYS. WE HAVE TO MOVE.
YOU SURE ABOUT THIS, LUKAS?
YES.
PAINFULLY CERTAIN.
gllt.
FRANKLIN!
GO.
GO.

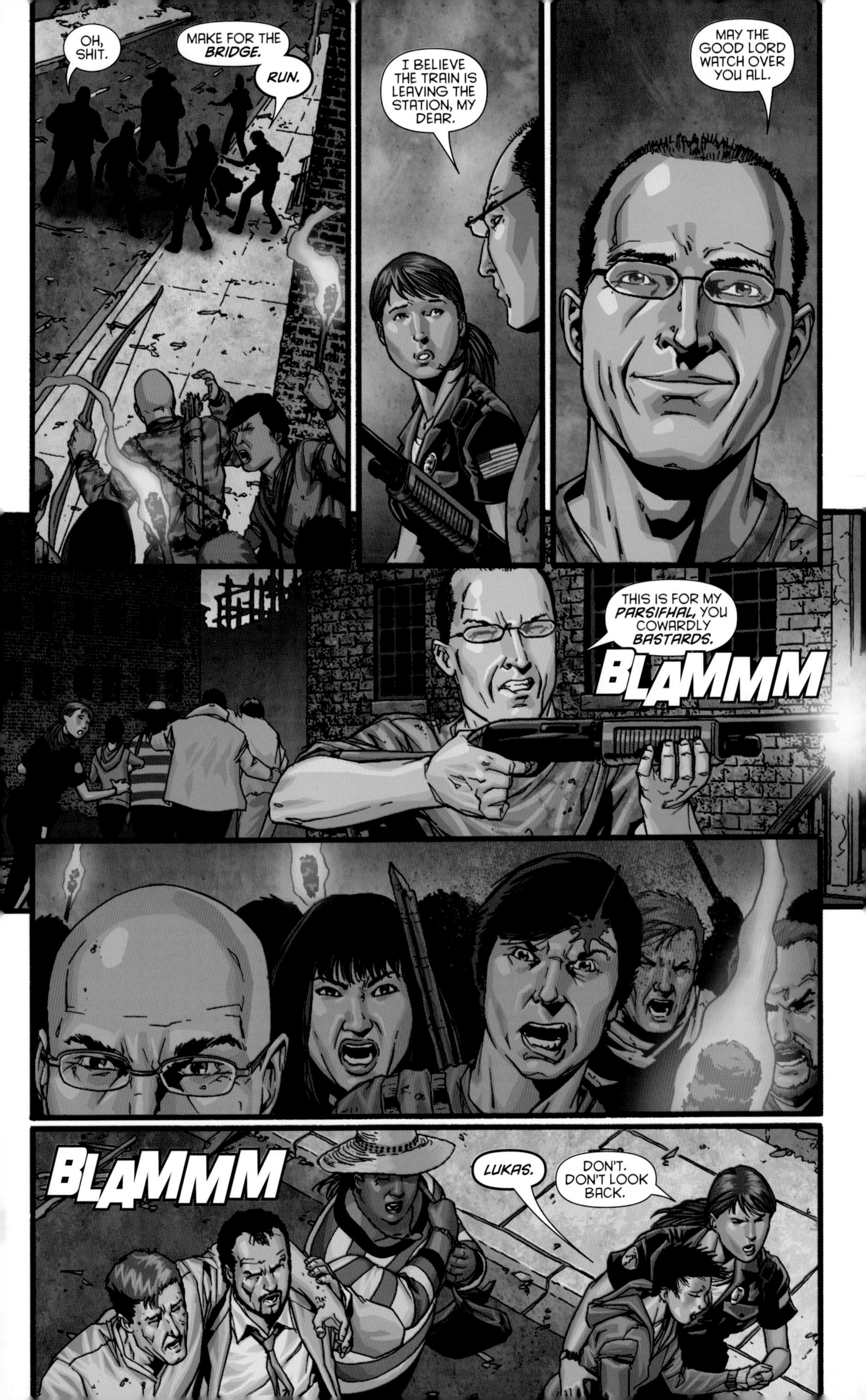

OH, SHIT.
MAKE FOR THE BRIDGE.
RUN.
I BELIEVE THE TRAIN IS LEAVING THE STATION, MY DEAR.
MAY THE GOOD LORD WATCH OVER YOU ALL.
THIS IS FOR MY PARSIFHAL, YOU COWARDLY BASTARDS.
BLAMMM
BLAMMM
LUKAS.
DON'T. DON'T LOOK BACK.

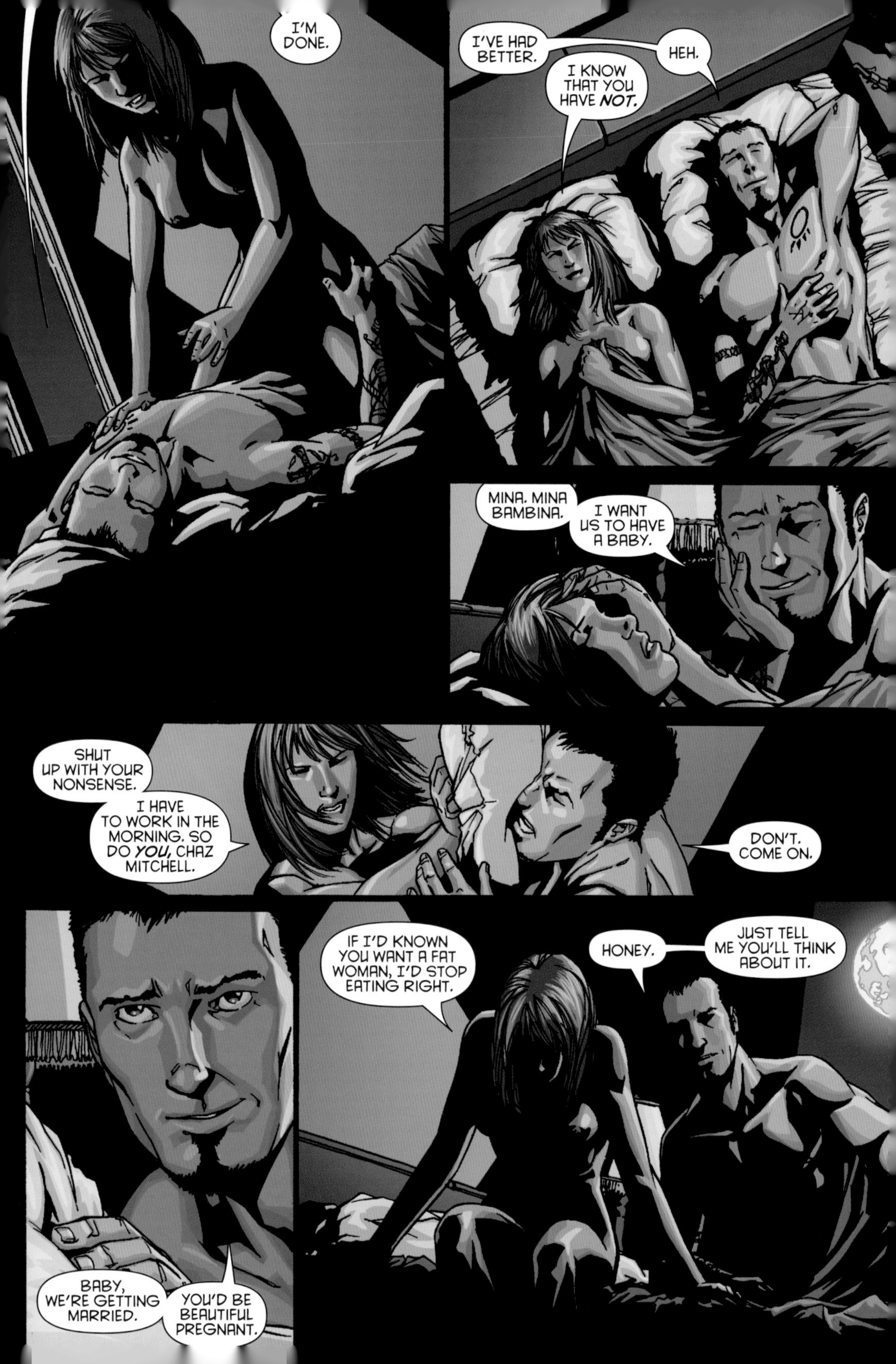
I'M DONE.
I'VE HAD BETTER.
HEH.
I KNOW THAT YOU HAVE *NOT.*
MINA. MINA BAMBINA.
I WANT US TO HAVE A BABY.
SHUT UP WITH YOUR NONSENSE.
I HAVE TO WORK IN THE MORNING. SO DO *YOU,* CHAZ MITCHELL.
DON'T. COME ON.
BABY, WE'RE GETTING MARRIED.
YOU'D BE BEAUTIFUL PREGNANT.
IF I'D KNOWN YOU WANT A FAT WOMAN, I'D STOP EATING RIGHT.
HONEY.
JUST TELL ME YOU'LL THINK ABOUT IT.

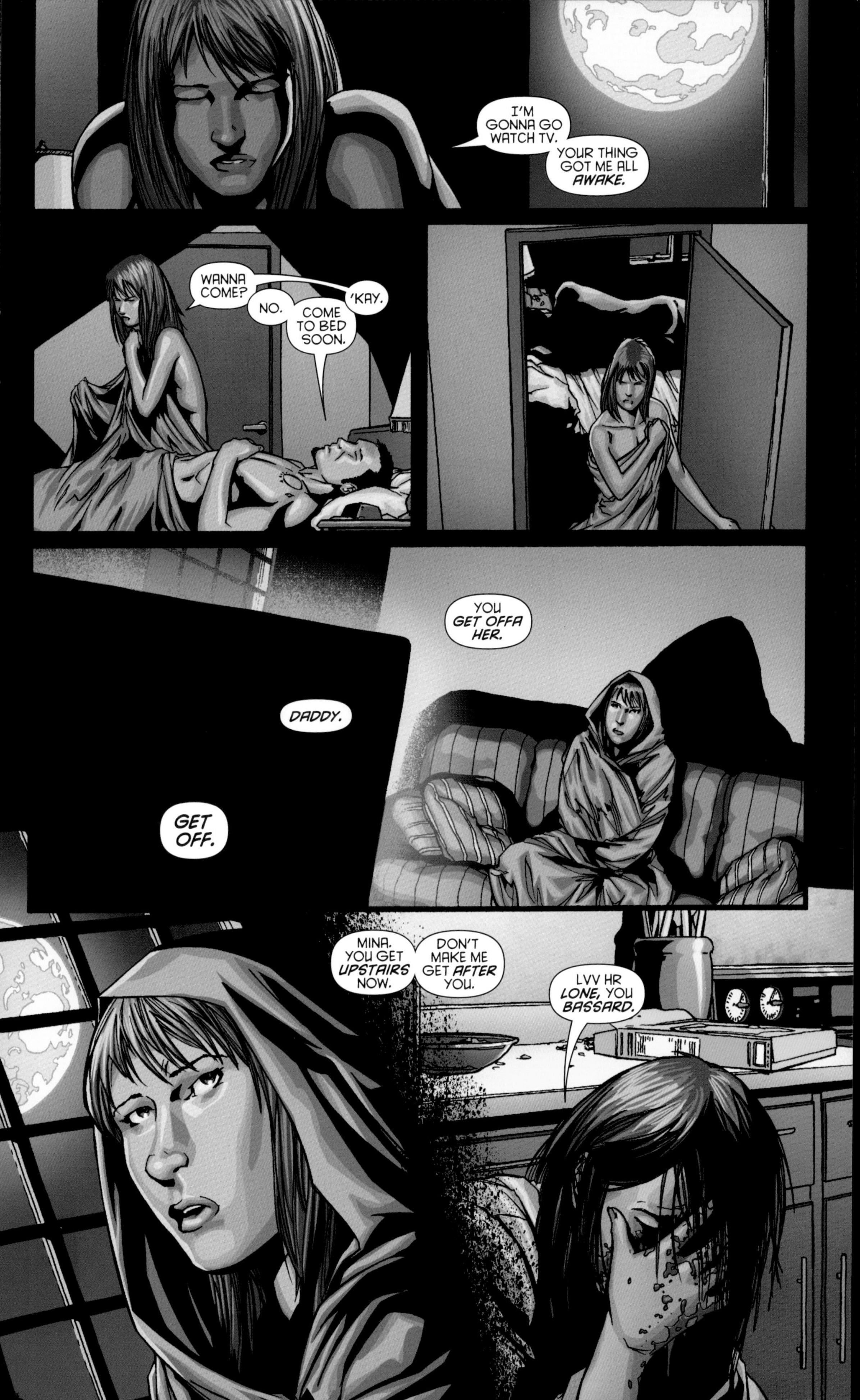
I'M GONNA GO WATCH TV.
YOUR THING GOT ME ALL *AWAKE.*
WANNA COME?
NO.
'KAY.
COME TO BED SOON.
YOU *GET OFFA HER.*
DADDY.
GET OFF.
MINA. YOU GET *UPSTAIRS* NOW.
DON'T MAKE ME GET *AFTER* YOU.
LVV HR *LONE,* YOU *BASSARD.*

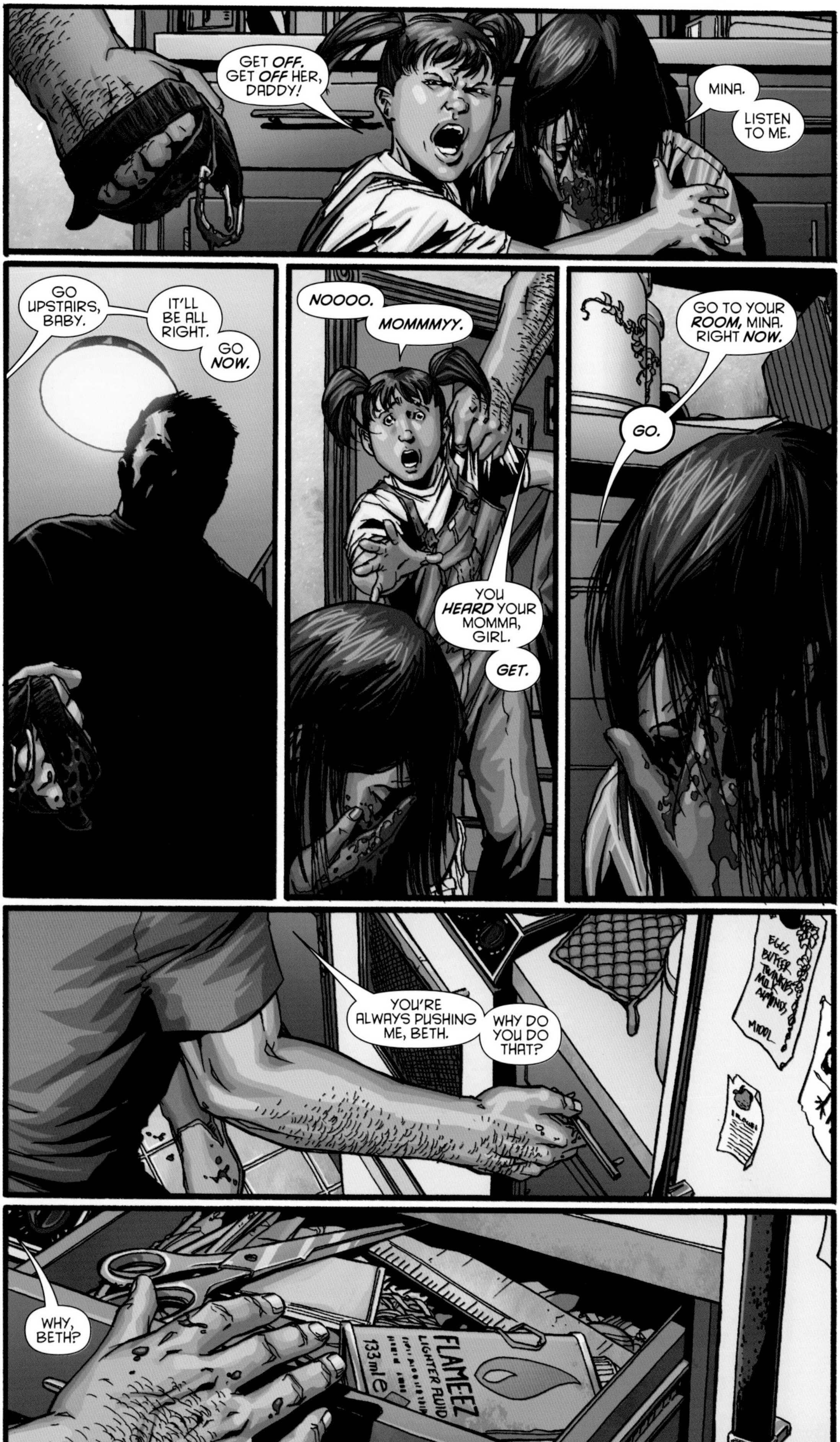

GET *OFF*. GET *OFF* HER, DADDY!
MINA.
LISTEN TO ME.
GO UPSTAIRS, BABY.
IT'LL BE ALL RIGHT.
GO *NOW.*
NOOOO.
MOMMMYY.
YOU *HEARD* YOUR MOMMA, GIRL.
GET.
GO TO YOUR *ROOM,* MINA. RIGHT *NOW.*
GO.
YOU'RE ALWAYS PUSHING ME, BETH.
WHY DO YOU DO THAT?
WHY, BETH?
FLAMEEZ
LIGHTER FLUID
133 ml ℮

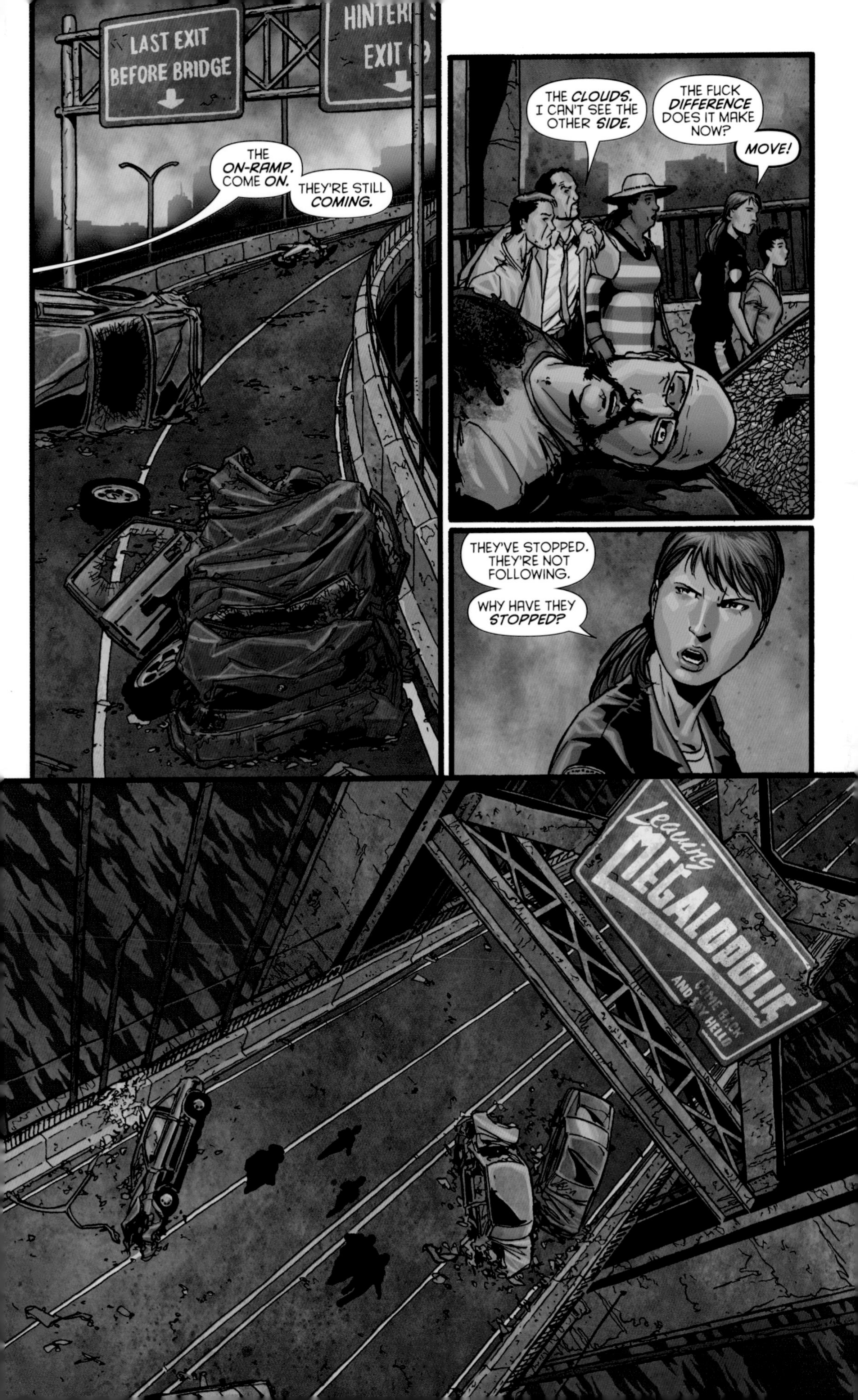
LAST EXIT BEFORE BRIDGE
THE ON-RAMP. COME ON.
THEY'RE STILL COMING.
THE CLOUDS. I CAN'T SEE THE OTHER SIDE.
THE FUCK DIFFERENCE DOES IT MAKE NOW?
MOVE!
THEY'VE STOPPED. THEY'RE NOT FOLLOWING.
WHY HAVE THEY STOPPED?
Leaving MEGALOPOLIS
COME BACK AND SAY HELLO

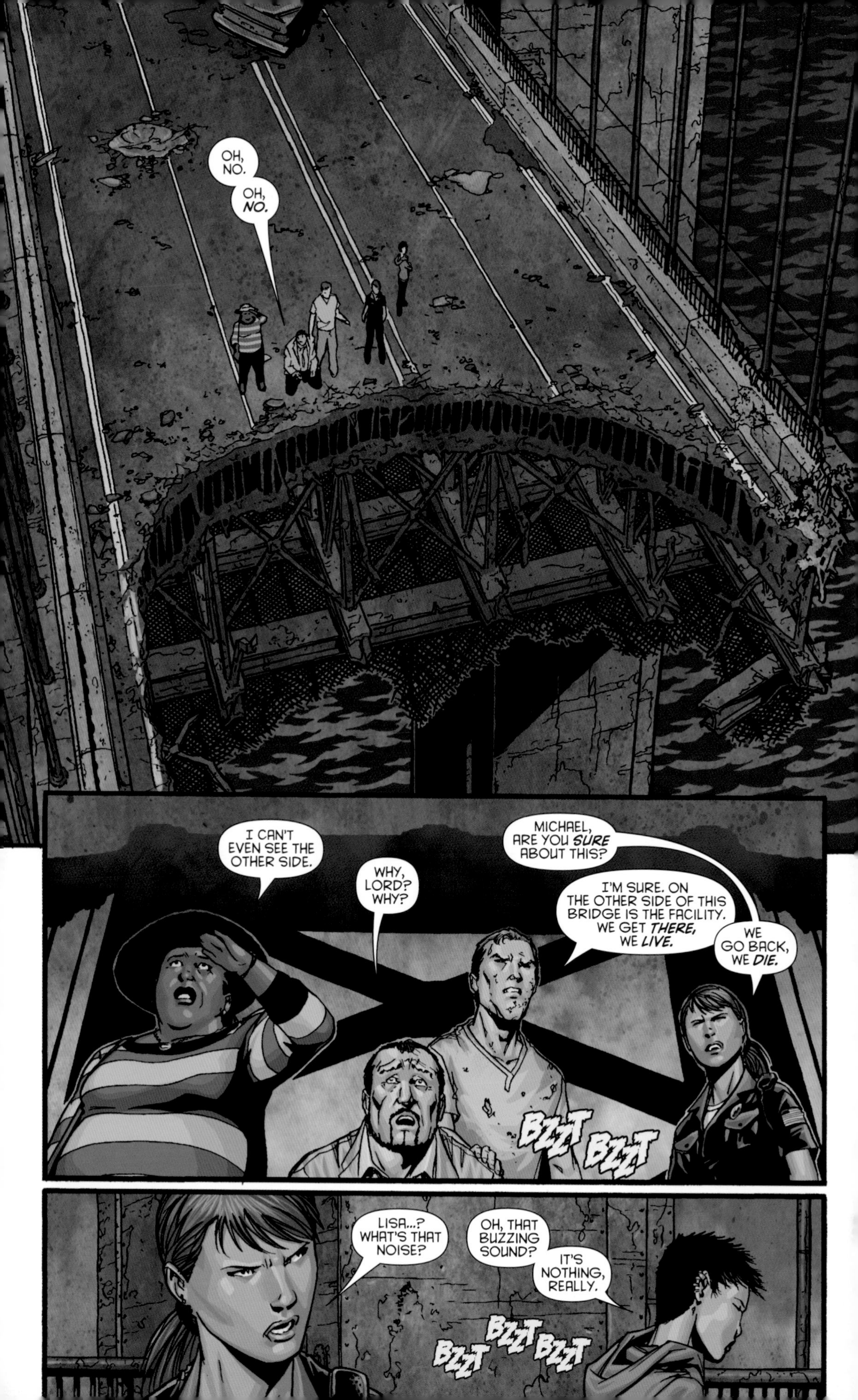
OH, NO.
OH, NO.
I CAN'T EVEN SEE THE OTHER SIDE.
WHY, LORD? WHY?
MICHAEL, ARE YOU SURE ABOUT THIS?
I'M SURE. ON THE OTHER SIDE OF THIS BRIDGE IS THE FACILITY. WE GET THERE, WE LIVE.
WE GO BACK, WE DIE.
BZZZT BZZZT
LISA...? WHAT'S THAT NOISE?
OH, THAT BUZZING SOUND?
IT'S NOTHING, REALLY.
BZZT BZZZT BZZZT

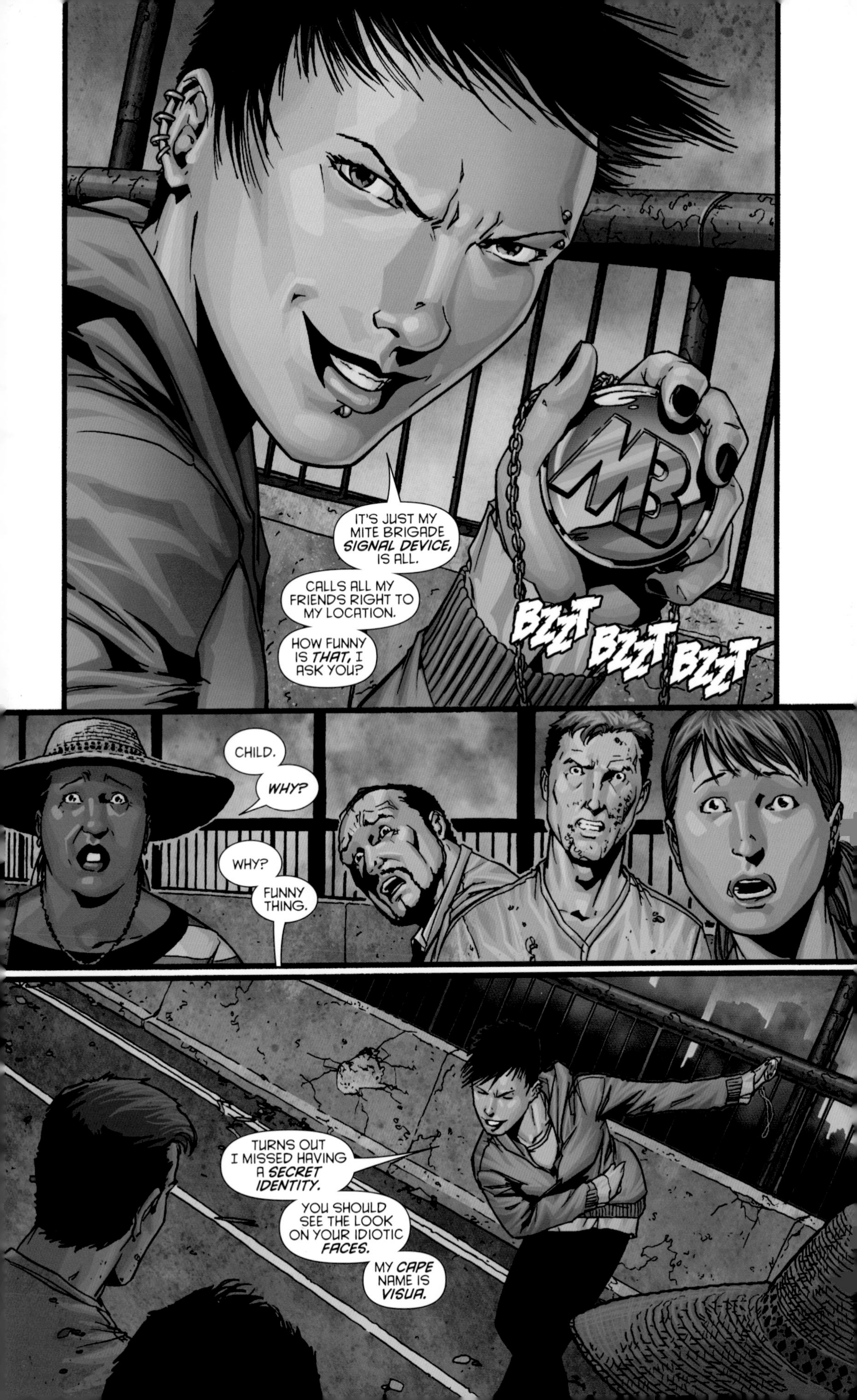
IT'S JUST MY MITE BRIGADE SIGNAL DEVICE, IS ALL.
CALLS ALL MY FRIENDS RIGHT TO MY LOCATION.
HOW FUNNY IS THAT, I ASK YOU?
BZZZT BZZZT BZZZT
CHILD.
WHY?
WHY?
FUNNY THING.
TURNS OUT I MISSED HAVING A SECRET IDENTITY.
YOU SHOULD SEE THE LOOK ON YOUR IDIOTIC FACES.
MY CAPE NAME IS VISUA.

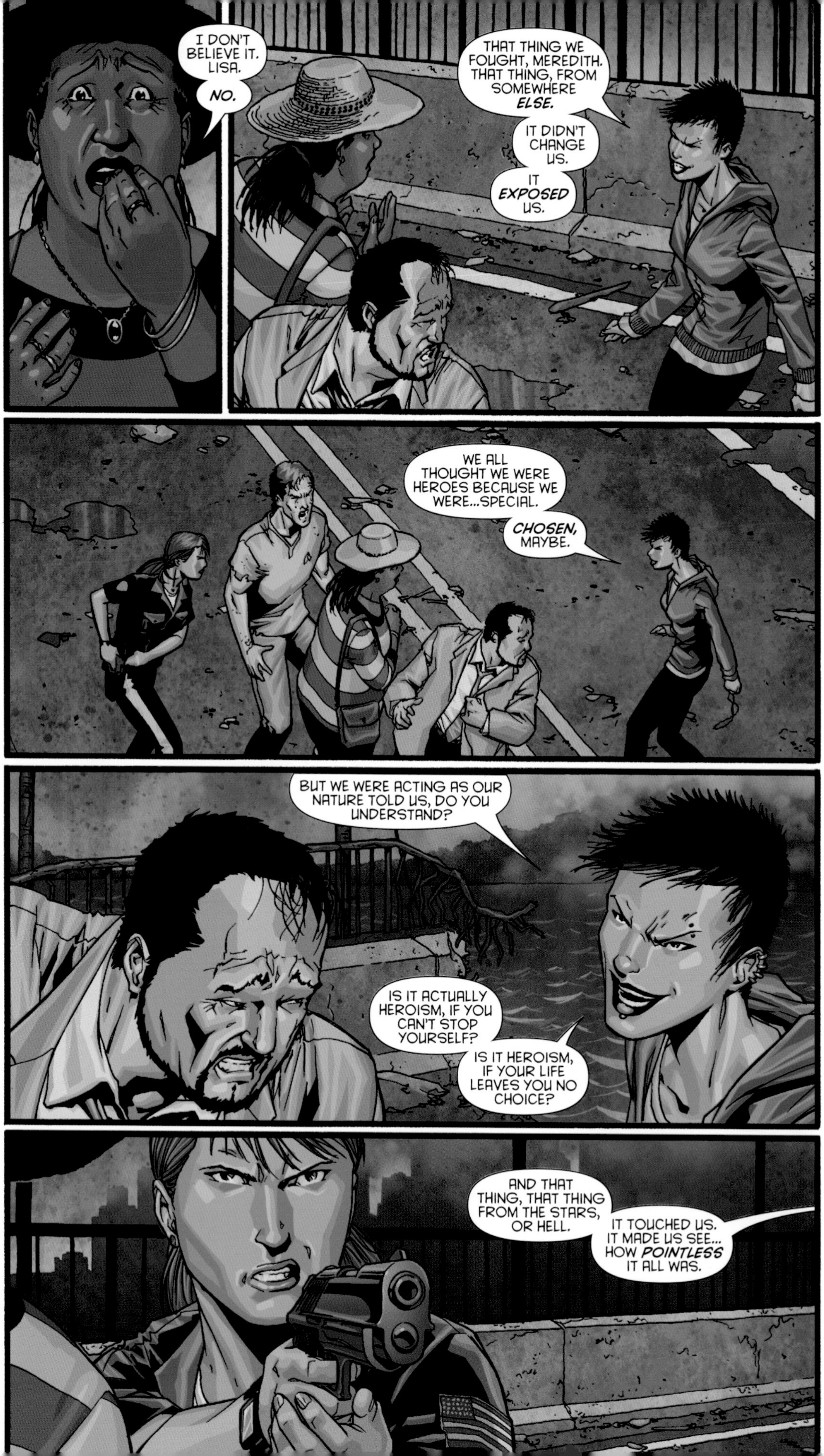

I DON'T BELIEVE IT. LISA.
NO.
THAT THING WE FOUGHT, MEREDITH. THAT THING, FROM SOMEWHERE ELSE.
IT DIDN'T CHANGE US.
IT EXPOSED US.
WE ALL THOUGHT WE WERE HEROES BECAUSE WE WERE...SPECIAL.
CHOSEN, MAYBE.
BUT WE WERE ACTING AS OUR NATURE TOLD US, DO YOU UNDERSTAND?
IS IT ACTUALLY HEROISM, IF YOU CAN'T STOP YOURSELF?
IS IT HEROISM, IF YOUR LIFE LEAVES YOU NO CHOICE?
AND THAT THING, THAT THING FROM THE STARS, OR HELL.
IT TOUCHED US. IT MADE US SEE... HOW POINTLESS IT ALL WAS.

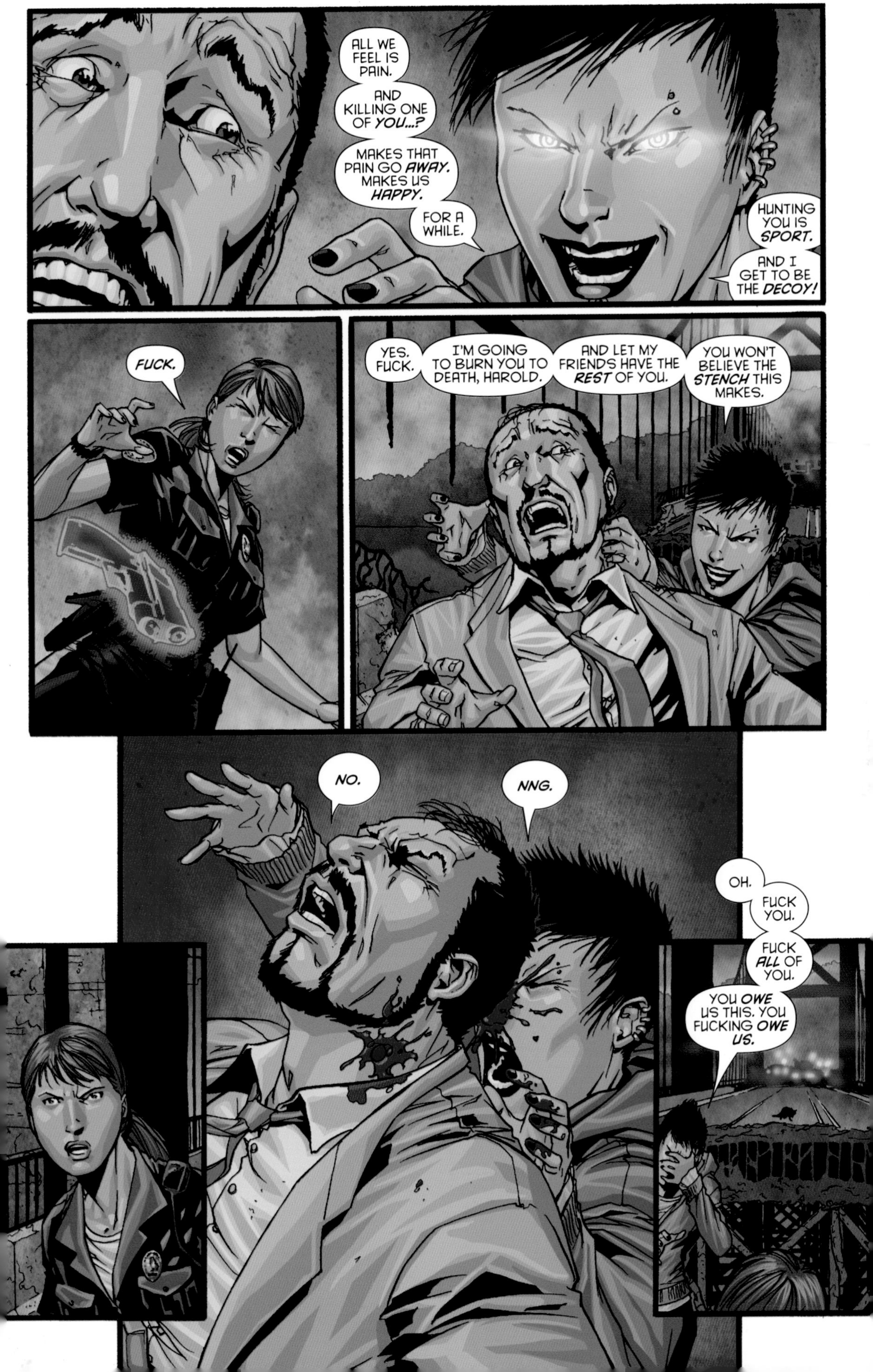
ALL WE FEEL IS PAIN.
AND KILLING ONE OF YOU...?
MAKES THAT PAIN GO AWAY. MAKES US HAPPY.
FOR A WHILE.
HUNTING YOU IS SPORT.
AND I GET TO BE THE DECOY!
FUCK.
YES. FUCK.
I'M GOING TO BURN YOU TO DEATH, HAROLD.
AND LET MY FRIENDS HAVE THE REST OF YOU.
YOU WON'T BELIEVE THE STENCH THIS MAKES.
NO.
NNG.
OH.
FUCK YOU.
FUCK ALL OF YOU.
YOU OWE US THIS. YOU FUCKING OWE US.

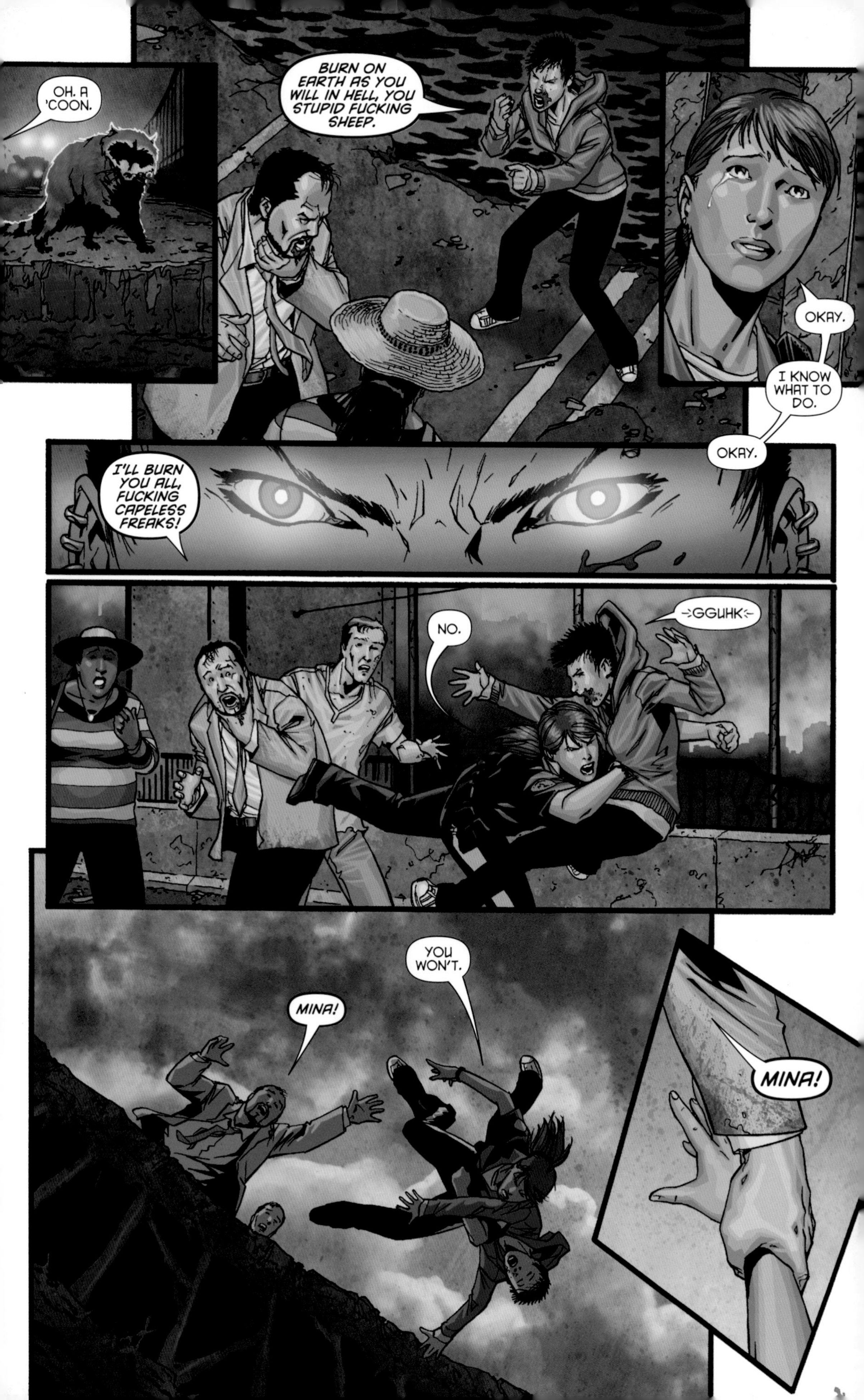
OH. A 'COON.
BURN ON EARTH AS YOU WILL IN HELL, YOU STUPID FUCKING SHEEP.
OKAY.
I KNOW WHAT TO DO.
OKAY.
I'LL BURN YOU ALL, FUCKING CAPELESS FREAKS!
NO.
GGUHK
MINA!
YOU WON'T.
MINA!

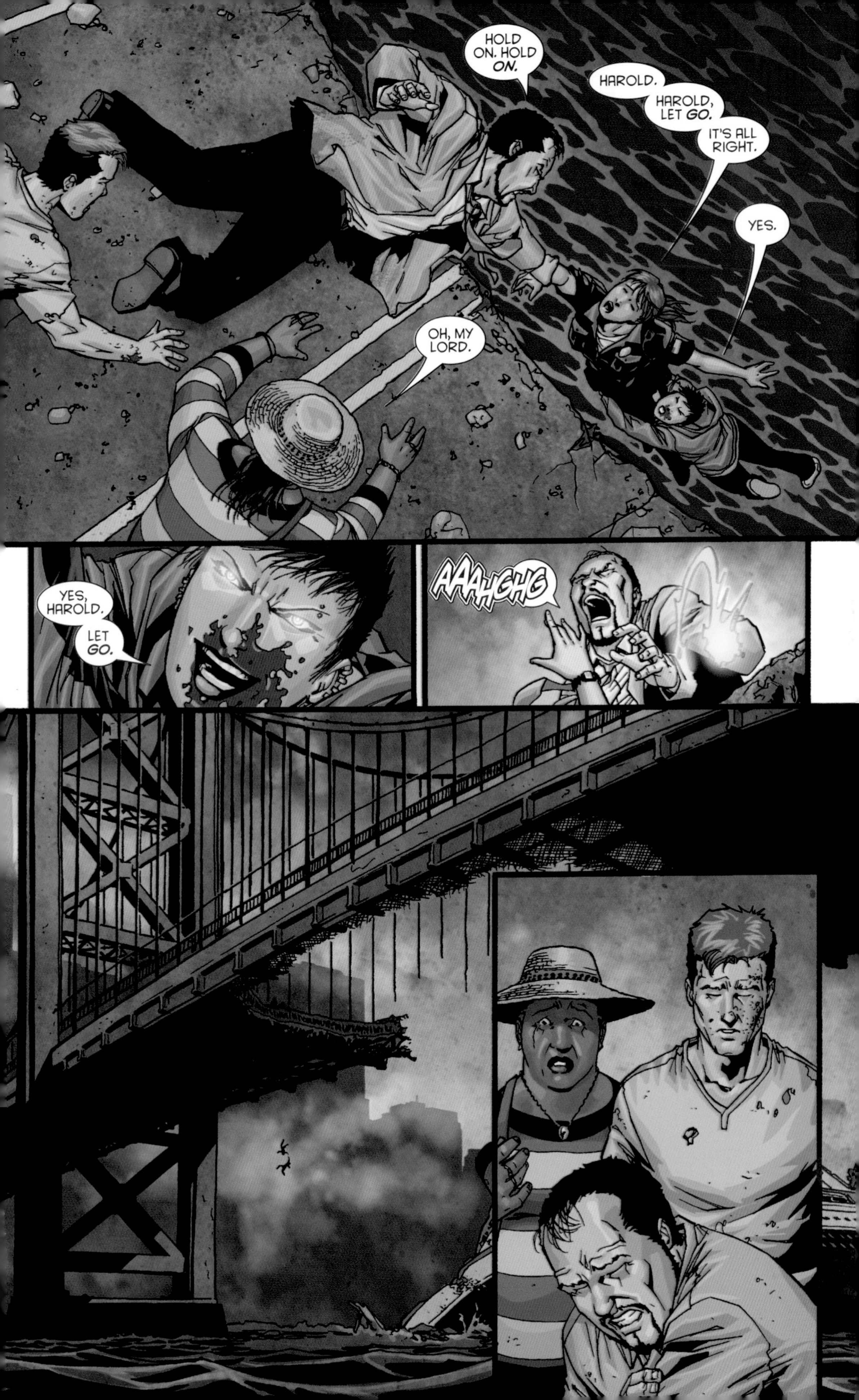
HOLD ON. HOLD ON.
HAROLD.
HAROLD, LET GO.
IT'S ALL RIGHT.
YES.
OH, MY LORD.
YES, HAROLD.
LET GO.
AAAHGHG

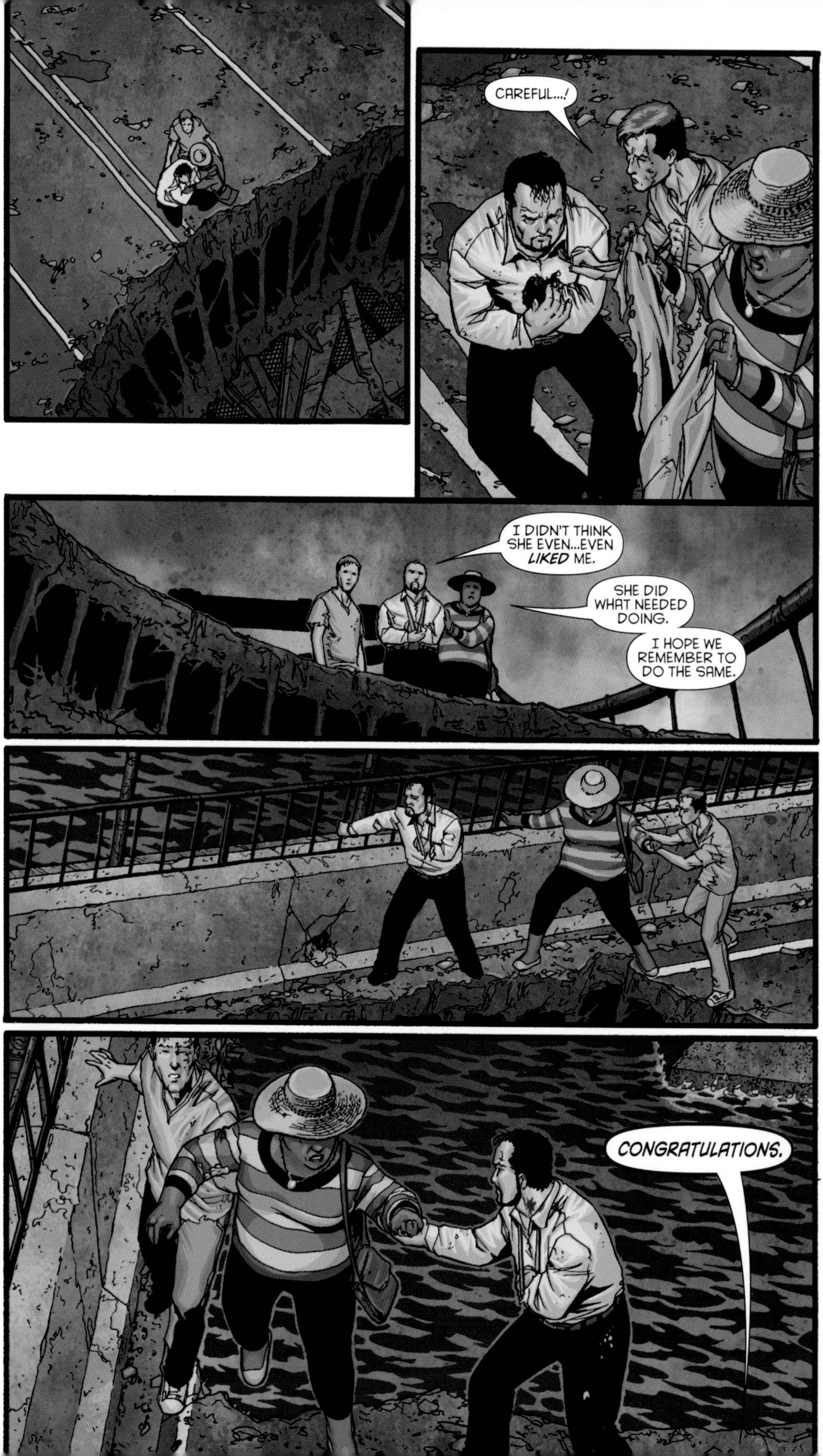
CAREFUL...!
I DIDN'T THINK SHE EVEN...EVEN LIKED ME.
SHE DID WHAT NEEDED DOING.
I HOPE WE REMEMBER TO DO THE SAME.
CONGRATULATIONS.

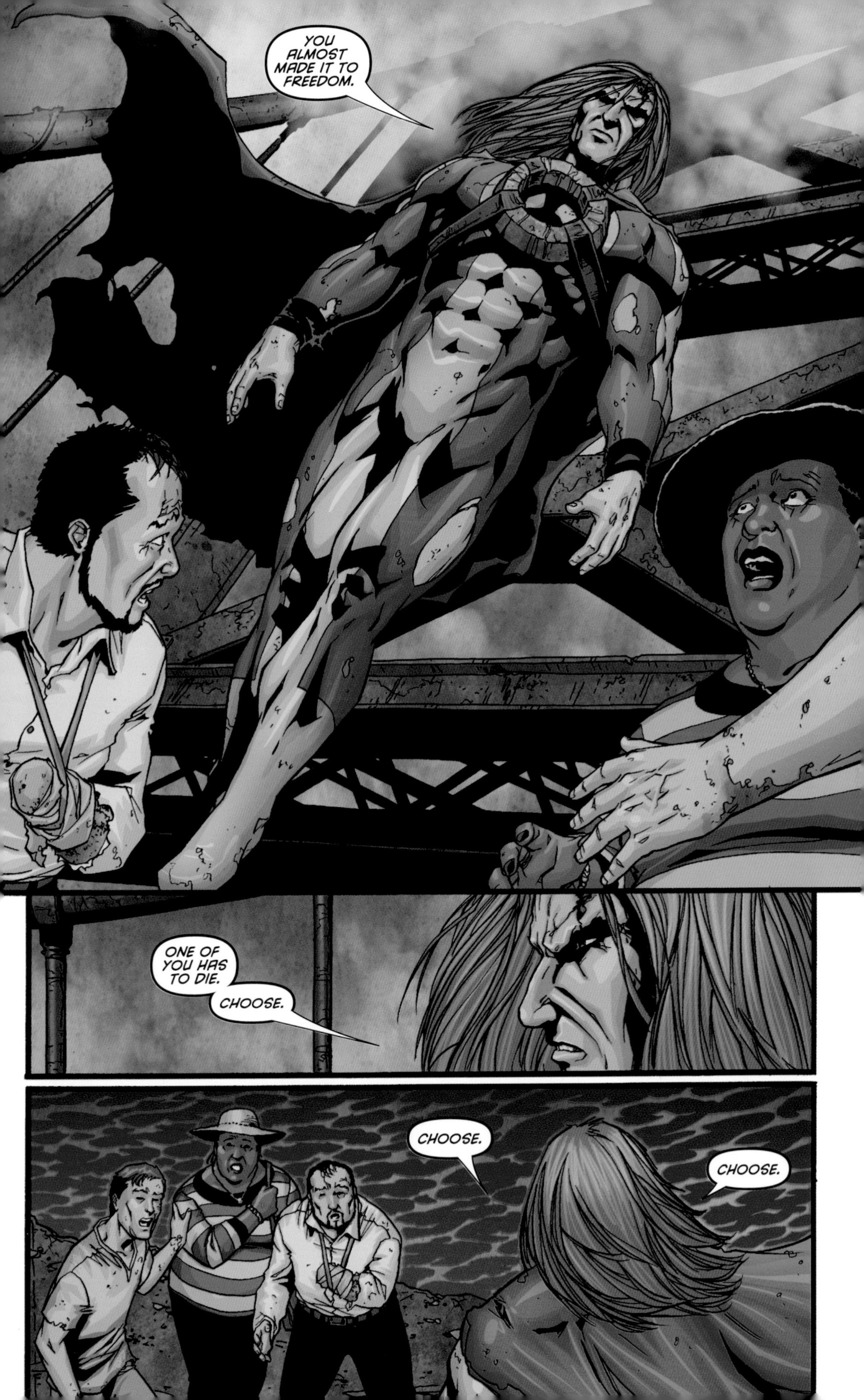
YOU ALMOST MADE IT TO FREEDOM.
ONE OF YOU HAS TO DIE.
CHOOSE.
CHOOSE.
CHOOSE.

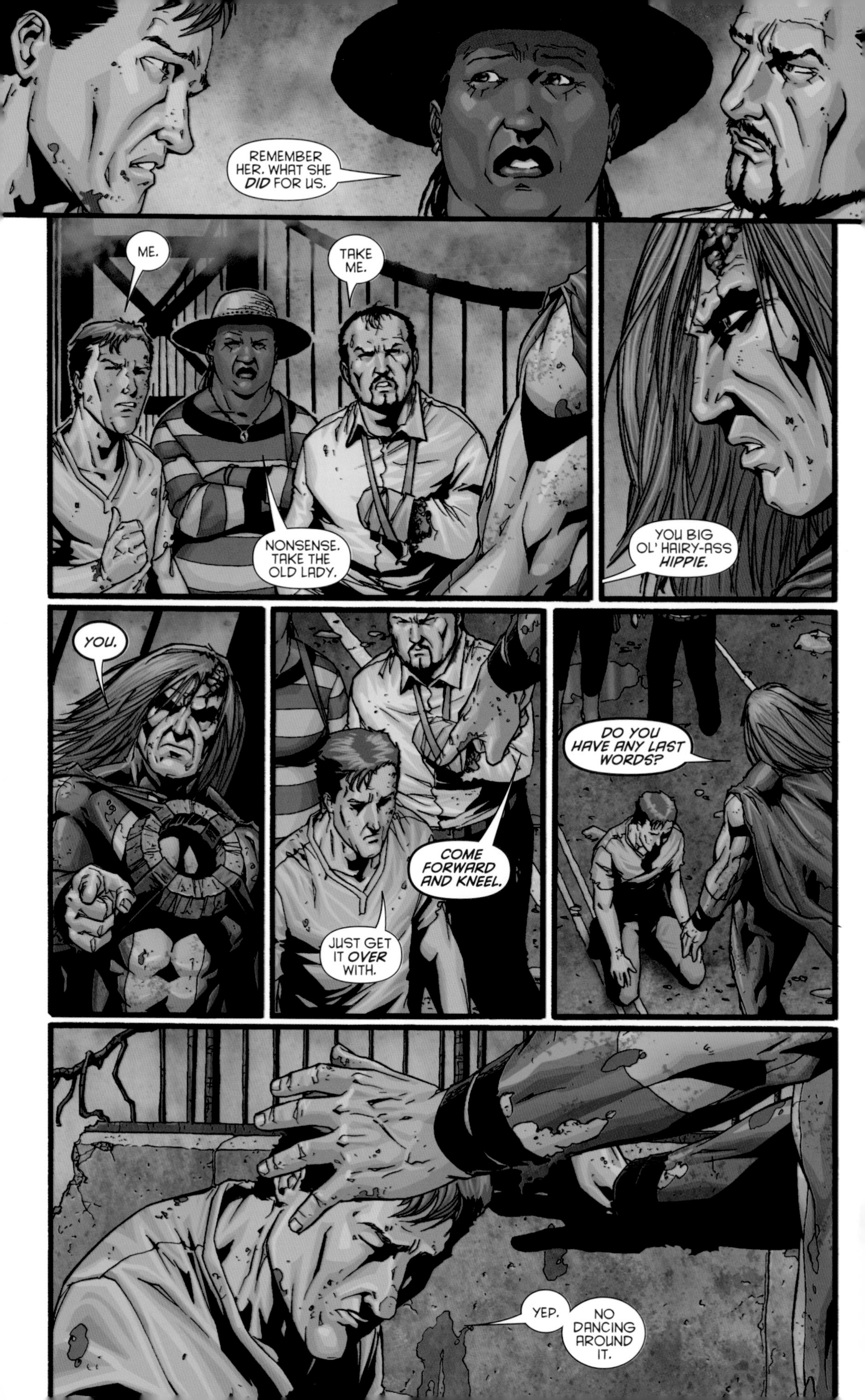
REMEMBER HER. WHAT SHE *DID* FOR US.
ME.
TAKE ME.
NONSENSE. TAKE THE OLD LADY.
YOU BIG OL' HAIRY-ASS *HIPPIE.*
YOU.
COME FORWARD AND KNEEL.
JUST GET IT *OVER* WITH.
DO YOU HAVE ANY LAST WORDS?
YEP.
NO DANCING AROUND IT.

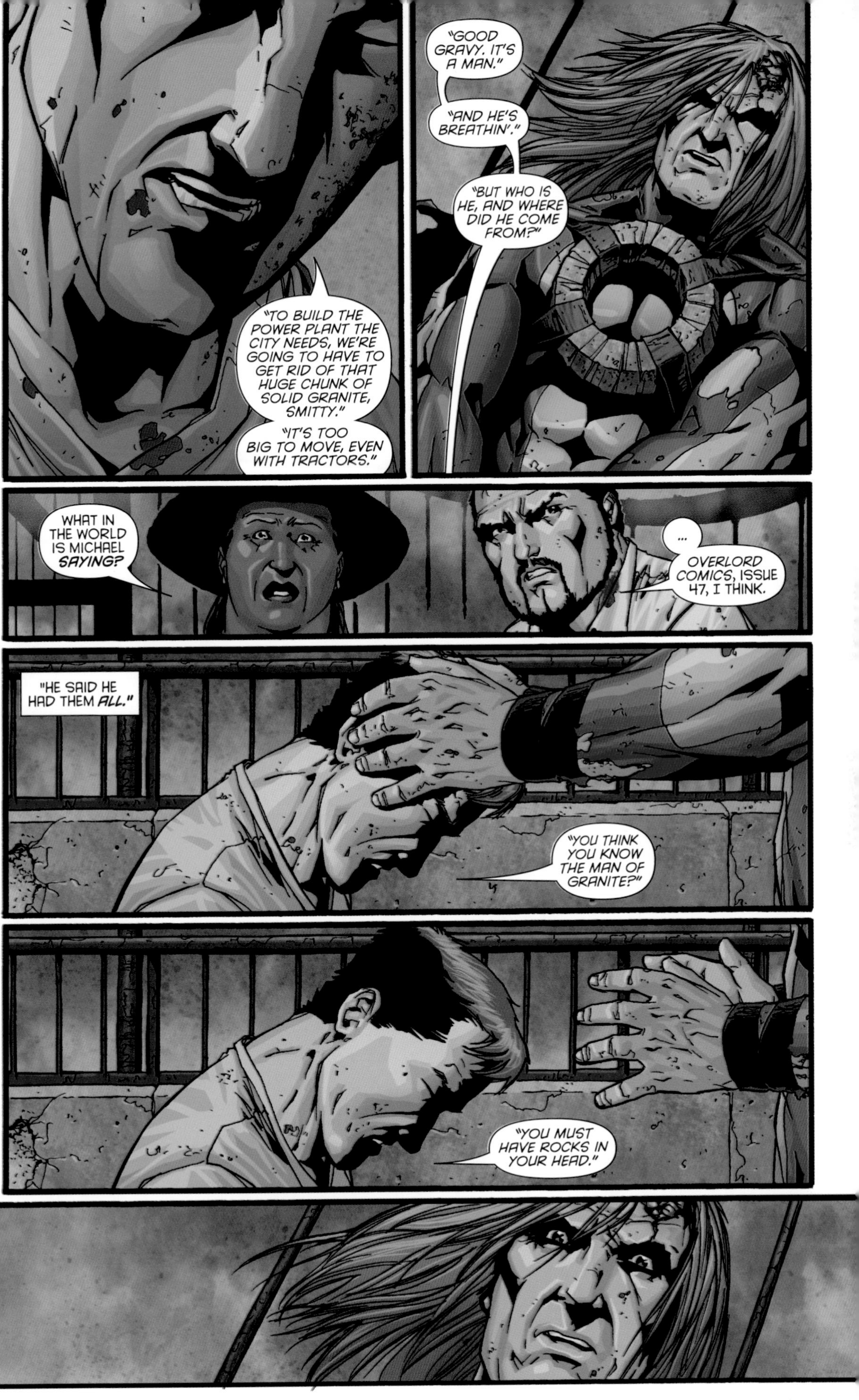
"TO BUILD THE POWER PLANT THE CITY NEEDS, WE'RE GOING TO HAVE TO GET RID OF THAT HUGE CHUNK OF SOLID GRANITE, SMITTY."
"IT'S TOO BIG TO MOVE, EVEN WITH TRACTORS."
"GOOD GRAVY. IT'S A MAN."
"AND HE'S BREATHIN'."
"BUT WHO IS HE, AND WHERE DID HE COME FROM?"
WHAT IN THE WORLD IS MICHAEL SAYING?
...
OVERLORD COMICS, ISSUE 47, I THINK.
"HE SAID HE HAD THEM ALL."
"YOU THINK YOU KNOW THE MAN OF GRANITE?"
"YOU MUST HAVE ROCKS IN YOUR HEAD."

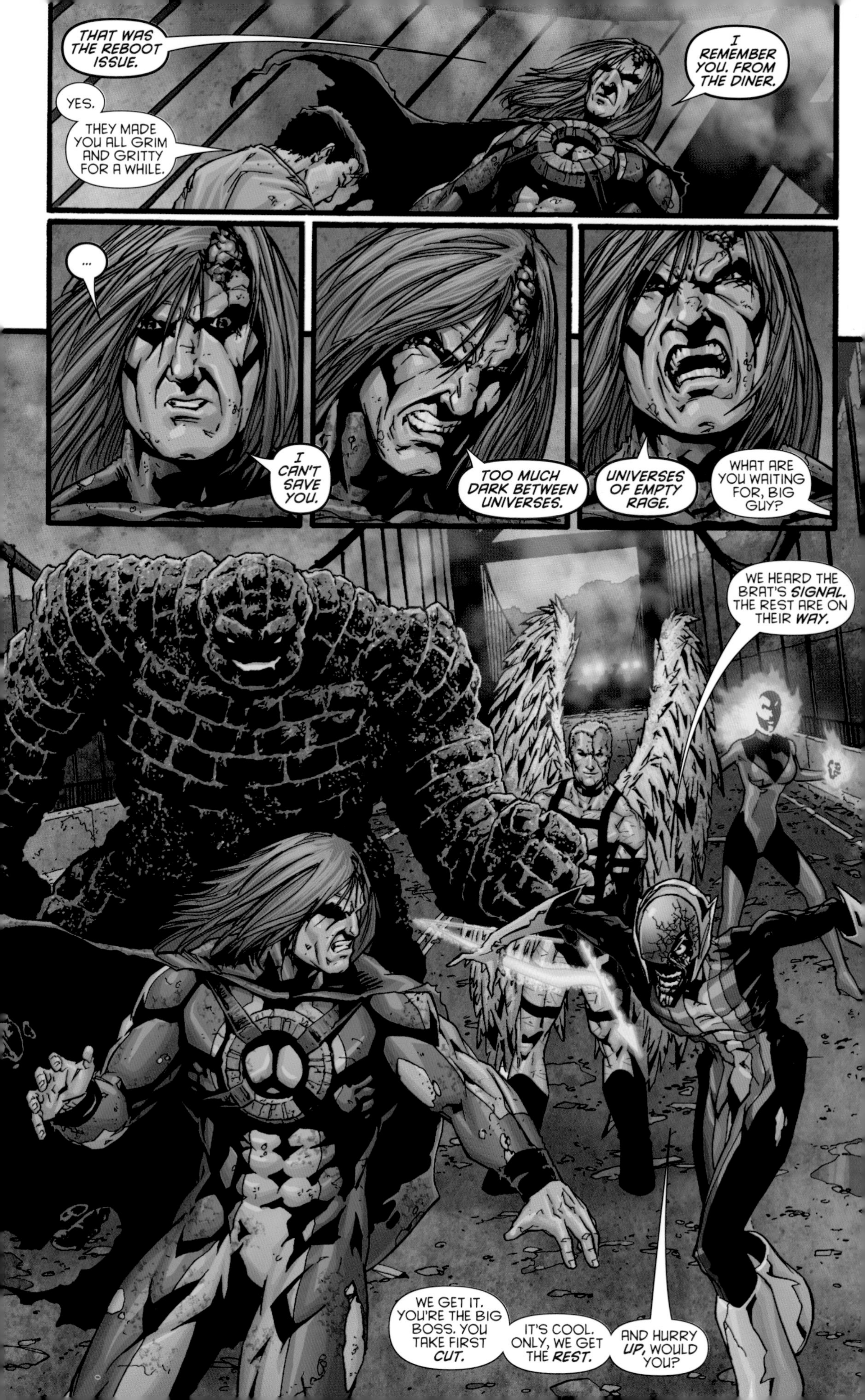
THAT WAS THE REBOOT ISSUE.
I REMEMBER YOU. FROM THE DINER.
YES.
THEY MADE YOU ALL GRIM AND GRITTY FOR A WHILE.
...
I CAN'T SAVE YOU.
TOO MUCH DARK BETWEEN UNIVERSES.
UNIVERSES OF EMPTY RAGE.
WHAT ARE YOU WAITING FOR, BIG GUY?
WE HEARD THE BRAT'S SIGNAL. THE REST ARE ON THEIR WAY.
WE GET IT. YOU'RE THE BIG BOSS. YOU TAKE FIRST CUT.
IT'S COOL. ONLY, WE GET THE REST.
AND HURRY UP, WOULD YOU?

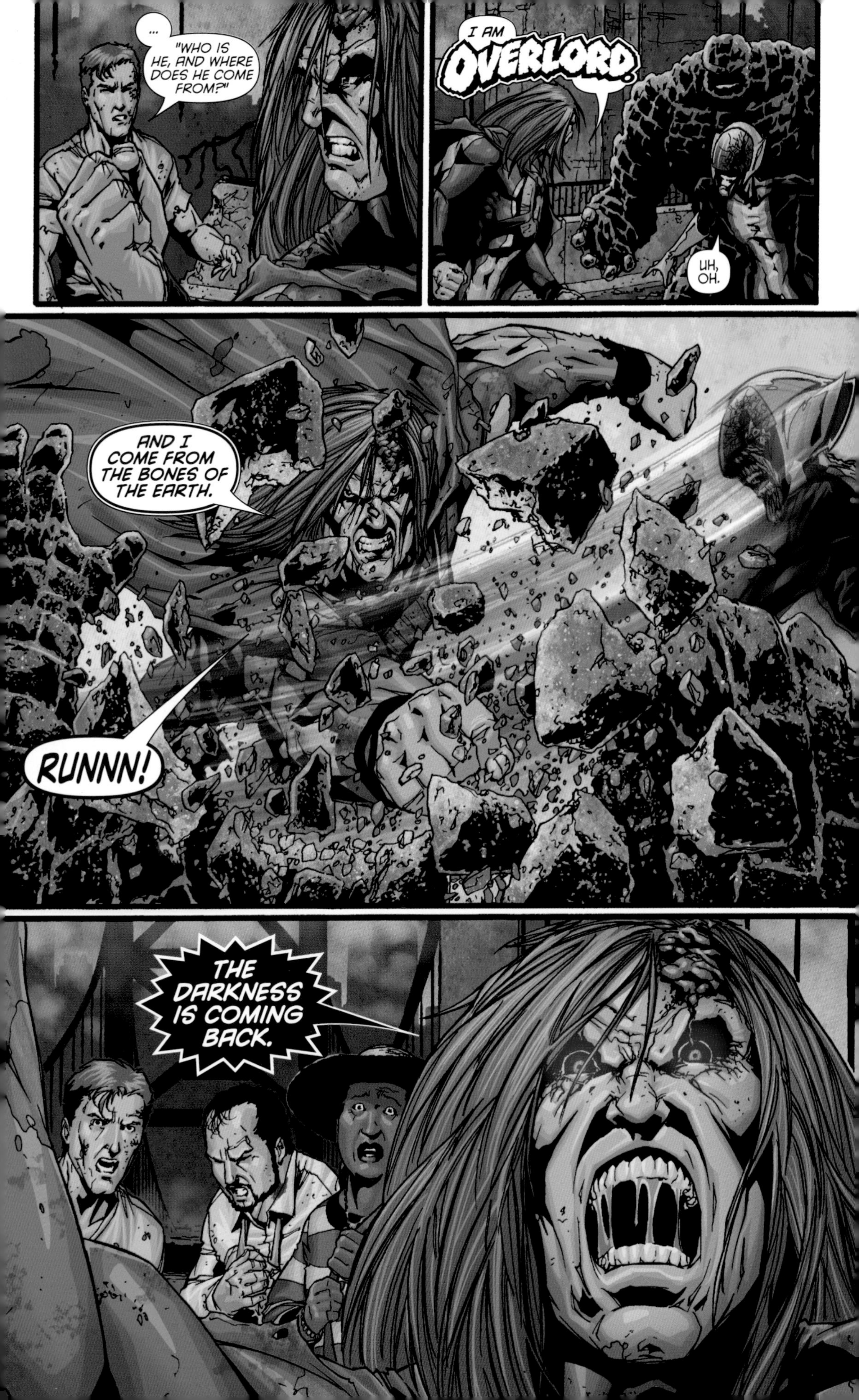
...
"WHO IS HE, AND WHERE DOES HE COME FROM?"
I AM OVERLORD.
UH, OH.
AND I COME FROM THE BONES OF THE EARTH.
RUNNN!
THE DARKNESS IS COMING BACK.

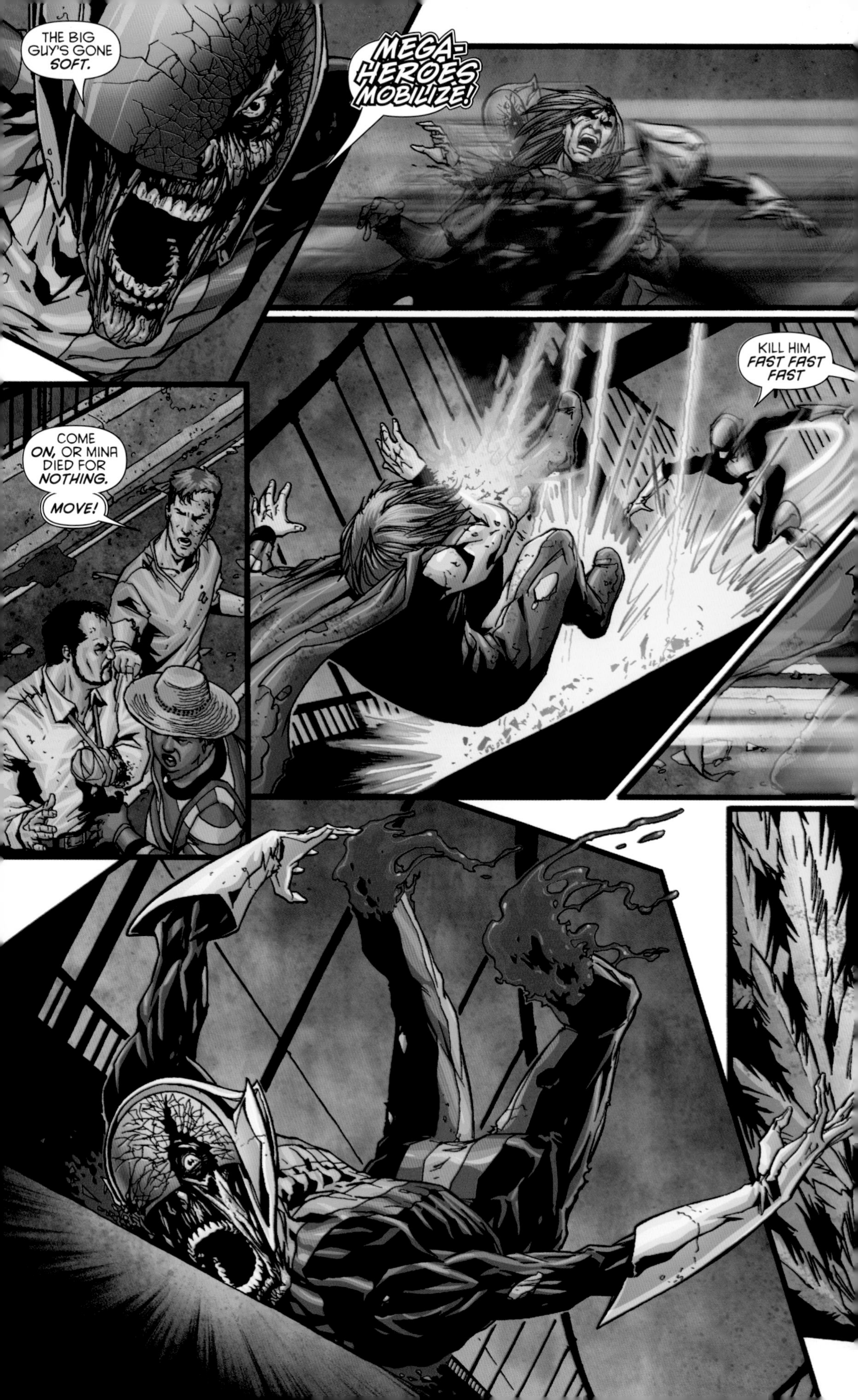
THE BIG GUY'S GONE SOFT.
MEGA-HEROES MOBILIZE!
KILL HIM FAST FAST FAST
COME ON, OR MINA DIED FOR NOTHING.
MOVE!

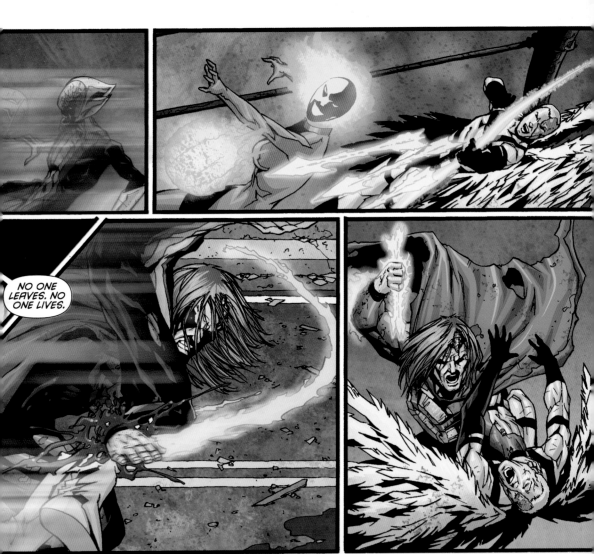

NO ONE LEAVES. NO ONE LIVES.

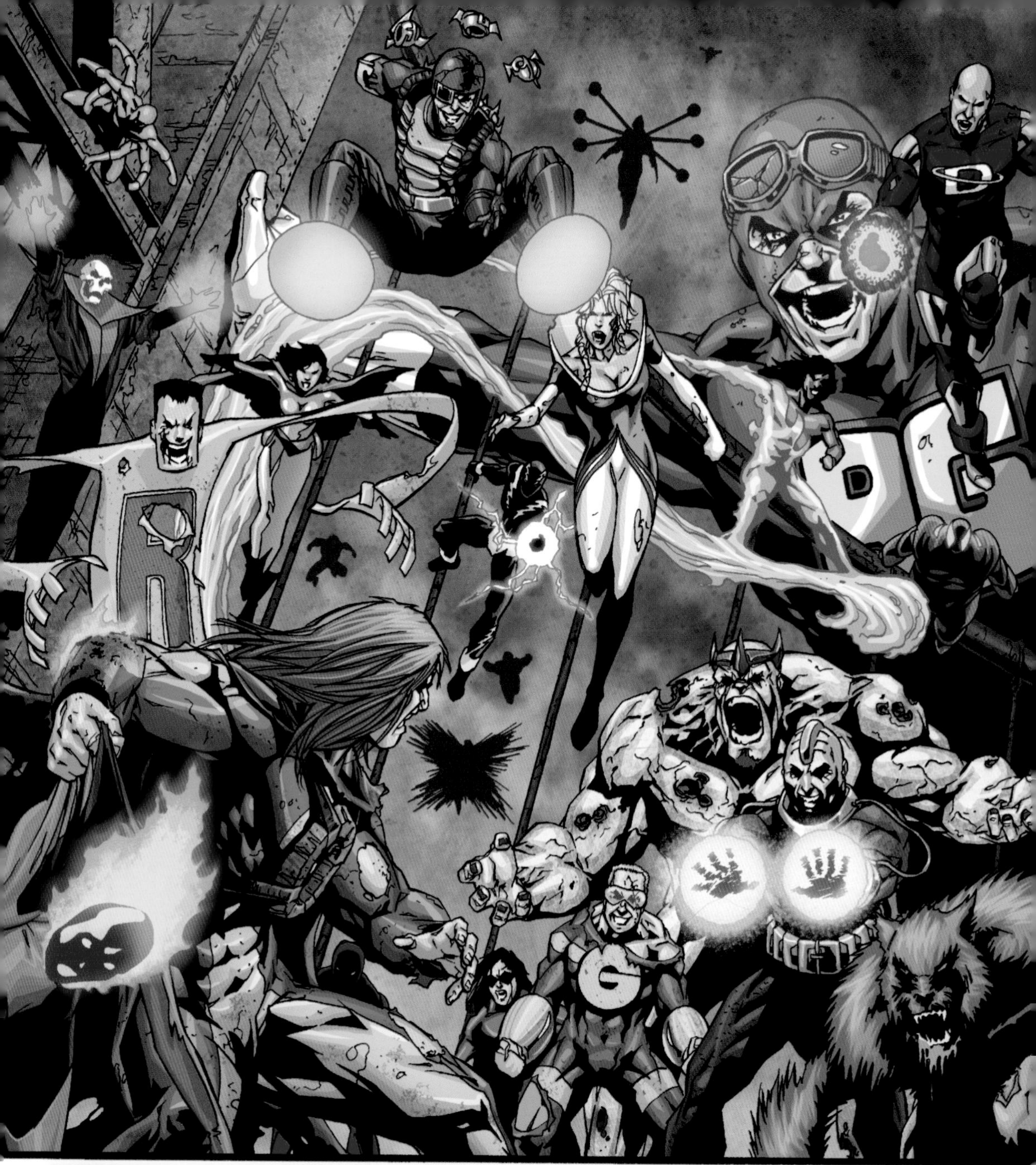

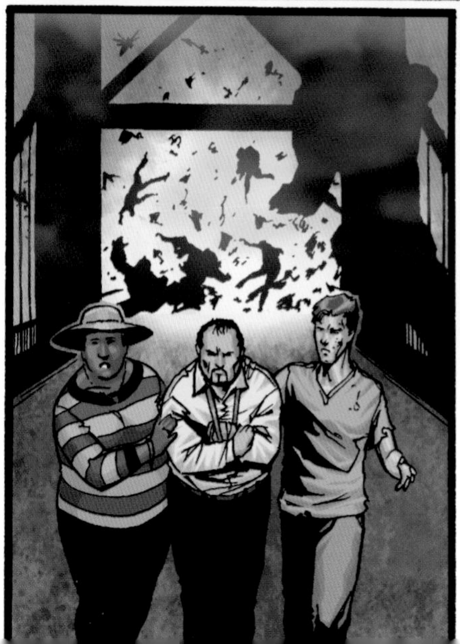

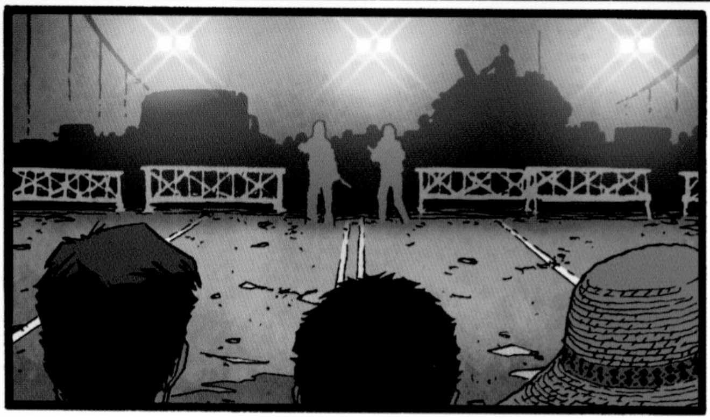

SENATOR BELL: And Colonel Culver, if I may ask one last question...

How LONG did you maintain the order to shoot any citizens attempting to leave Megalopolis?

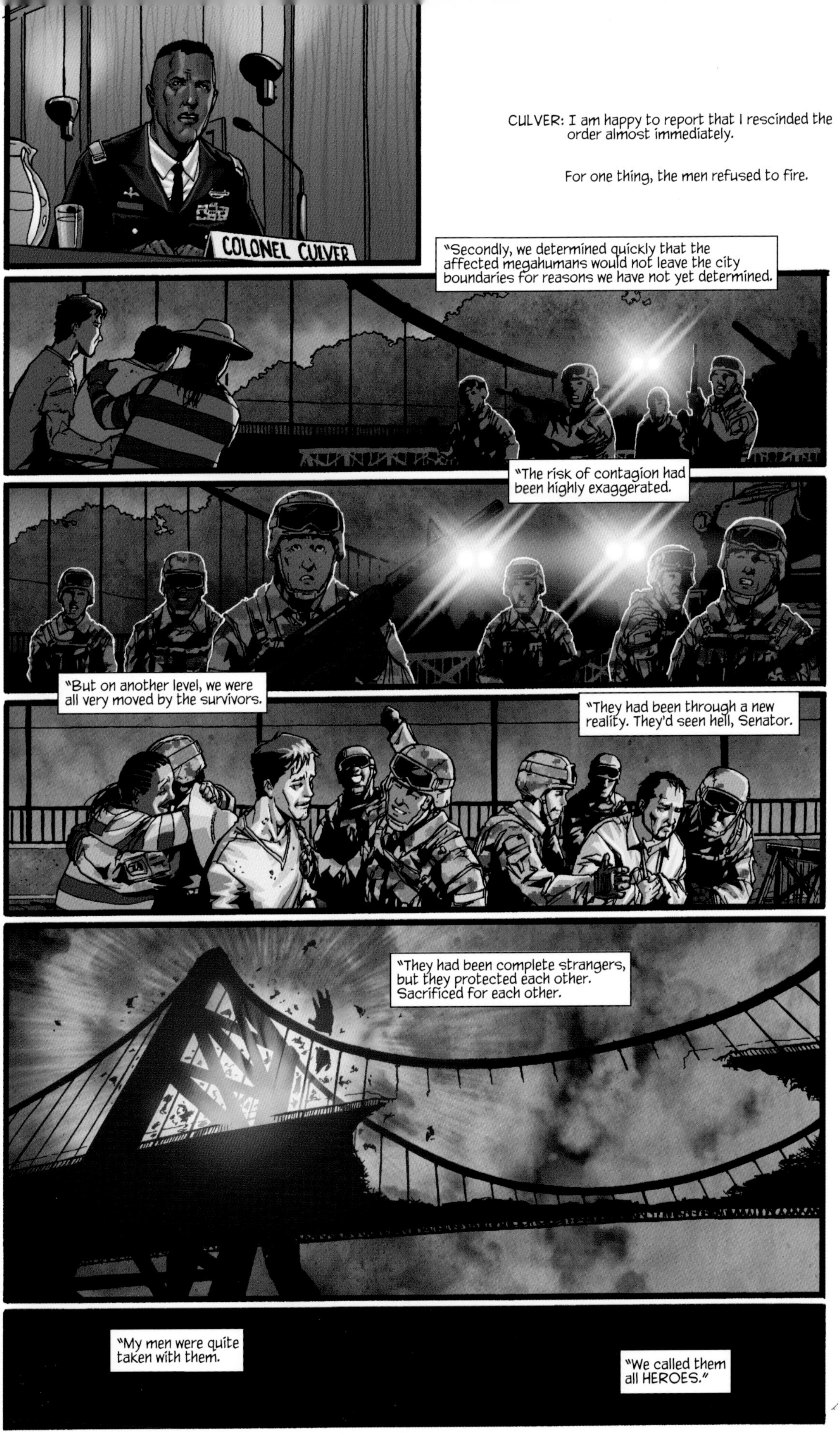
COLONEL CULVER
CULVER: I am happy to report that I rescinded the order almost immediately.
For one thing, the men refused to fire.
"Secondly, we determined quickly that the affected megahumans would not leave the city boundaries for reasons we have not yet determined.
"The risk of contagion had been highly exaggerated.
"But on another level, we were all very moved by the survivors.
"They had been through a new reality. They'd seen hell, Senator.
"They had been complete strangers, but they protected each other. Sacrificed for each other.
"My men were quite taken with them.
"We called them all HEROES."

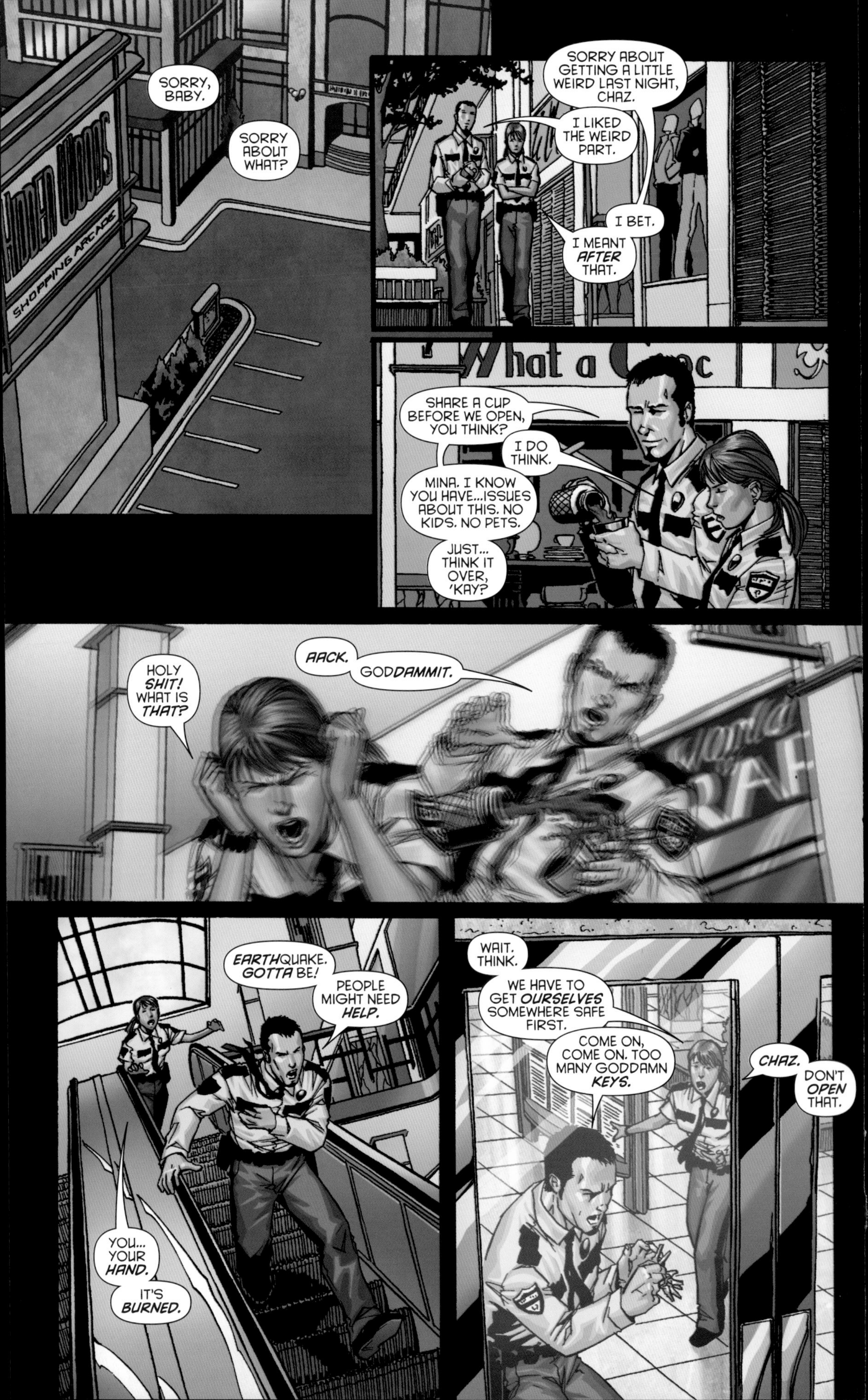
HIDDEN WOODS
SHOPPING ARCADE
SORRY, BABY.
SORRY ABOUT WHAT?
SORRY ABOUT GETTING A LITTLE WEIRD LAST NIGHT, CHAZ.
I LIKED THE WEIRD PART.
I BET.
I MEANT *AFTER* THAT.
What a C... c
SHARE A CUP BEFORE WE OPEN, YOU THINK?
I DO THINK.
MINA. I KNOW YOU HAVE...ISSUES ABOUT THIS. NO KIDS. NO PETS.
JUST... THINK IT OVER, 'KAY?
HOLY *SHIT!* WHAT IS *THAT?*
AACK.
GOD*DAMMIT.*
*EARTH*QUAKE. *GOTTA* BE!
PEOPLE MIGHT NEED *HELP.*
YOU... YOUR *HAND.*
IT'S *BURNED.*
WAIT. THINK.
WE HAVE TO GET *OURSELVES* SOMEWHERE SAFE FIRST.
COME ON, COME ON. TOO MANY GODDAMN *KEYS.*
CHAZ.
DON'T *OPEN* THAT.

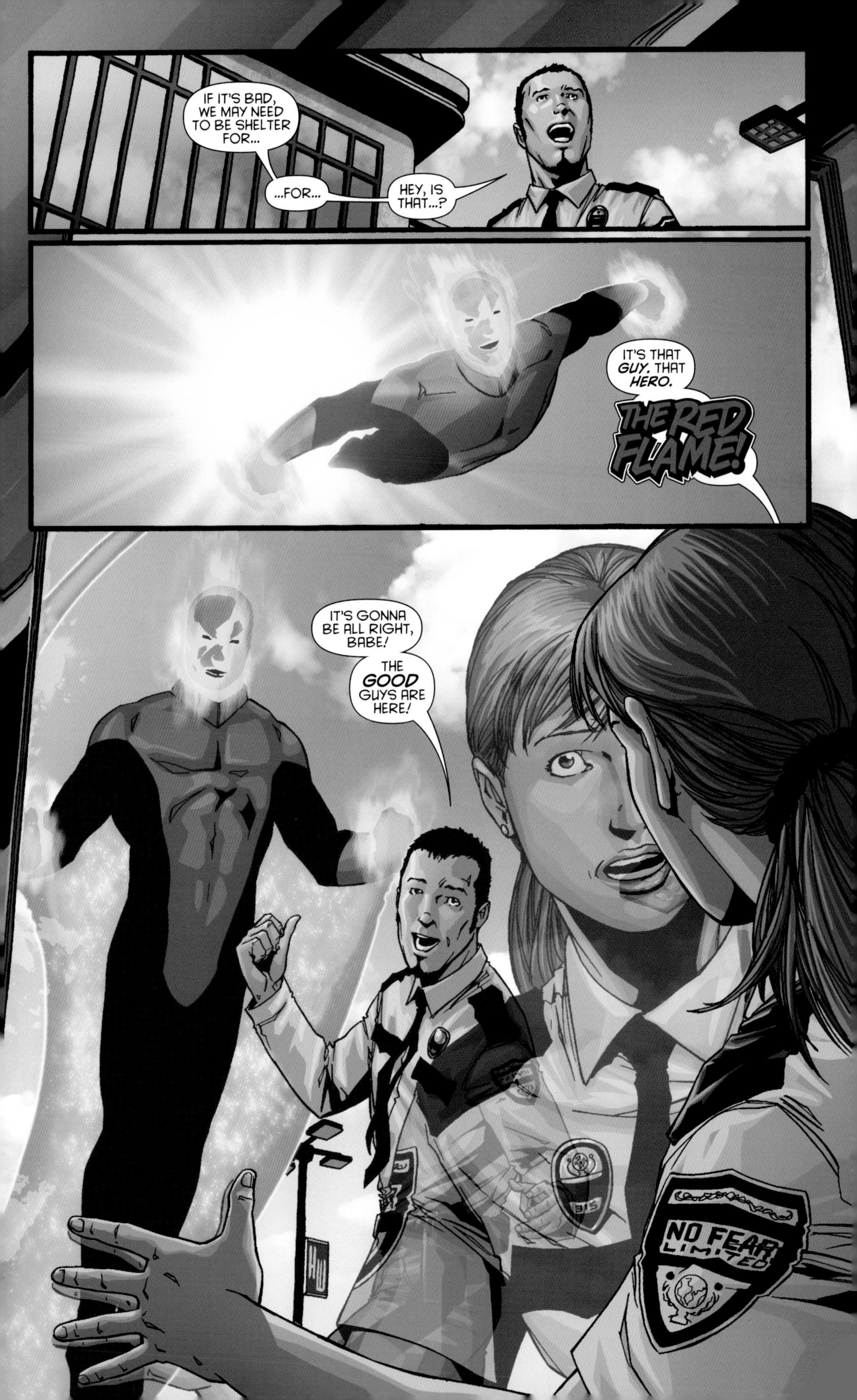
IF IT'S BAD, WE MAY NEED TO BE SHELTER FOR...
...FOR...
HEY, IS THAT...?
IT'S THAT GUY. THAT HERO.
THE RED FLAME!
IT'S GONNA BE ALL RIGHT, BABE!
THE GOOD GUYS ARE HERE!
NO FEAR LIMITED

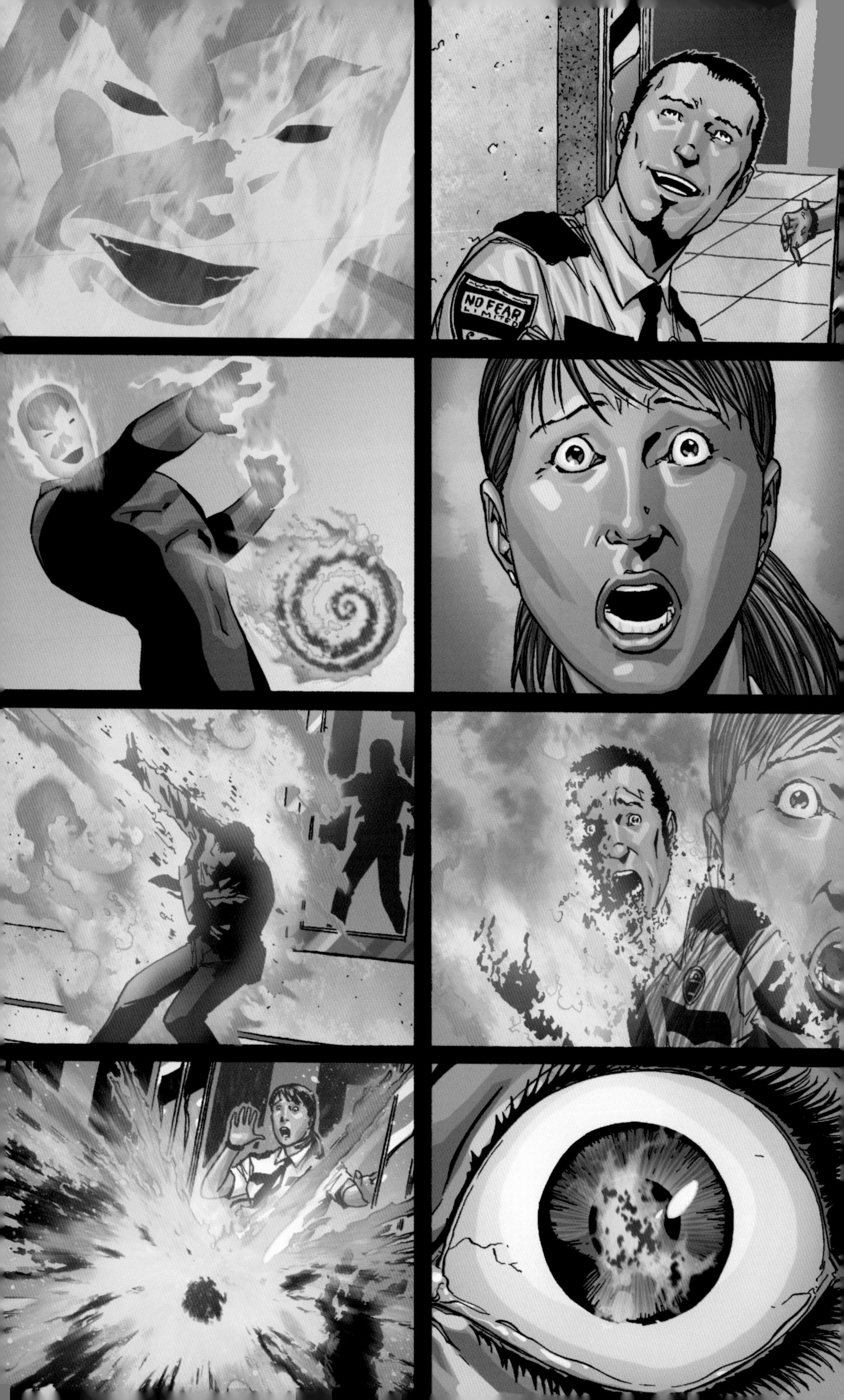
NO FEAR
LIMITED

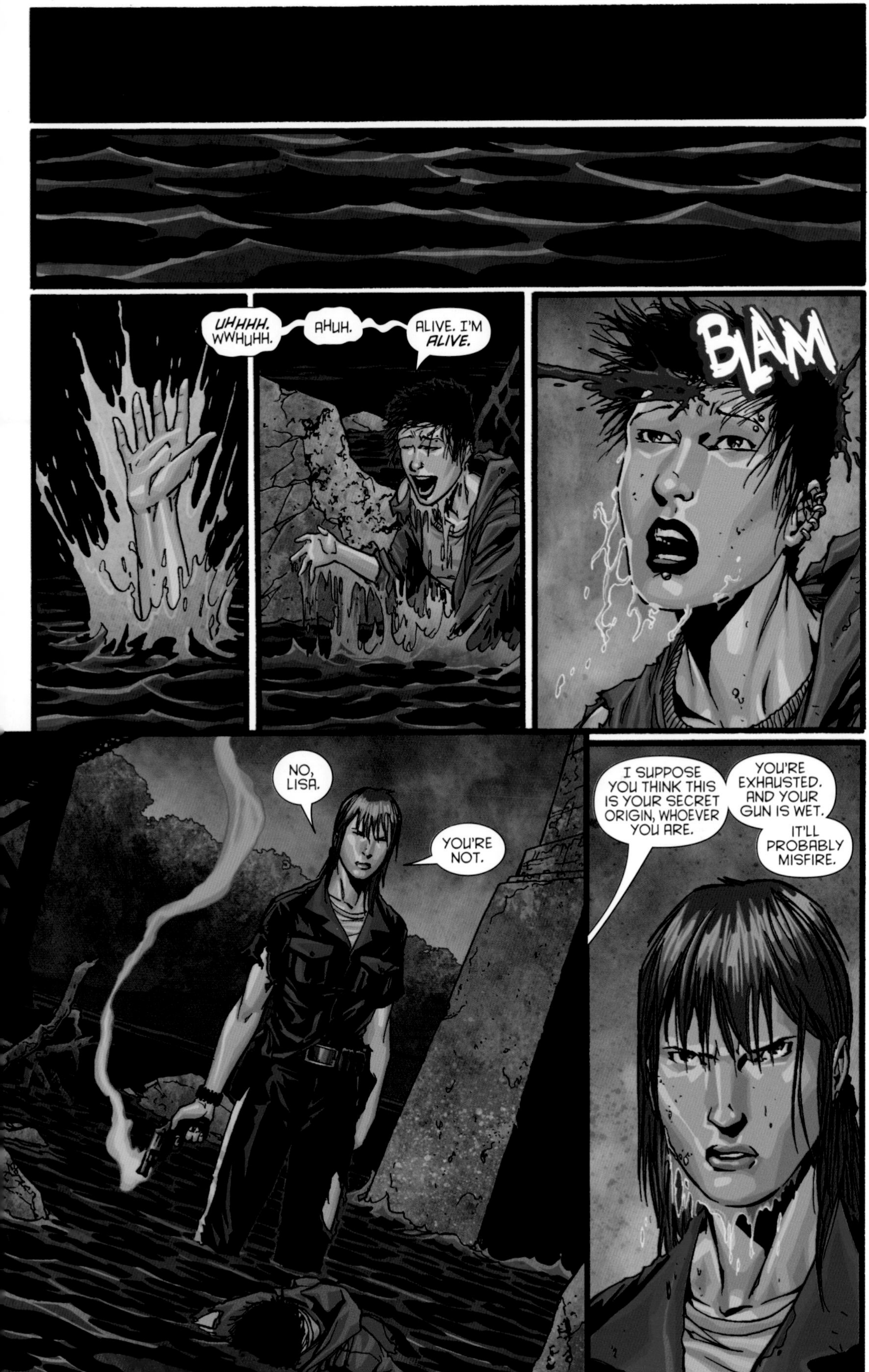
UHHHH. WWHUHH.
AHUH.
ALIVE. I'M ALIVE.
BLAM
NO, LISA.
YOU'RE NOT.
I SUPPOSE YOU THINK THIS IS YOUR SECRET ORIGIN, WHOEVER YOU ARE.
YOU'RE EXHAUSTED. AND YOUR GUN IS WET.
IT'LL PROBABLY MISFIRE.

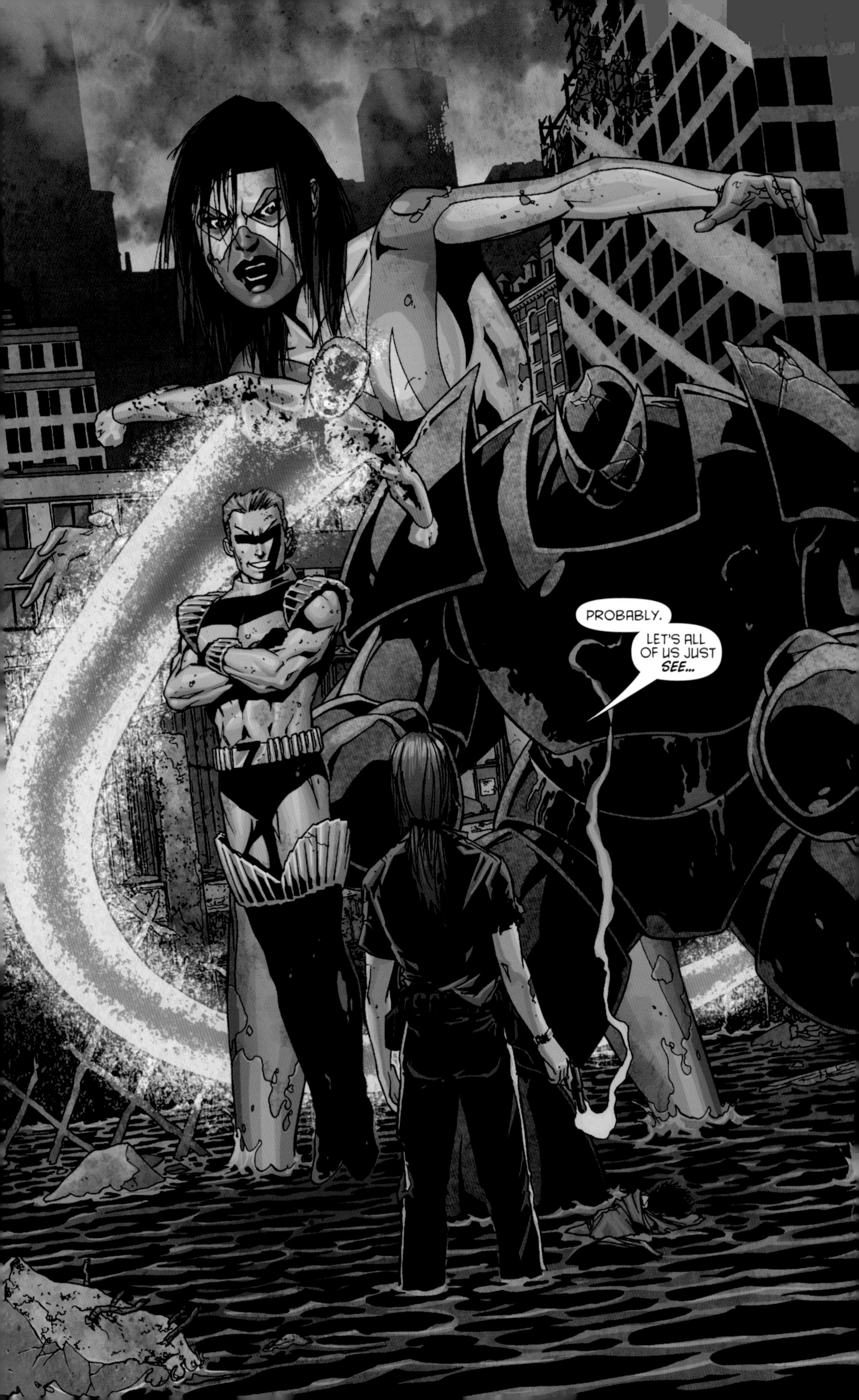

PROBABLY.
LET'S ALL OF US JUST *SEE...*

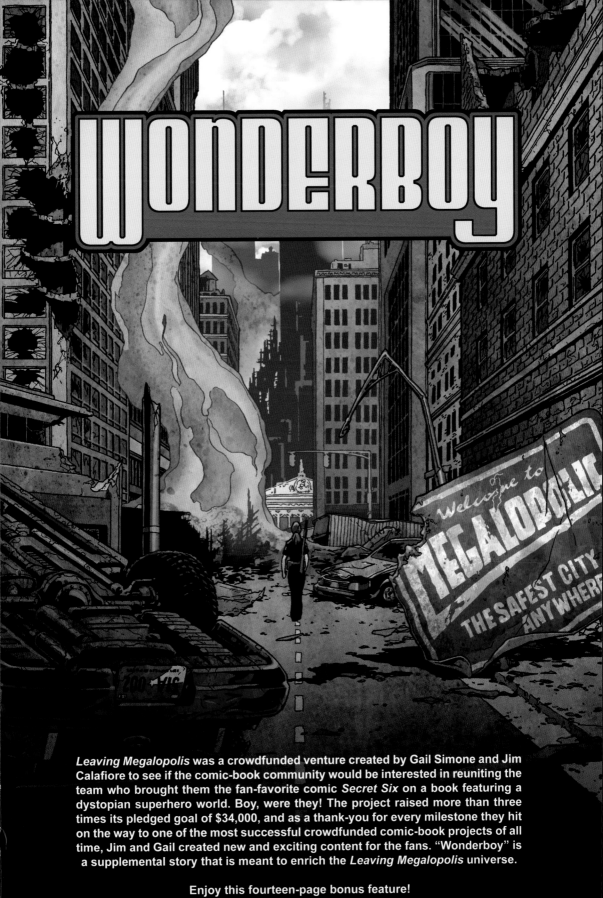

WONDERBOY

Leaving Megalopolis was a crowdfunded venture created by Gail Simone and Jim Calafiore to see if the comic-book community would be interested in reuniting the team who brought them the fan-favorite comic *Secret Six* on a book featuring a dystopian superhero world. Boy, were they! The project raised more than three times its pledged goal of $34,000, and as a thank-you for every milestone they hit on the way to one of the most successful crowdfunded comic-book projects of all time, Jim and Gail created new and exciting content for the fans. "Wonderboy" is a supplemental story that is meant to enrich the *Leaving Megalopolis* universe.

Enjoy this fourteen-page bonus feature!

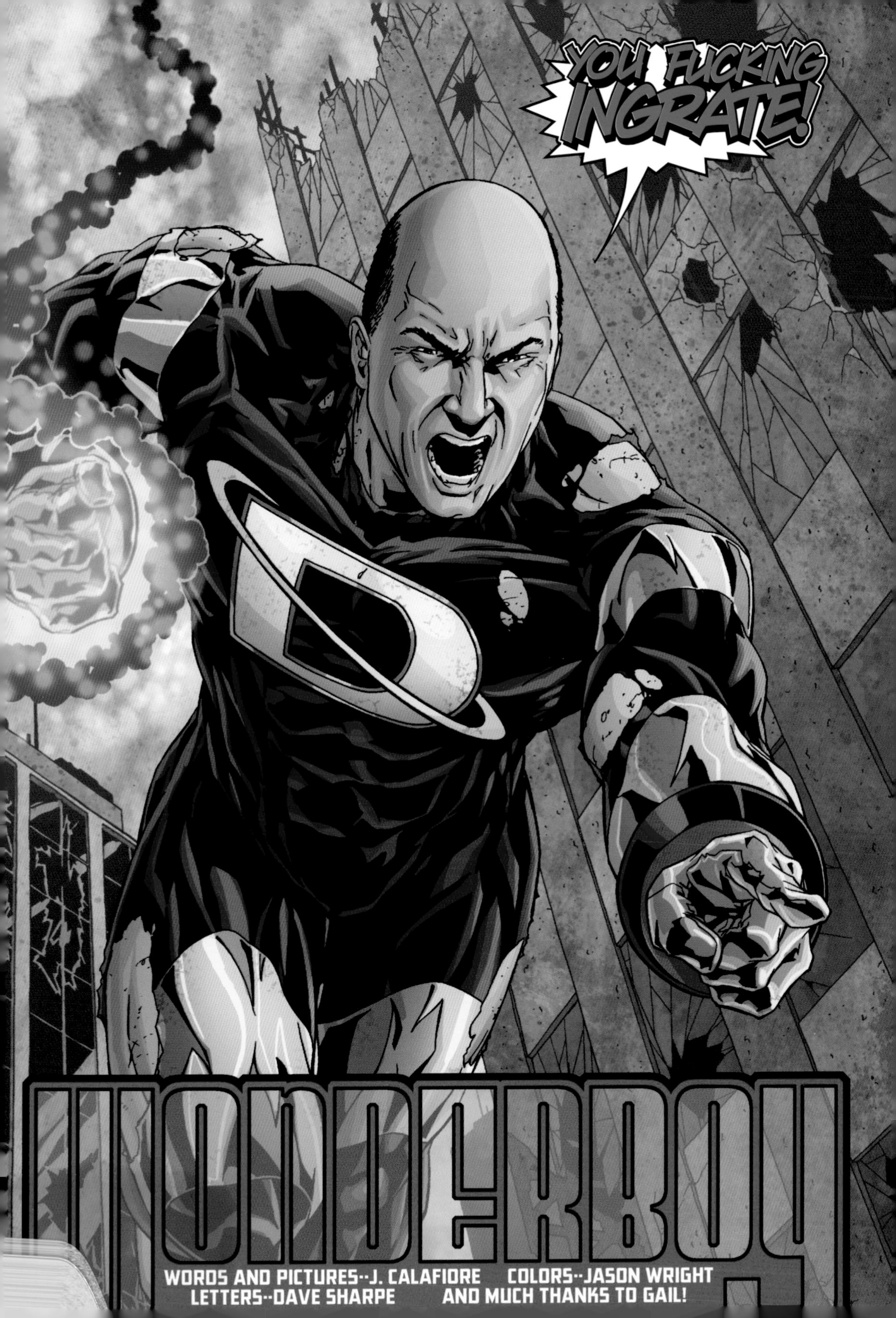
YOU FUCKING INGRATE!
WONDERBOY
WORDS AND PICTURES--J. CALAFIORE COLORS--JASON WRIGHT
LETTERS--DAVE SHARPE AND MUCH THANKS TO GAIL!

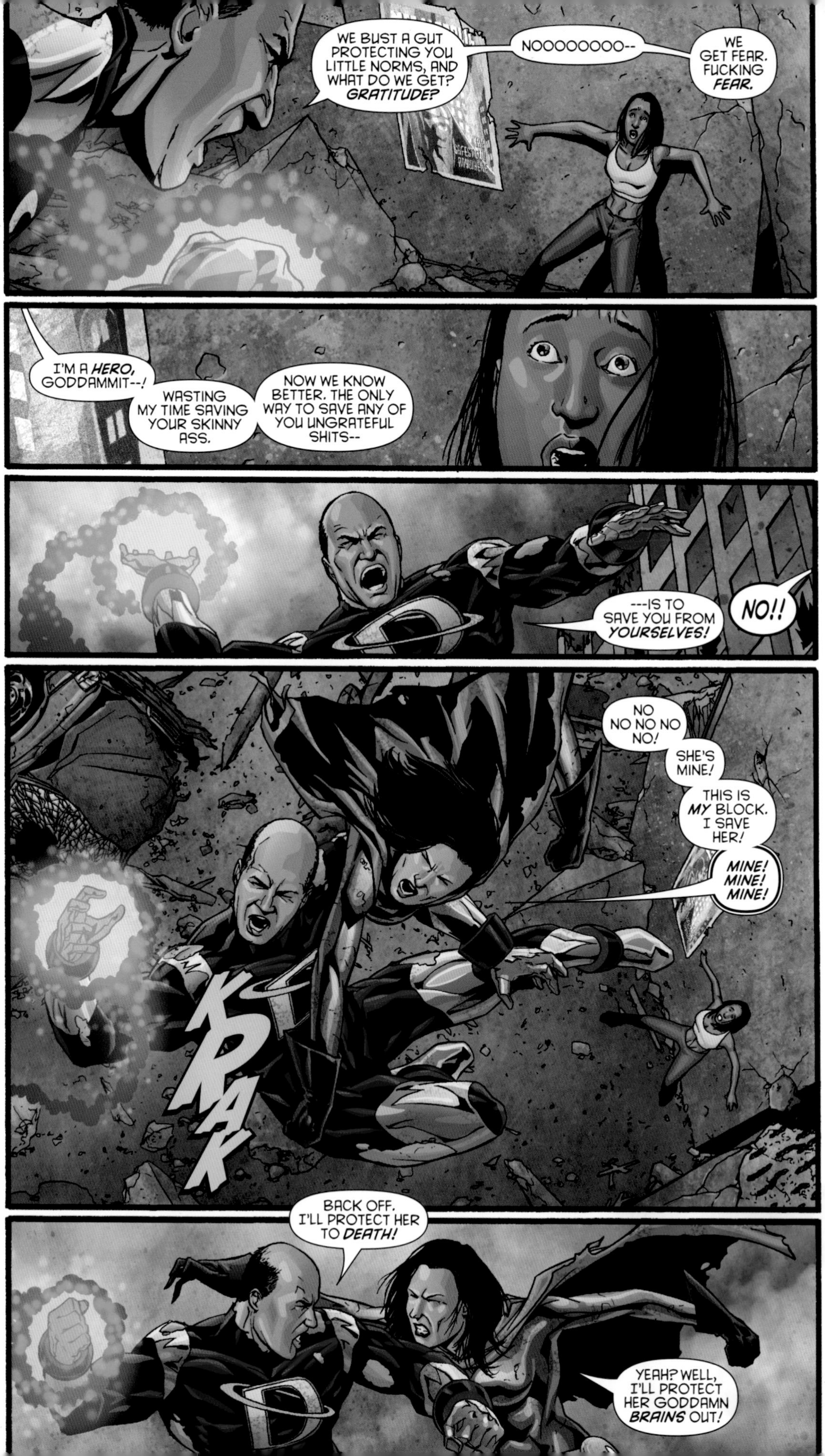
WE BUST A GUT PROTECTING YOU LITTLE NORMS, AND WHAT DO WE GET? GRATITUDE?
NOOOOOOOO--
WE GET FEAR. FUCKING FEAR.
I'M A HERO, GODDAMMIT--!
WASTING MY TIME SAVING YOUR SKINNY ASS.
NOW WE KNOW BETTER. THE ONLY WAY TO SAVE ANY OF YOU UNGRATEFUL SHITS--
---IS TO SAVE YOU FROM YOURSELVES!
NO!!
NO NO NO NO NO!
SHE'S MINE!
THIS IS MY BLOCK. I SAVE HER!
MINE! MINE! MINE!
KRAK
BACK OFF. I'LL PROTECT HER TO DEATH!
YEAH? WELL, I'LL PROTECT HER GODDAMN BRAINS OUT!

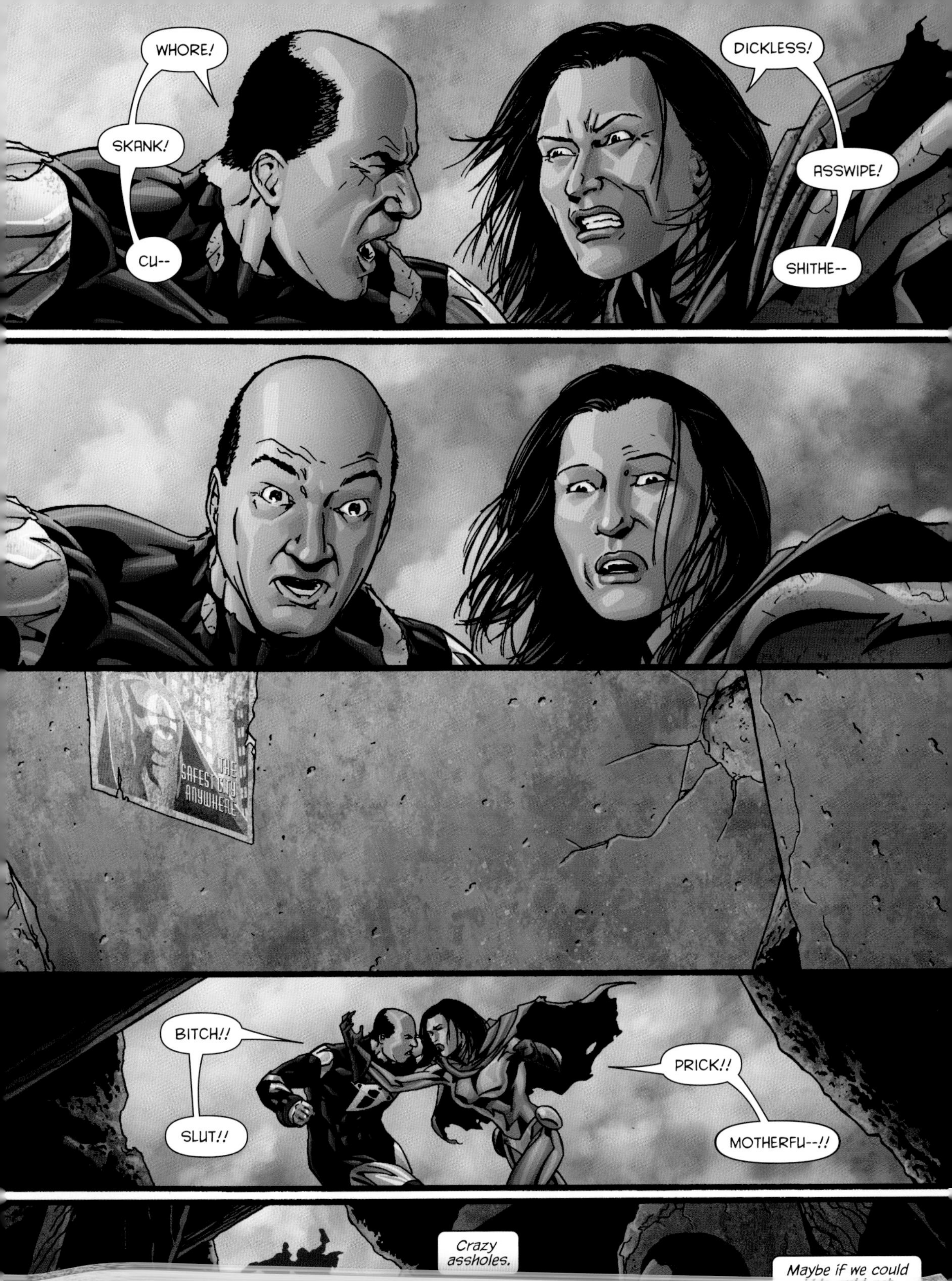
WHORE!
SKANK!
CU--
DICKLESS!
ASSWIPE!
SHITHE--
THE SAFEST CITY ANYWHERE
BITCH!!
SLUT!!
PRICK!!
MOTHERFU--!!
Crazy assholes.
Maybe if we could

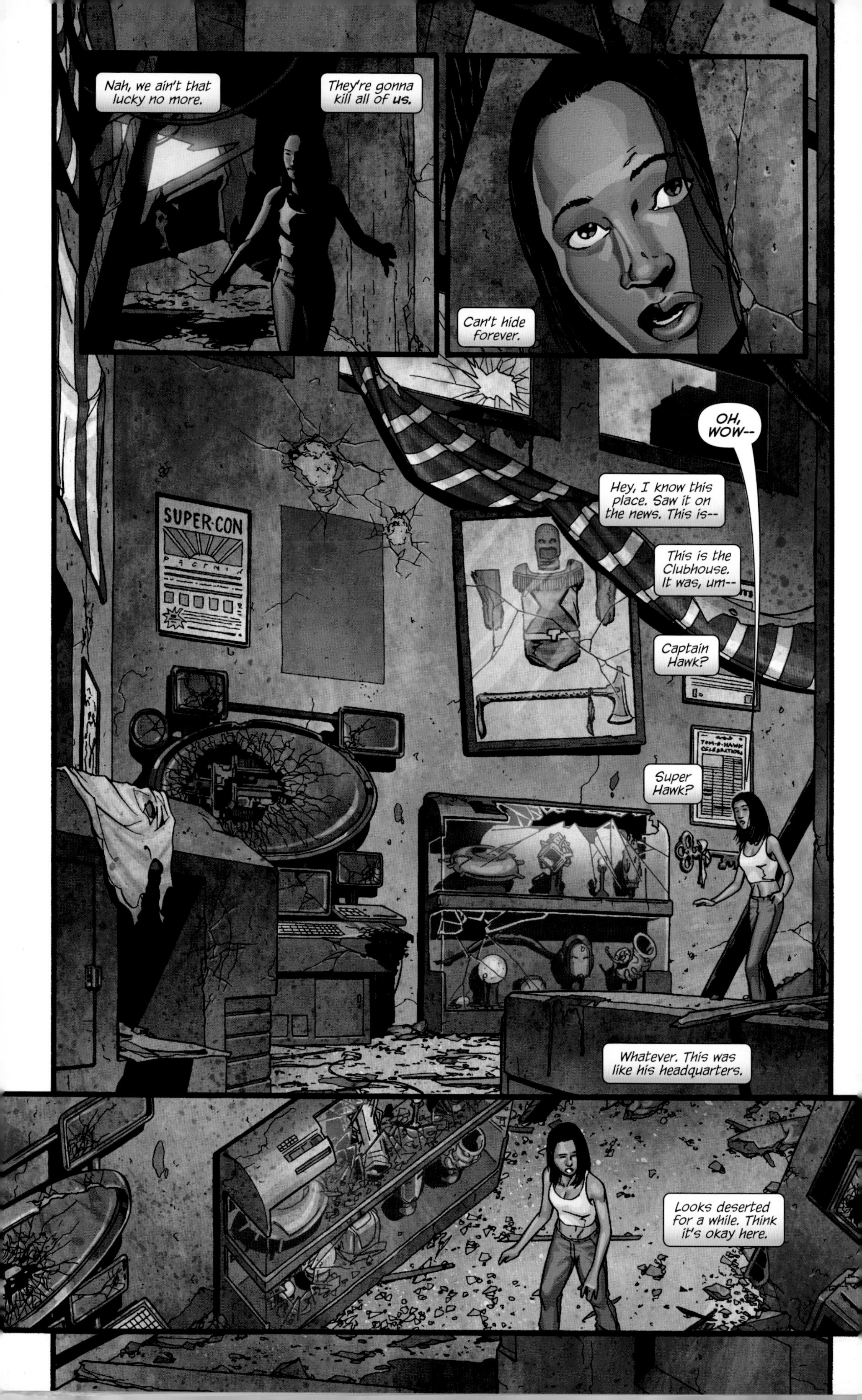

Nah, we ain't that lucky no more.
They're gonna kill all of **us.**
Can't hide forever.
OH, WOW--
Hey, I know this place. Saw it on the news. This is--
This is the Clubhouse. It was, um--
Captain Hawk?
Super Hawk?
SUPER-CON
Whatever. This was like his headquarters.
Looks deserted for a while. Think it's okay here.

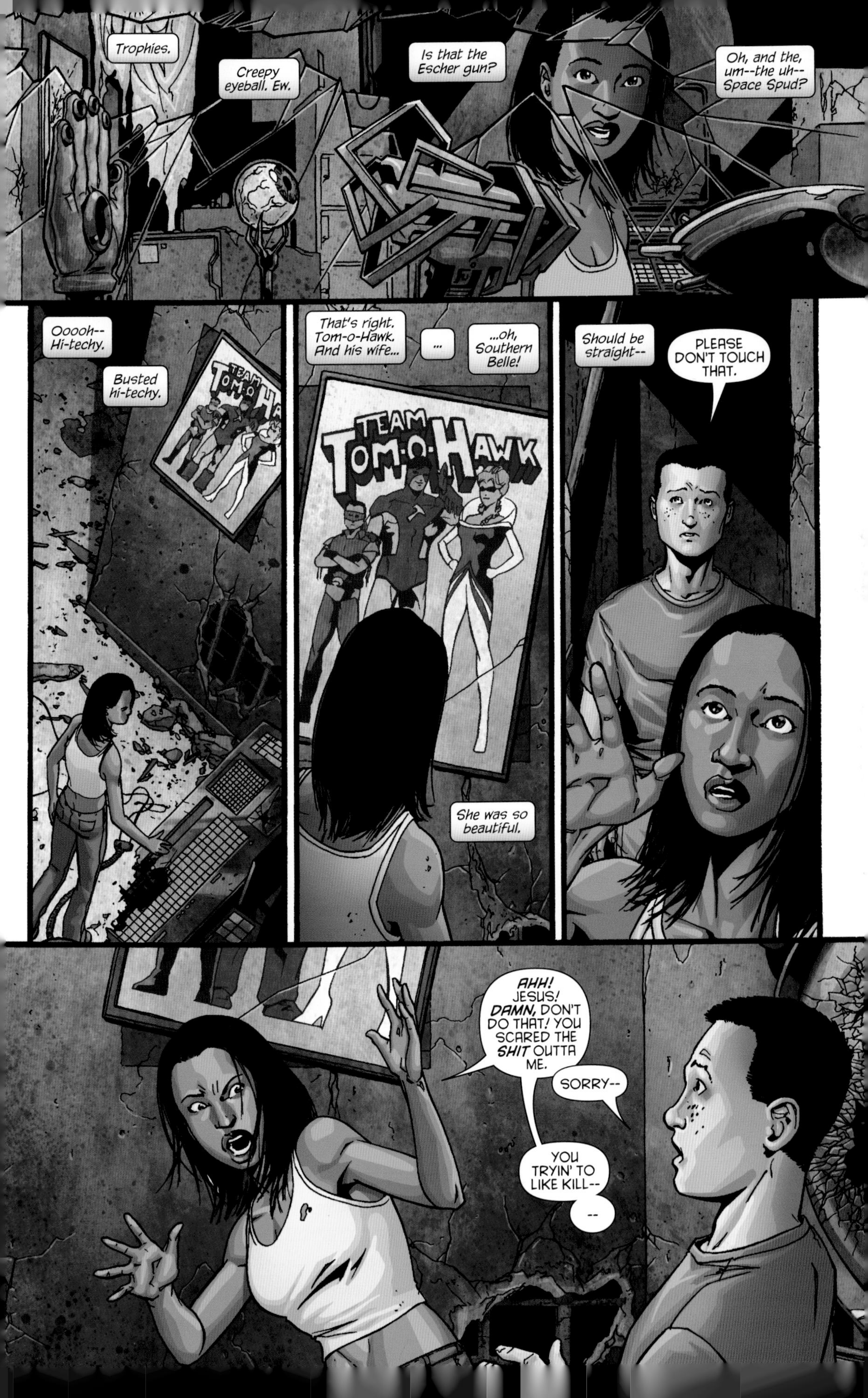
Trophies.
Creepy eyeball. Ew.
Is that the Escher gun?
Oh, and the, um--the uh--Space Spud?
Ooooh--Hi-techy.
Busted hi-techy.
TEAM TOM-O-HAWK
That's right. Tom-o-Hawk. And his wife...
...
...oh, Southern Belle!
TEAM TOM-O-HAWK
She was so beautiful.
Should be straight--
PLEASE DON'T TOUCH THAT.
AHH! JESUS! DAMN, DON'T DO THAT! YOU SCARED THE SHIT OUTTA ME.
SORRY--
YOU TRYIN' TO LIKE KILL--
--

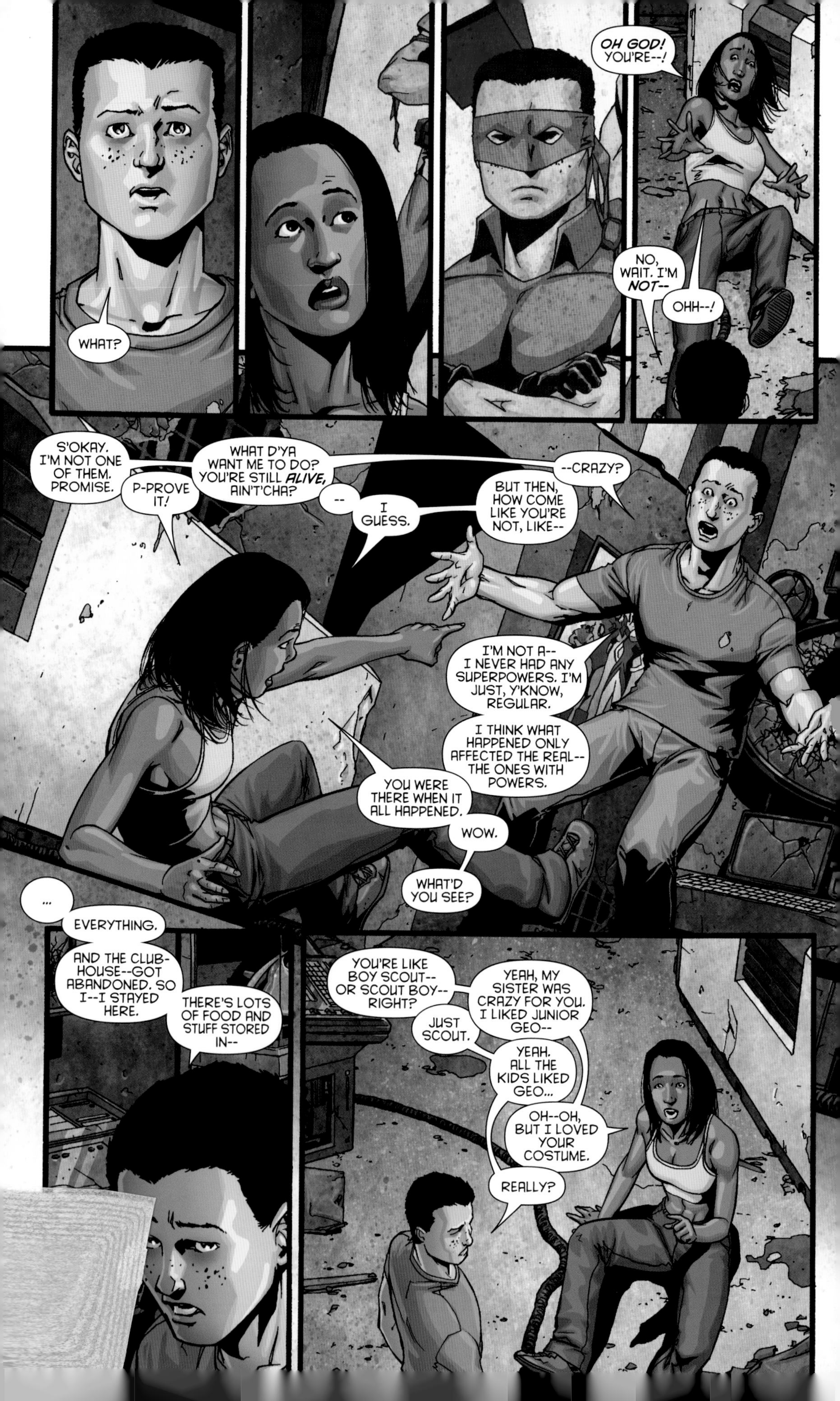
WHAT?
OH GOD! YOU'RE--!
NO, WAIT. I'M NOT--
OHH--!
S'OKAY. I'M NOT ONE OF THEM. PROMISE.
P-PROVE IT!
WHAT D'YA WANT ME TO DO? YOU'RE STILL ALIVE, AIN'T'CHA?
--
I GUESS.
--CRAZY?
BUT THEN, HOW COME LIKE YOU'RE NOT, LIKE--
I'M NOT A-- I NEVER HAD ANY SUPERPOWERS. I'M JUST, Y'KNOW, REGULAR.
I THINK WHAT HAPPENED ONLY AFFECTED THE REAL-- THE ONES WITH POWERS.
YOU WERE THERE WHEN IT ALL HAPPENED.
WOW.
WHAT'D YOU SEE?
...
EVERYTHING.
AND THE CLUB-HOUSE--GOT ABANDONED. SO I--I STAYED HERE.
THERE'S LOTS OF FOOD AND STUFF STORED IN--
YOU'RE LIKE BOY SCOUT-- OR SCOUT BOY-- RIGHT?
JUST SCOUT.
YEAH, MY SISTER WAS CRAZY FOR YOU. I LIKED JUNIOR GEO--
YEAH. ALL THE KIDS LIKED GEO...
OH--OH, BUT I LOVED YOUR COSTUME.
REALLY?

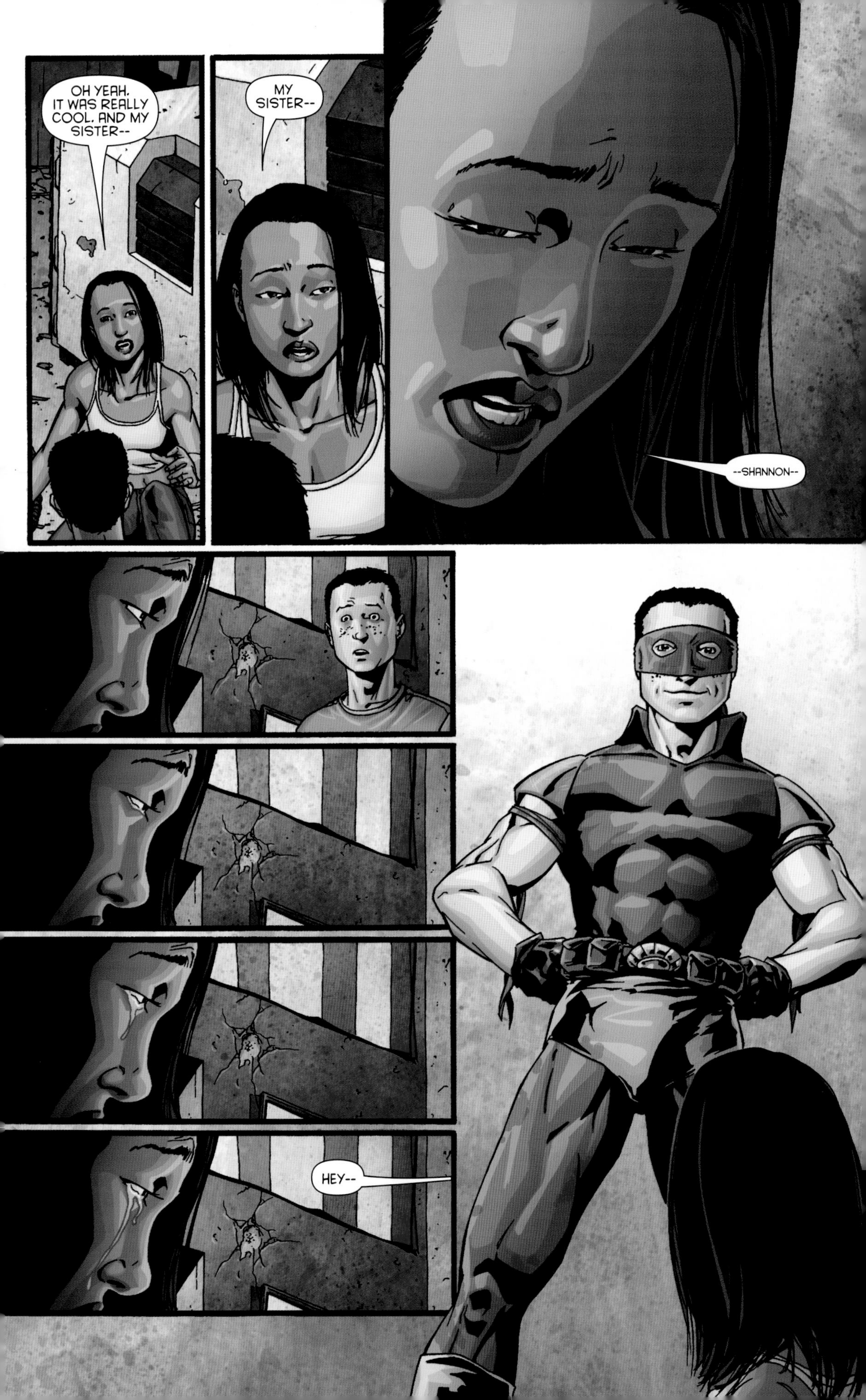
OH YEAH. IT WAS REALLY COOL. AND MY SISTER--
MY SISTER--
--SHANNON--
HEY--

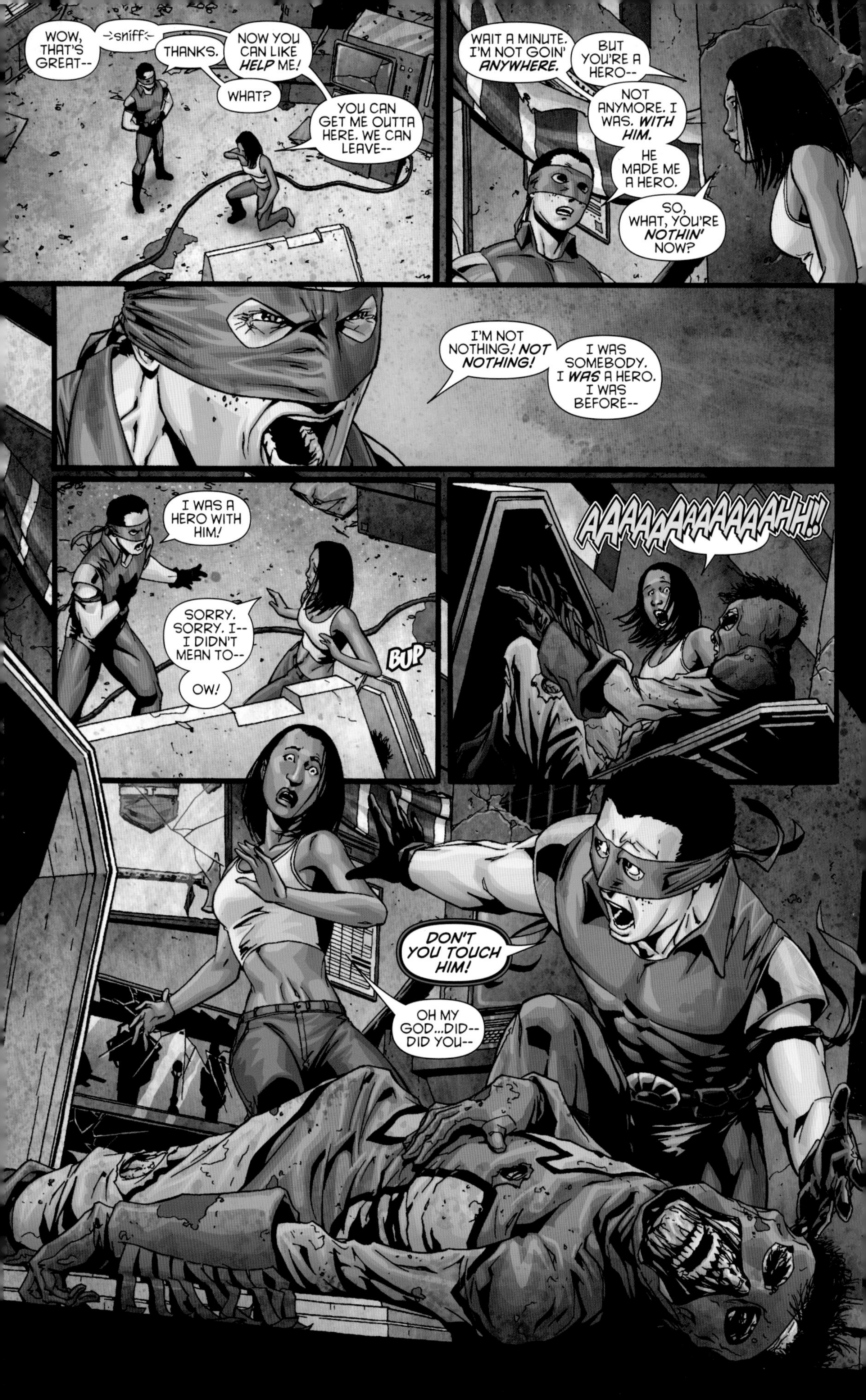
WOW, THAT'S GREAT--
~sniff~
THANKS.
NOW YOU CAN LIKE HELP ME!
WHAT?
YOU CAN GET ME OUTTA HERE. WE CAN LEAVE--
WAIT A MINUTE. I'M NOT GOIN' ANYWHERE.
BUT YOU'RE A HERO--
NOT ANYMORE. I WAS. WITH HIM.
HE MADE ME A HERO.
SO, WHAT, YOU'RE NOTHIN' NOW?
I'M NOT NOTHING! NOT NOTHING!
I WAS SOMEBODY. I WAS A HERO. I WAS BEFORE--
I WAS A HERO WITH HIM!
SORRY. SORRY. I-- I DIDN'T MEAN TO--
OW!
BUP
AAAAAAAAAAAAHH!!
DON'T YOU TOUCH HIM!
OH MY GOD...DID-- DID YOU--

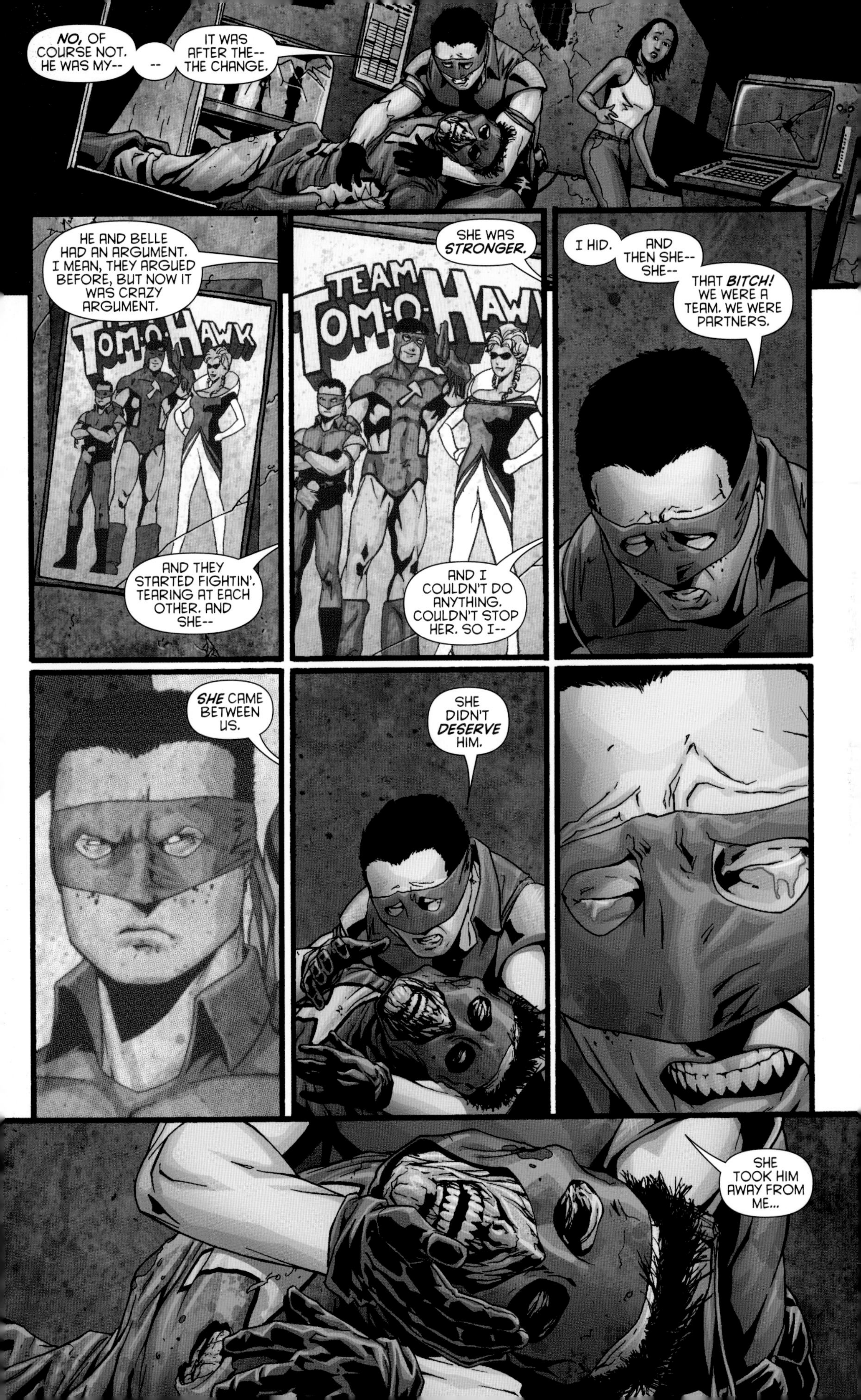
NO, OF COURSE NOT. HE WAS MY--
--
IT WAS AFTER THE-- THE CHANGE.
HE AND BELLE HAD AN ARGUMENT. I MEAN, THEY ARGUED BEFORE, BUT NOW IT WAS CRAZY ARGUMENT.
TOM-O-HAWK
AND THEY STARTED FIGHTIN'. TEARING AT EACH OTHER. AND SHE--
SHE WAS STRONGER.
TEAM TOM-O-HAWK
AND I COULDN'T DO ANYTHING. COULDN'T STOP HER. SO I--
I HID.
AND THEN SHE-- SHE--
THAT BITCH! WE WERE A TEAM. WE WERE PARTNERS.
SHE CAME BETWEEN US.
SHE DIDN'T DESERVE HIM.
SHE TOOK HIM AWAY FROM ME...

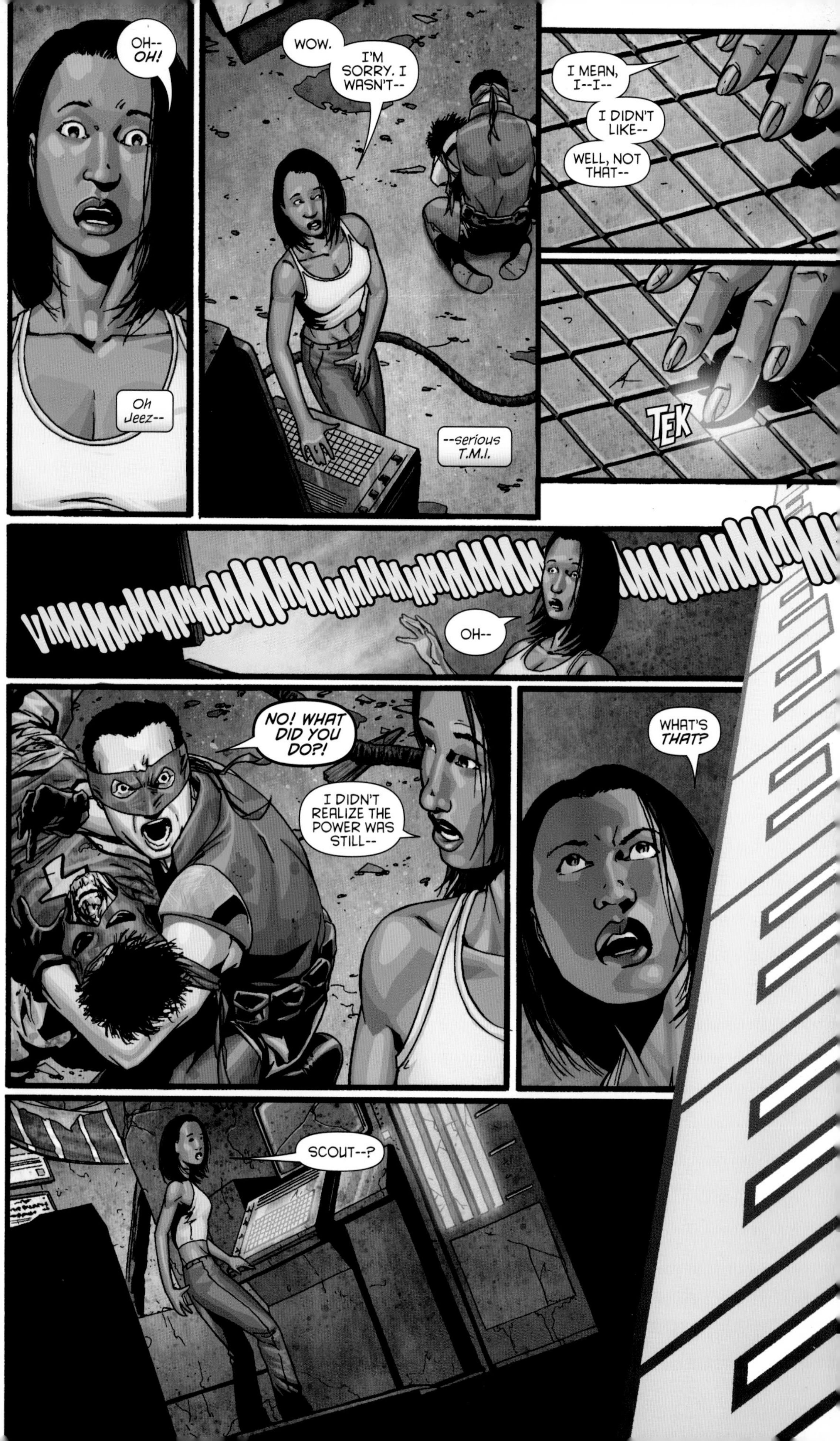
OH--
OH!
Oh Jeez--
WOW.
I'M SORRY. I WASN'T--
--serious T.M.I.
I MEAN, I--I--
I DIDN'T LIKE--
WELL, NOT THAT--
TEK
VMMMMMMMMMMMMMMMMMMMMMMMMMMMMMMMMMMMMMMMMMMMMM
OH--
NO! WHAT DID YOU DO?!
I DIDN'T REALIZE THE POWER WAS STILL--
WHAT'S THAT?
SCOUT--?

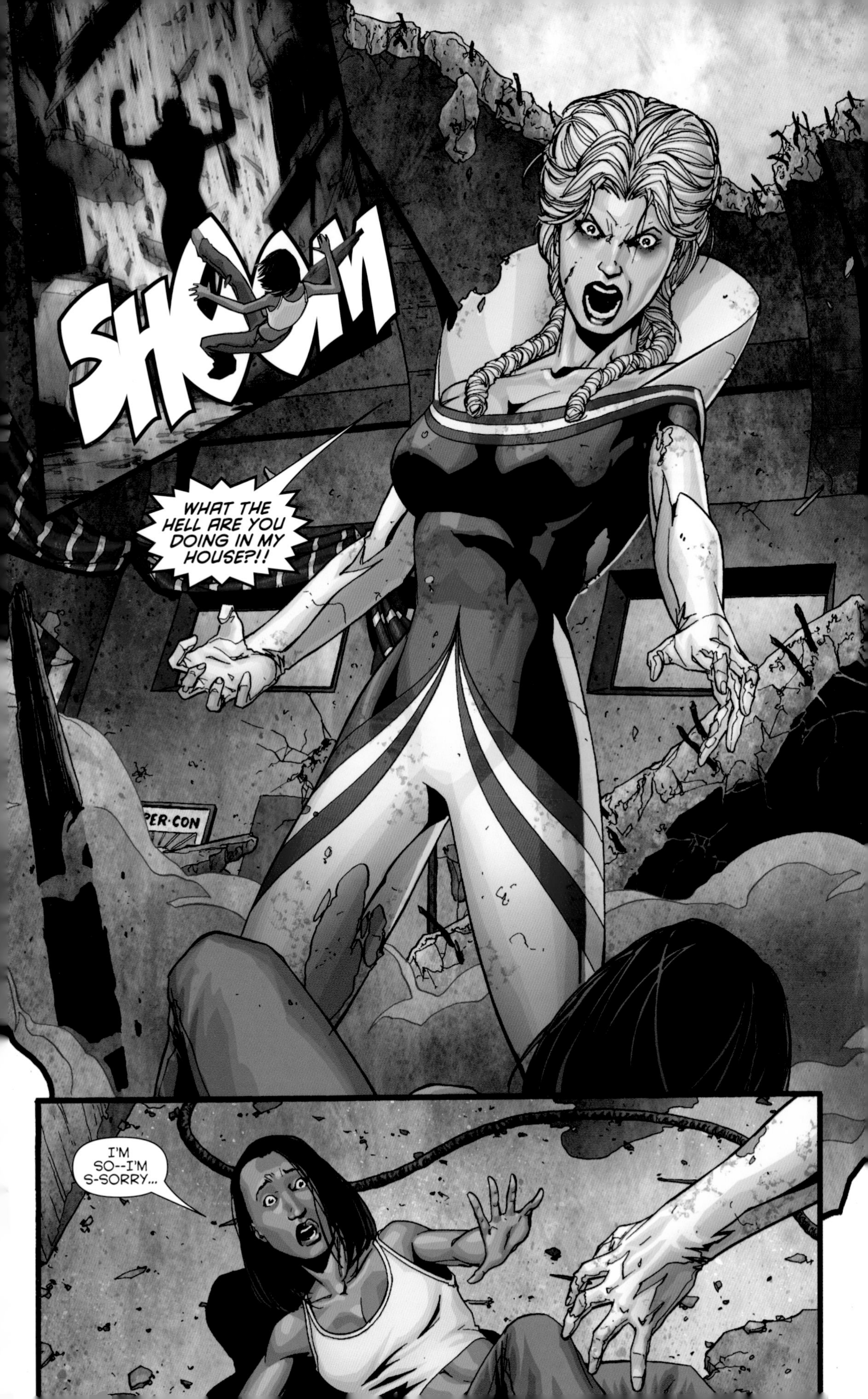
WHAT THE HELL ARE YOU DOING IN MY HOUSE?!!
I'M SO--I'M S-SORRY...

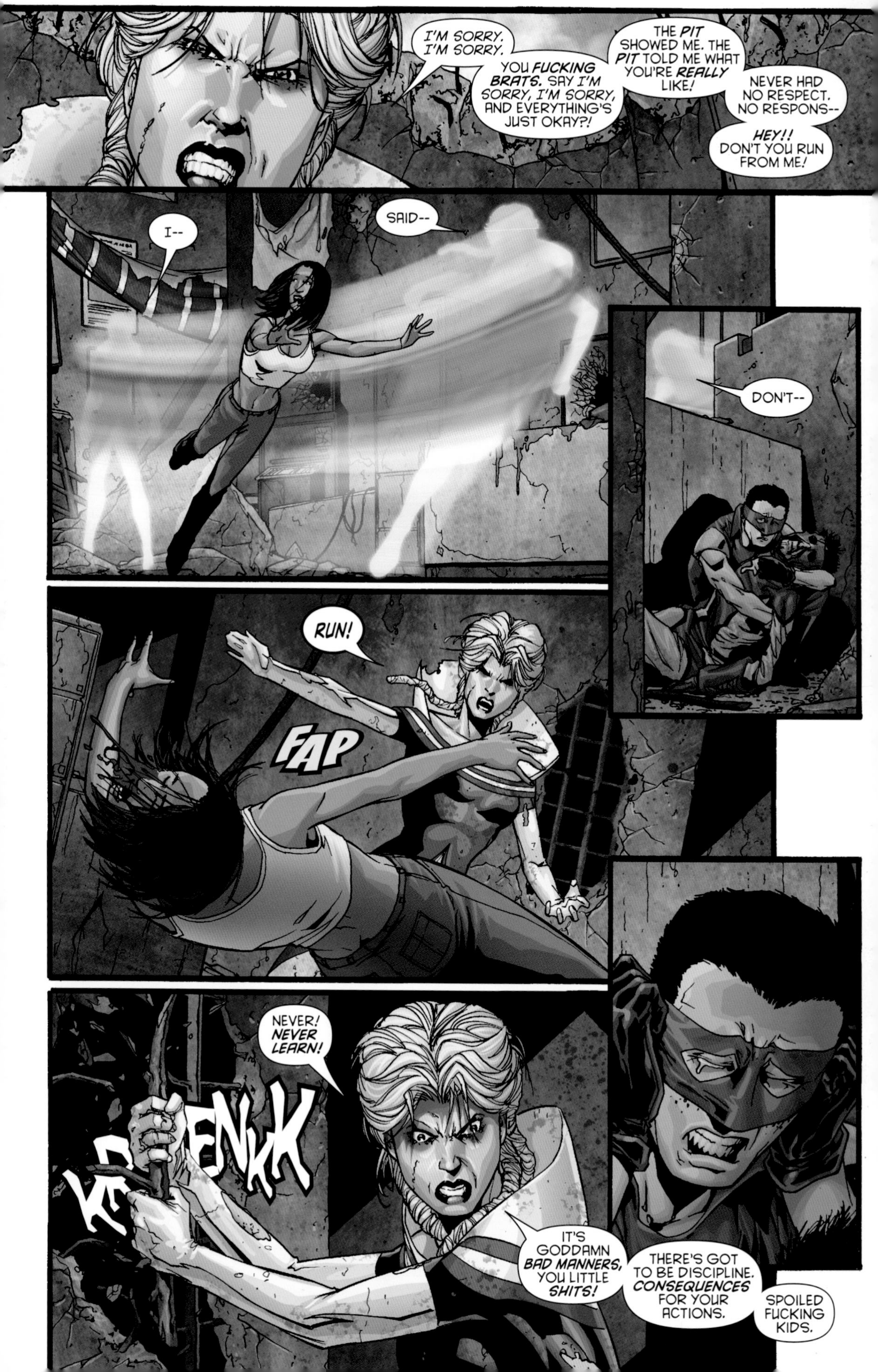
I'M SORRY. I'M SORRY.
YOU FUCKING BRATS. SAY I'M SORRY, I'M SORRY, AND EVERYTHING'S JUST OKAY?!
THE PIT SHOWED ME. THE PIT TOLD ME WHAT YOU'RE REALLY LIKE!
NEVER HAD NO RESPECT. NO RESPONS--
HEY!! DON'T YOU RUN FROM ME!
I--
SAID--
DON'T--
RUN!
FAP
NEVER! NEVER LEARN!
IT'S GODDAMN BAD MANNERS, YOU LITTLE SHITS!
THERE'S GOT TO BE DISCIPLINE. CONSEQUENCES FOR YOUR ACTIONS.
SPOILED FUCKING KIDS.

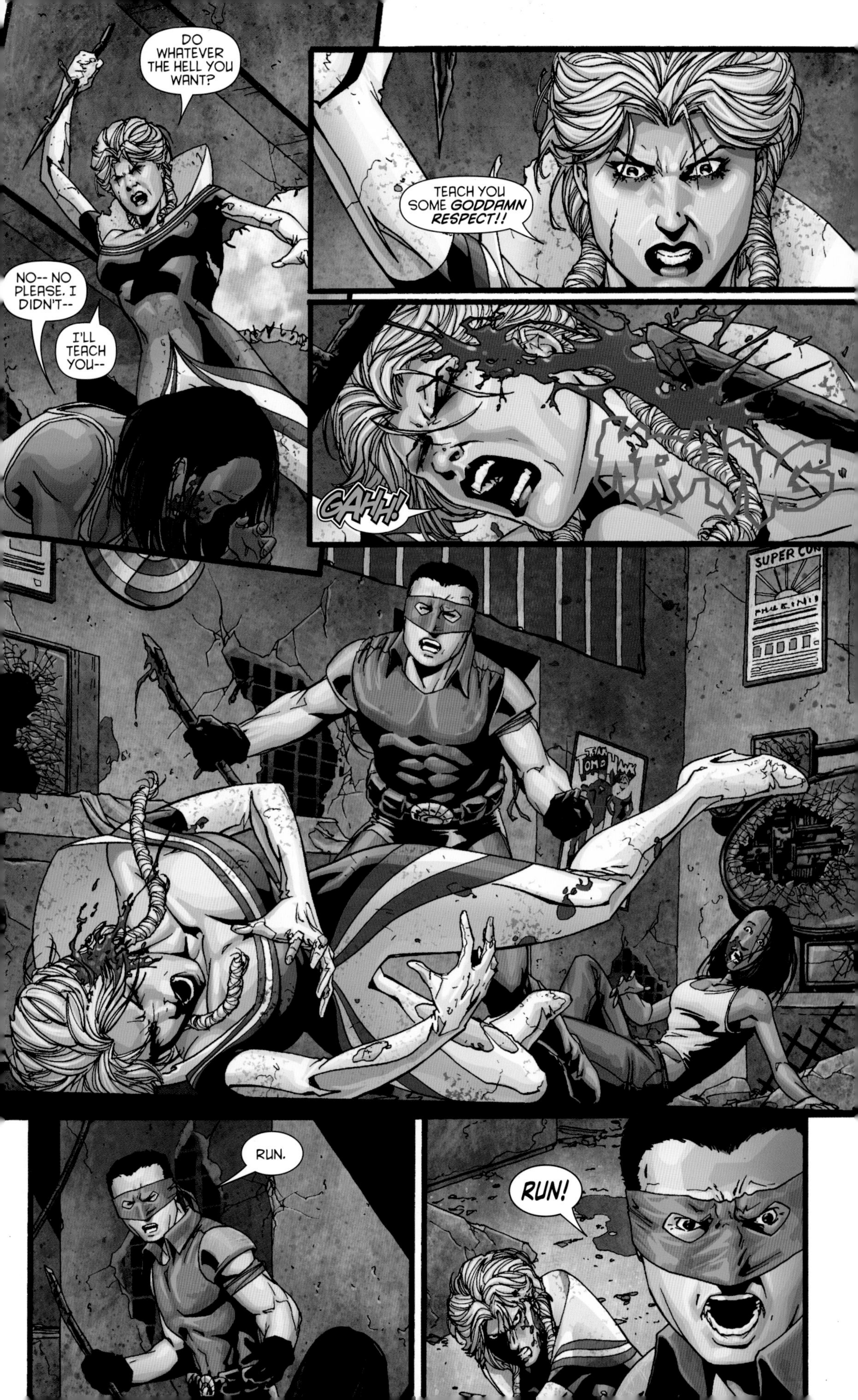
DO WHATEVER THE HELL YOU WANT?
NO-- NO PLEASE. I DIDN'T--
I'LL TEACH YOU--
TEACH YOU SOME GODDAMN RESPECT!!
GAHH!
RUN.
RUN!

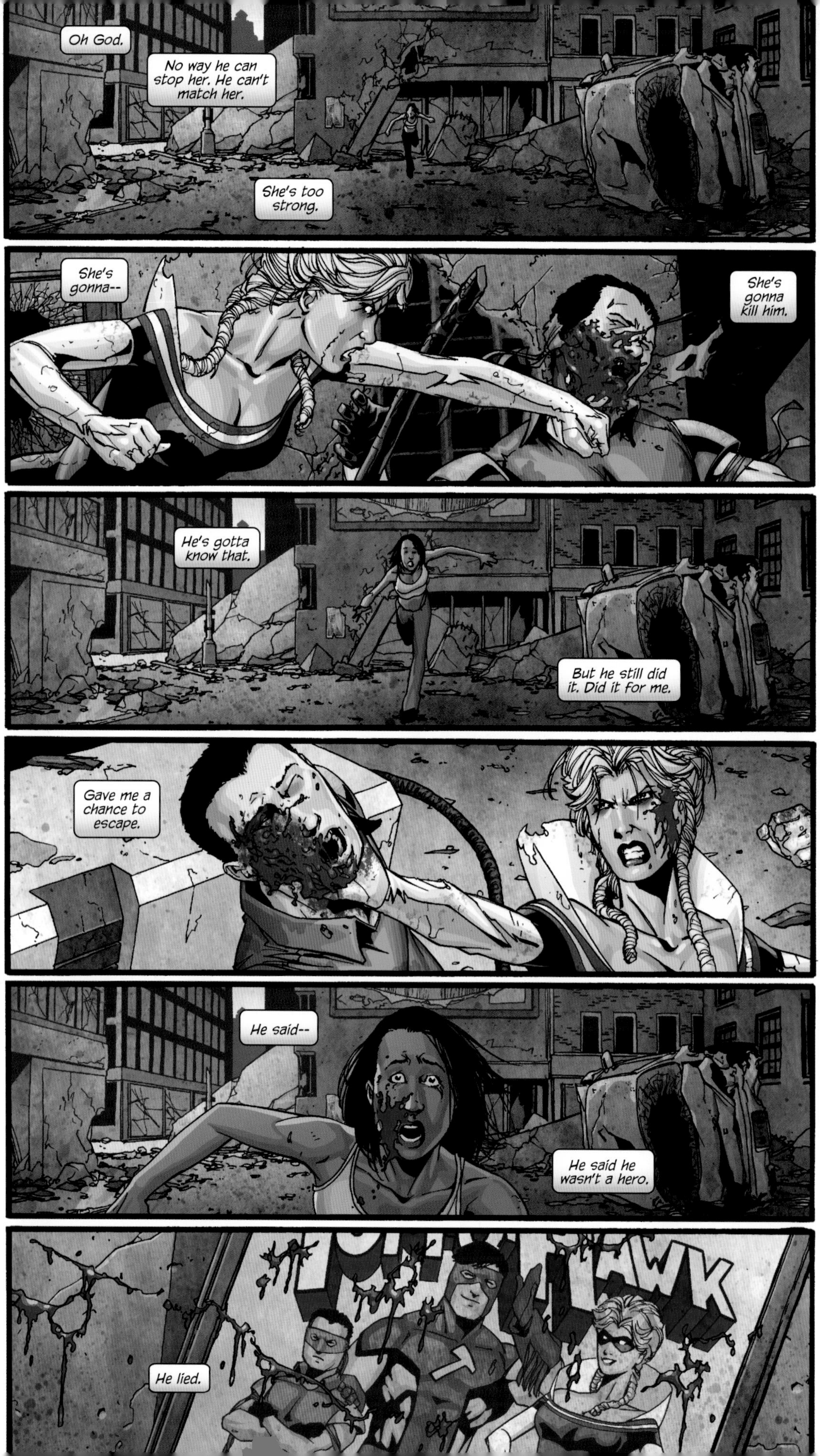
Oh God.
No way he can stop her. He can't match her.
She's too strong.
She's gonna--
She's gonna kill him.
He's gotta know that.
But he still did it. Did it for me.
Gave me a chance to escape.
He said--
He said he wasn't a hero.
He lied.

CHARACTERS

GAIL: It's an industry secret that even some of the best artists are not great designers. In our previous book together, I didn't give Jim much opportunity, sadly, to design new characters; it just didn't come up that often. That said, I don't remember asking for a single major revision of Jim's designs for *Megalopolis*; everything felt just RIGHT coming from his pencil. I will add that neither of us wanted to do the typical "homage" characters, as I kind of hate that whole concept. I didn't want you to look and say, oh, that's Spider-Man, that's Batman. We wanted the characters to capture the spirit of certain eras in comics, but not specific characters. Jim nailed this.

JIM: I usually design characters on the fly as they're needed in a story. RED FLAME was designed this way. And even when I do preliminary sketches, I don't do a lot of revisions. I try to do most of that in my head.

OVERLORD

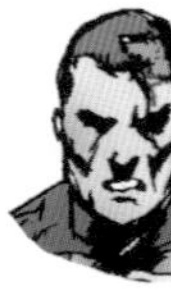

Overlord's original hair

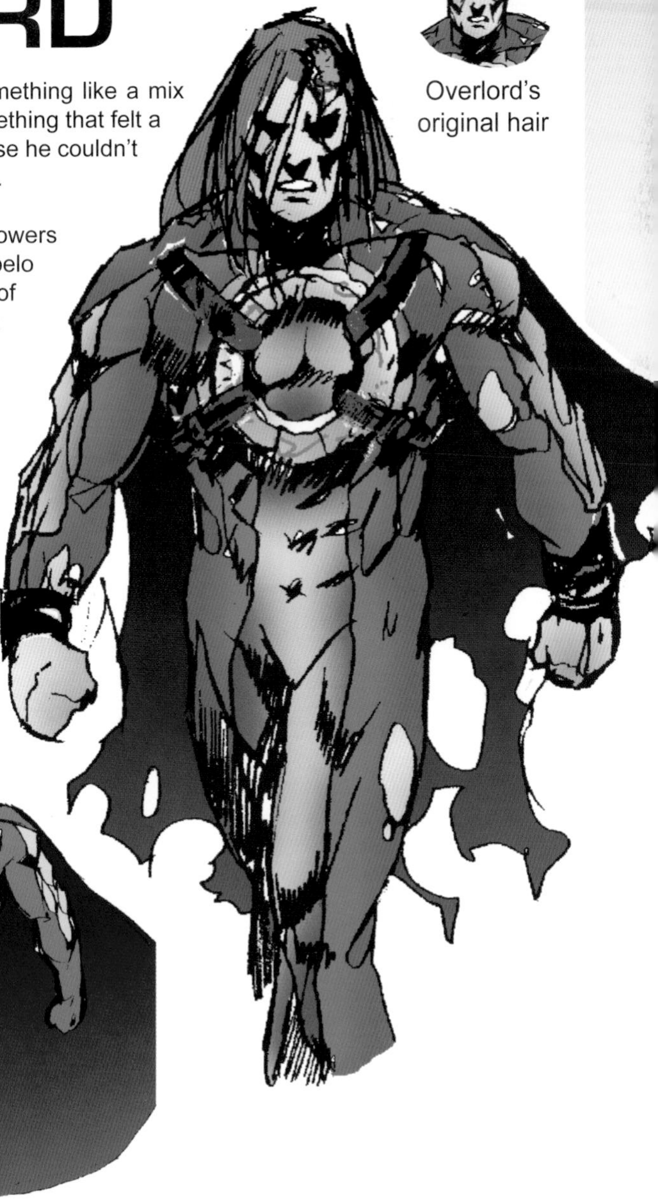

GAIL: The idea here, to me, was something like a mix of Marvel and early Image styles, something that felt a bit uncomfortable to the reader, because he couldn't quite be placed as an exact archetype.

Interestingly, the idea for his granite powers came from a Van Morrison song, "Tupelo Honey," where he talks about "men of insight, men in granite." That line stuck with me, and years later, here he is.

JIM: With all the crazy heroes in *Megalopolis*, I sort of reverse engineered the costumes. I decided how I wanted the crazy version to look first. That's why OVERLORD's costume is mostly green. I thought the green would tint well to olive and ocher, to show the sweat and stains.

Gail didn't take to the first, short-haired version, and she was right. The long straggly hair is a much better look. The big *O* of granite on his chest was Gail's main request for the design, relating to his origin.

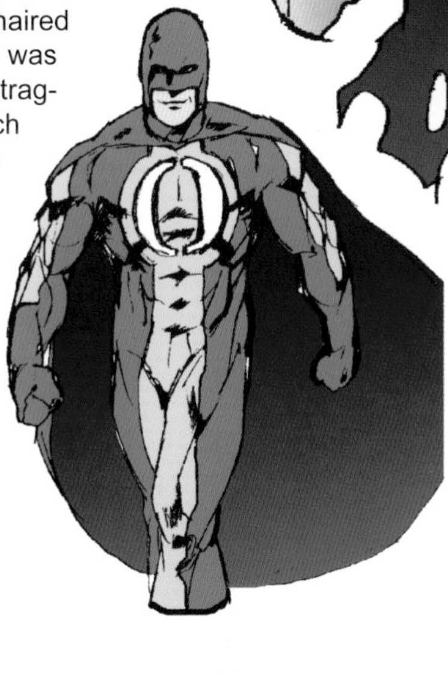

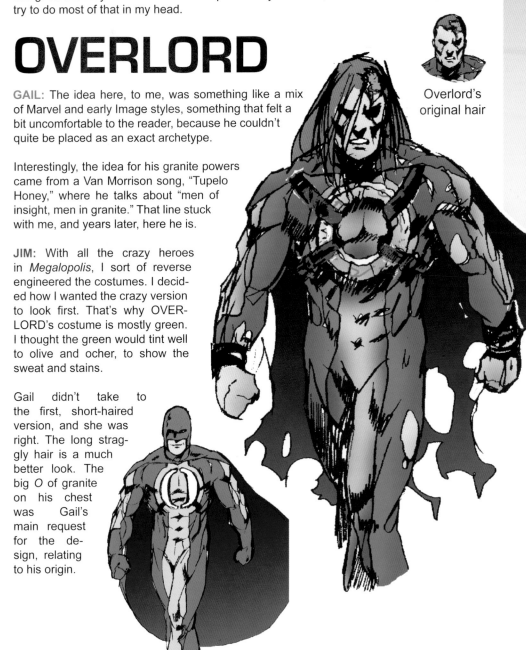

CHARACTERS

MINA

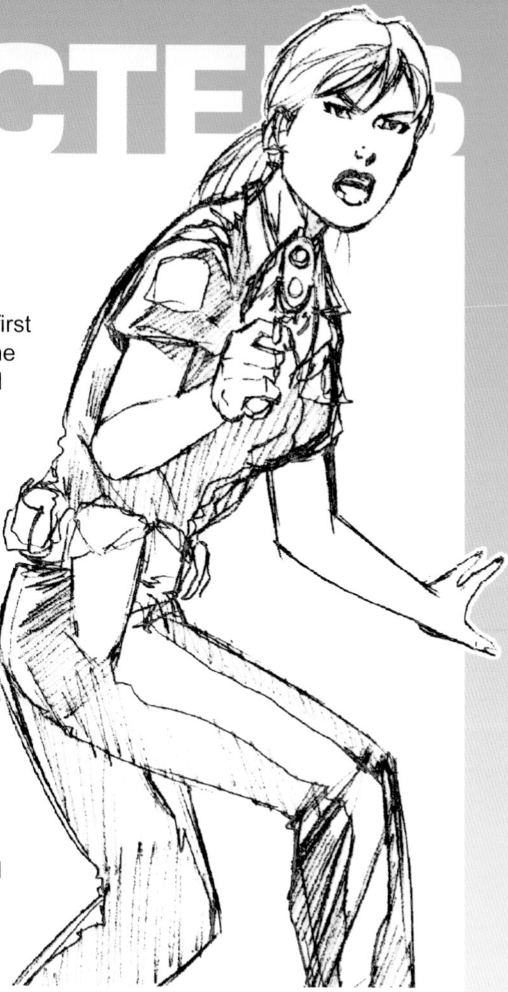

GAIL: Mina is clearly our key character in this first book, and we wanted someone who rises to the threat and the occasion. Mina could have lived her entire life as a mall security guard, living an existence where she never had to show what she was made of . . . Instead, people immediately are drawn to her, and rely on her, and even if it's because of a deception, she rises.

I love the way Jim makes her acting so convincing, and I love how she could be someone you wouldn't look at twice on the street, because she doesn't want to be noticed . . . but you end up missing the person who could change your life forever.

JIM: Gail had some specifics on Mina. Besides her nationality, she wanted her cute/attractive, but not over-the-top sexy, and I think we hit that pretty well. I put her hair back in a ponytail to avoid the big flowing comic-booky hair.

MICHAEL

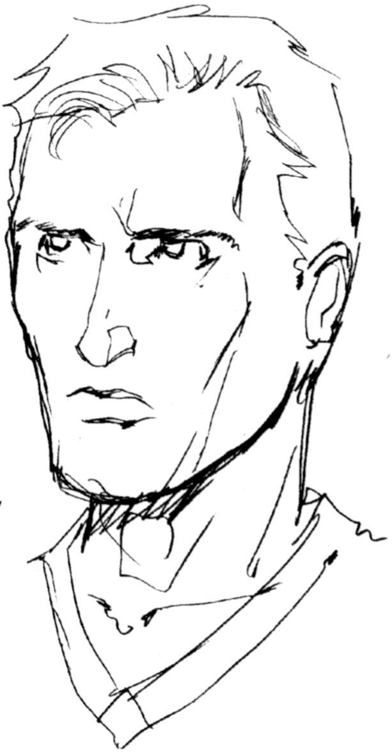

JIM: I rarely base characters on actors, and even then it's just sort of my impression of the person. I may look at a photo briefly, but I try not to make characters look photo referenced. Just not my style. Michael was based on Patrick Wilson, who played Nite Owl in *Watchmen*, and was the lead in the TV series *A Gifted Man* (a show my wife really liked).

In this first sketch of Michael, the features are a little more severe than I settled on for his final look.

GAIL: This is interesting. I didn't even know that. My idea for Michael was fairly simple: I have a lot of male nurses who are readers, for some reason, and they routinely complain about how they are portrayed in the media. Having seen the care and kindness nurses give made me want to portray them with more grace.

CHARACTERS

HAROLD

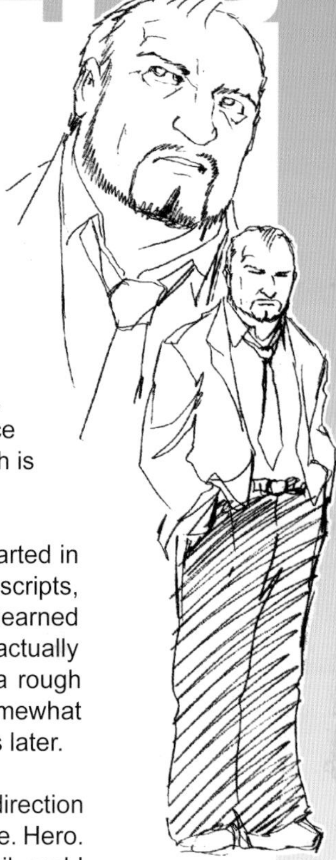

GAIL: For the surface story, Harold is the second most important character in the plot, as he reveals himself only through the decisions he makes, rather than through dialogue. But thematically, Harold represents Free Will, which is why characters react to him with varying degrees of hostility in direct relation to the amount of free will that they themselves possess. Lisa, who is under the influence of the Event, has no free will, and thus hates Harold's guts, while Mina, who believes she is swept along by circumstance with very little choice of her own, also dislikes him on sight. Later, he pays a huge cost, which is often what happens when we act as conscience dictates.

I didn't ask for too specific a look for Harold, I don't believe. When I started in comics, I was annoyingly specific about the look of everything in my scripts, but as I gained experience and trust in the artists I have worked with, I learned that they are far better at visuals than I am, which sounds obvious but actually takes a bit of learning. With Jim, he is fantastic at design, and just a rough hint of a mental sketch always produces something lovely. Harold's somewhat schlubby look and body language are perfect for the choices he makes later.

JIM: My original file is labeled BALD; middle-aged balding was the direction from Gail. Written, Harold is so many different things in the book. Weenie. Hero. He's the least guarded; his look was the easiest to "find" with my pencil, and I really enjoyed drawing his expressive face.

FLEET

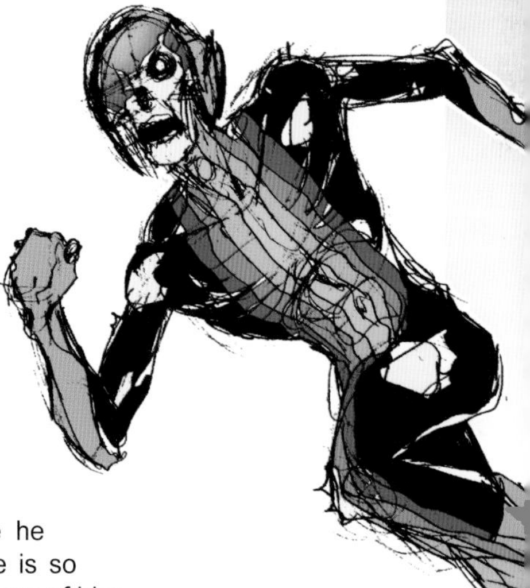

JIM: One of the best parts of the project was coming up with the Crazy Capes, just throwing out ideas and names and seeing what stuck. This was one of those. Gail just wrote "Fleet, our speedster" and I ran with it. My idea was that he never stops running, not even to eat, so he's drastically undernourished. And here again, the only reason he wears a helmet is for the crazy-version visual. I wanted it cracked and revealing that one insane, sunken eyeball.

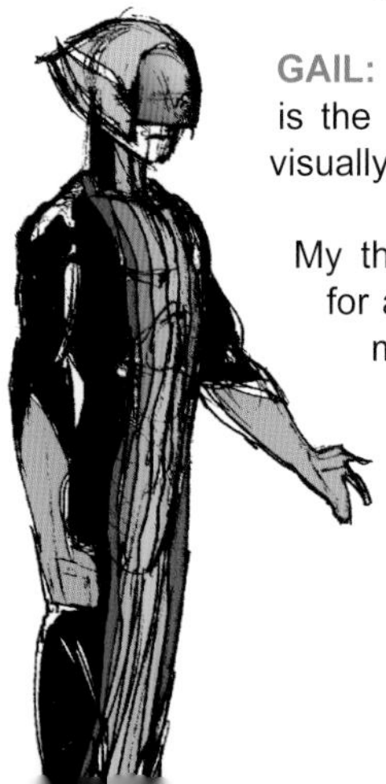

GAIL: Fleet became a key visual, because he is the first of the converted "heroes," and he is so visually charismatic that you just want to see more of him.

My thought with Fleet was that he was a metaphor for addiction, in this case, to bloodshed. The quirky movements, the skinny form, the complexion, the jumpiness, it was meant to invoke a fear, but also a bit of sadness . . . Almost everyone has been touched by addiction, either themselves or a loved one. It's painful, it stings.

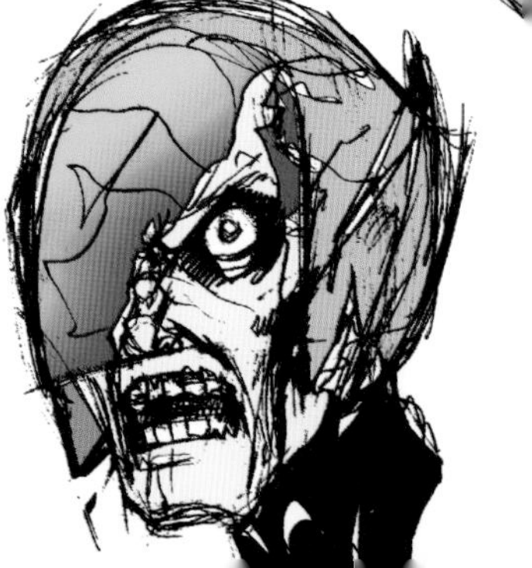

CUPID

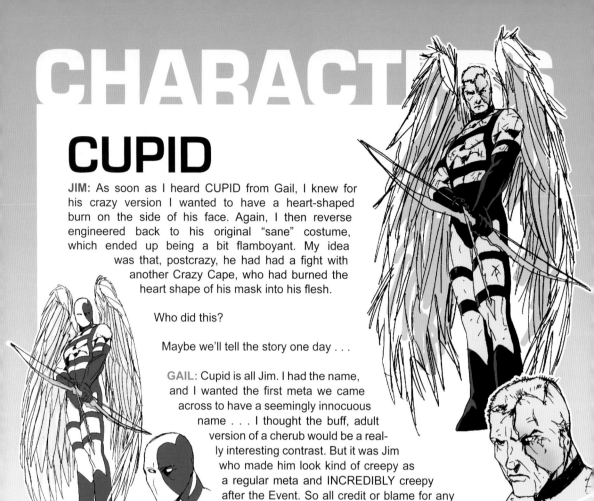

JIM: As soon as I heard CUPID from Gail, I knew for his crazy version I wanted to have a heart-shaped burn on the side of his face. Again, I then reverse engineered back to his original "sane" costume, which ended up being a bit flamboyant. My idea was that, postcrazy, he had had a fight with another Crazy Cape, who had burned the heart shape of his mask into his flesh.

Who did this?

Maybe we'll tell the story one day . . .

GAIL: Cupid is all Jim. I had the name, and I wanted the first meta we came across to have a seemingly innocuous name . . . I thought the buff, adult version of a cherub would be a really interesting contrast. But it was Jim who made him look kind of creepy as a regular meta and INCREDIBLY creepy after the Event. So all credit or blame for any nightmares is completely the artist's fault.

SOUTHERN BELLE

GAIL: This is Jim's character, and I have to say, I dearly love her. From her design, I just instantly knew how I felt she should talk, and how I wanted her portrayed. Probably my favorite design in the book.

JIM: Unlike a lot of the others, Southern Belle's "sane" costume was designed first. Besides the patriotic motif, I tried to emulate a real old-time southern belle dress. The collar and neckline, the evening gloves. I couldn't have her in a big hoop skirt, but the lines on her legs get the feel, I hope.

When I did the color guide for her crazy version, I had a lot of trouble. She still looked sane no matter how I roughed her up. That was until I gave her the purple stains around her eyes, like smeared mascara.

Then she looked good and nuts.

THE LIFE OF A PAGE

Gail: To me, there is no more important tool in the suspense writer's toolbox than the Reveal, and its often neglected kid sister, Dawning Realization. I live for writing those moments, where you have played fair the whole way, but the story suddenly shows you something that wasn't on the expected playlist.

Up until this moment, we've seen nothing but vicious brutality from all the heroes, not a single moment of mercy or compassion. And Overlord has done more damage than any of them . . . He's our Bruce the Shark from the film version of *Jaws*. When his theme music starts, things are about to go terribly wrong.

But something in Michael's speech finds that tiny spark of light buried in darkness. Is it ego? Is it nostalgia? Why does this particular speech unveil a hidden spark of human empathy?

I'll leave that to the reader to decide, but I love that we see the pain and confusion on Overlord's face as he gets it, as he realizes what he's become, and like an addict who can't stay out of his gear, he knows this realization is fleeting.

JIM: The first thing I do with a new script is print it out, one script page to a sheet, leaving room for notes and a small thumbnail sketch of the page as I figure the panel layout.

Page 84 is big. Gail's got this great moment that I wanted to emphasize. You can see the note "telescope" in red near panel 2's action text. I wanted to extend this conflicted moment, Overlord fighting with his insanity—let the moment fill the space so the reader focuses on it. So I turned that one panel into three.

9

PAGE EIGHTY-FOUR: 84

(1) PANEL ONE: Overlord stands on the ground now, not floating.

OVERLOAD: THAT WAS THE REBOOT ISSUE.

MICHAEL: Yes.

MICHAEL: They made you all grim and gritty for a while.

OVERLORD: I REMEMBER YOU. FROM THE DINER.

(2) PANEL TWO: Overlord's face, dark. But not angry. More sad, or blank. — MORE TENSE / CONFLICTED

OVERLORD: ...

OVERLORD: I CAN'T SAVE YOU.

OVERLORD: TOO MUCH DARK BETWEEN. UNIVERSES. — TELESCOPE

OVERLORD: UNIVERSES OF EMPTY RAGE.

VOICE (off-panel): What are you waiting for, big guy?

(3) PANEL THREE: Big panel...it's several remaining Megalopolis heroes.

Jim, the three characters that have to be here are Cupid, a FEMALE version of the Red Flame (same outfit, but sexier, in that dumbass slutty way of old Image comics) and FLEET.

They all look cruel, ready to be cruel, ready to kill. Smiling.

Now, we can HAVE a couple more heroes, we should have, in fact, but I wanted to get your opinion on who they should be. If you have no one you want, that's fine, if you want someone from your story, that's fine, but be aware that they will either die or get maimed here. Whoever you want is fine, and how they fight is whatever you think looks coolest. We want a big, HORRENDOUS superhero fight, bloody, violent beyond words, more scary than thrilling.

The characters we DON'T want are anyone from the Mite Brigade, okay? Anyone else, or new, made-up characters, it's up to you. I can adjust dialog if need be, but I want you to pull out all the stops on this sequence, and make it as powerful as possible, and I want you to feel completely not obligated by my suggestions, okay?

One of them may be a man made out of bricks, literal red bricks and mortar. We'll call him BARRICADE for now.

They come out of the fog. Behind Overlord, who turns to face them.

Fleet seems to be in charge, here.

FLEET: We heard the brat's SIGNAL. The rest are on their WAY.

FLEET: We get it, you're the big boss. You take first CUT.

FLEET: It's cool. Only, we get the REST.

FLEET: And hurry UP, would you?

(1) FLEET
(2) CUPID
(3) LADY FLAME
(4) BARRICADE
(5) ELECTROLUX

(84)

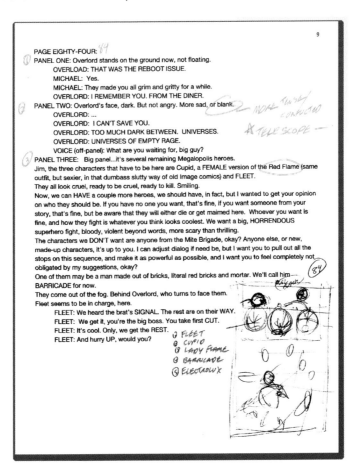

THE LIFE OF A PAGE

JIM: Next is approximately half-sized pencil layouts. I don't do much sketching on the final board, instead working out all the rough drawing here. When done, I photocopy it up to full board size (11" x 17"), and move to a lightbox with the photocopy taped behind the board.

(Yes, I still work on boards, not digitally.)

This technique also allows me to resize anything when photocopying. I can make panels, or just specific elements, larger or smaller.

GAIL: It's important that it not feel phony or forced. The smiling unmasking of Vader in *Return of the Jedi* springs to mind; that isn't what I wanted. I wanted the pain of the man who realizes his parachute is faulty, but jumps anyway because he has no choice.

This is also where we see how important Jim's ideas are to the story. There are several noteworthy things here—he's made one scripted panel of Overlord's struggle into three, which gives a much better feel for the internals of the scene. And a favorite bit: Overlord's head is cracked open, his brains are showing. There's something darkly amusing and sad about that, like having your zipper open in class while giving a speech. Overlord is unaware . . . He's too deep in his own universe. That's all Jim.

JIM: And here's the pencils. There weren't a lot of adjustments from the layout, just some figure repositioning. Since I've been inking myself, the pencils are a little looser. Blacks are just sort of indicated since I know where I'm going in the inks.

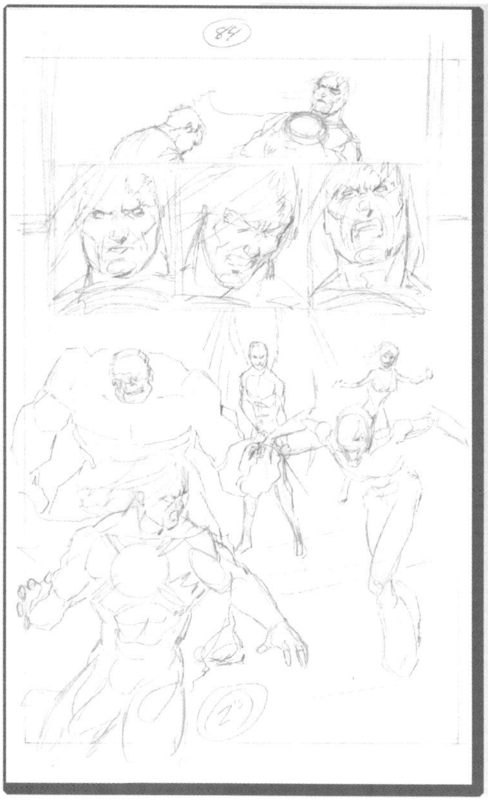
84

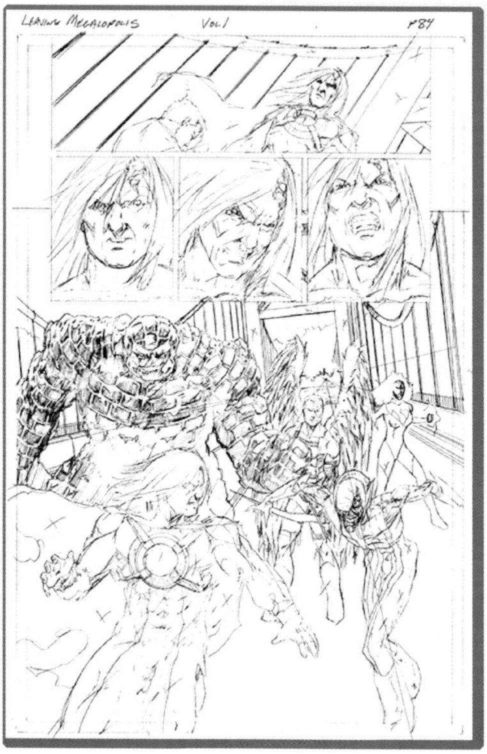
LEAVING MEGALOPOLIS
Vol 1
P84

THE LIFE OF A PAGE

JIM: And the finish line—here's the final inks compared to the final colored and lettered page.

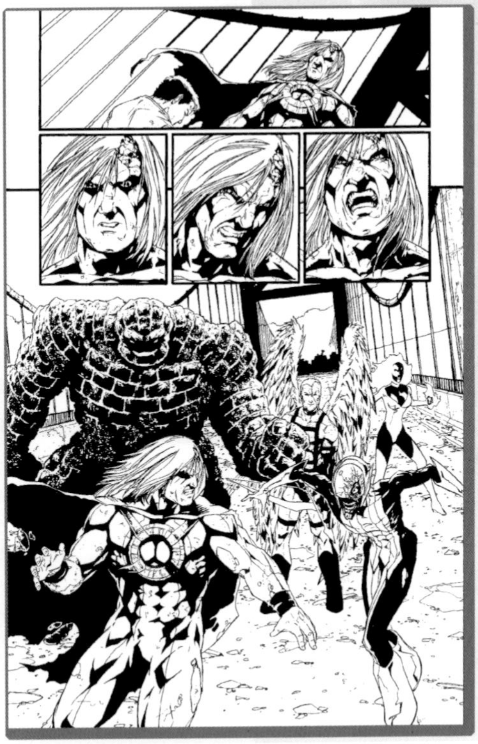

My main concern for black-and-white art that's going to be colored is whether it can stand without the color. I've always felt that any page should be clear and legible, the reader able to understand what's going on if color is never added. I don't want to lay on a colorist the problem of having to save my mistakes.

That being said, working with Jason Wright has always been a blast. His colors are excellent, and since we had already built a good working relationship on *Secret Six*, we were on the same page right off.

The only aspect we went back and forth on was a general palette for the series. We tried first a slightly yellow tint, reflecting the sickness in the city. But we eventually agreed that it needed a harder feel, a steely gray to it. I felt it reflected the ever-present clouds shrouding the city.

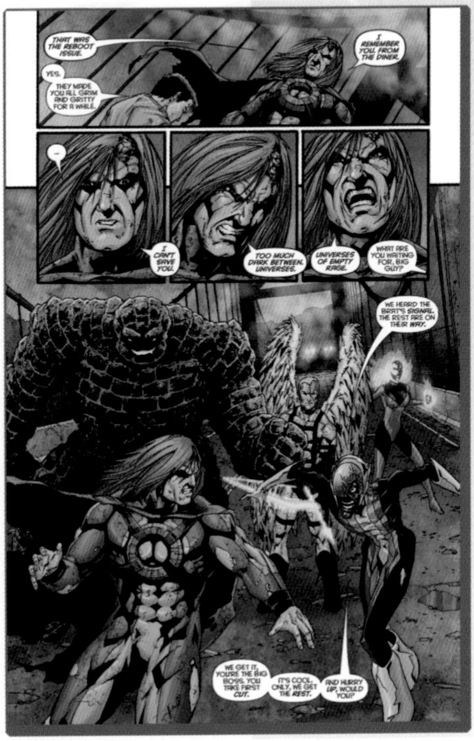
THAT WAS THE REBOOT ISSUE.
YES.
THEY MADE YOU ALL GRIM AND GRITTY FOR A WHILE.
I REMEMBER YOU FROM THE DINER.
I CAN'T SAVE YOU.
TOO MUCH DARK BETWEEN. UNIVERSES.
UNIVERSES OF EMPTY RAGE.
WHAT ARE YOU WAITING FOR, BIG GUY?
WE HEARD THE BRAT'S SIGNAL. THE REST ARE ON THEIR WAY.
WE GET IT, YOU'RE THE BIG BOSS. YOU TAKE FIRST CUT.
IT'S COOL. ONLY, WE GET THE REST.
AND HURRY UP, WOULD YOU?

GAIL: Comics partnerships are always a crapshoot; there are writers who can't write for visuals and artists who can't convey a theme. When you get an artist that you trust, that thinks and adds and improves, it's the best feeling; it gives you license to ask for more, to go subtle instead of bombastic. This is a terrific page to show what you get when you have a great artist interpreting and adding to the story.

WHO THE HELL ARE THESE PEOPLE ANYWAY?

JIM: Like I said, coming up with the Crazy Capes was a blast, especially page 88. Gail just said, "There are two dozen 'heroes' on the bridge," so I had fun . . . and sometimes got a little silly. As evidence, check out this character key. (None of the names are official, or permanent. They're just the names I gave them as I drew to keep them straight. And if any names infringe on anyone's copyright anywhere, then they're definitely not their names!)

1 - LADY FLAME—Female version of RED FLAME from earlier in the story. There's a reason he's not here . . . and it ain't because he's dead.

2 - HUSHPUPPY—Just a were-guy, with a really silly name.

3 - PURPLE HAZE—Ditto on the silly. This guy didn't have a name until I saw him colored by Jason in the big flashback spread.

4 - PHULK—Okay, so sue me. The Hulk's my favorite character, so I had to put in a big nod to him. But I gave him a different color, a goatee, and that weird red crown. (At least I didn't just throw a fin on his head.)

5 - GEO—Big *G* on his chest. His sidekick, Junior Geo, is mentioned in the backup story "Wonderboy" but not seen here.

6 & 7 - LONGHAIR and RED GUY—Not a clue; sorry, some are just filler . . .

8 - With some of the tiny figures I was just drawing interesting silhouettes without much specific thought.

9 - SOUTHERN BELLE—Enough said about her already.

10 - THE RIBBON—I wanted a stretchy guy with holes torn in him. And so . . . tadaaa, THE RIBBON! Even has a big *R* on his costume. Clever, right?

11 - WIDGET—This guy has a bunch of little flying mechanical doohickies with him. Not a clue what they do.

12a & 12b - These were two of the cameo backers, from the backup story "Wonderboy": my friends Dave (hence the *D* on his chest) and his wife, Liz. (And, no, in real life they don't call each other those nasty names like in the story . . . Well, not all the time.)

13 - SHOCK-O—Also seen in part on the flashback spread. Do I need to say electrical powers?

14 - HYDRO—This was supposed to be water-guy, but I forgot to tell Jason, and he colored him as ice-guy. He looks better as ice-guy already.

15 - WEIRD ROBOT—Just that, a weird robot.

16 - BIG GUY—He's just a big guy; has a *B* and a *G* on his chest (sensing a trend) to prove it.

17 - ORNITHOPTER—Those are air cups at the end of his "wings."

18 - Never gave this guy a name. But every city needs a mystic character; and someone has to have a skull head, right? So the two-birds-with-one-stone thing applies.

19 - SPIDERMAN—What? Taken? How about LOTS-O-ARMS . . .

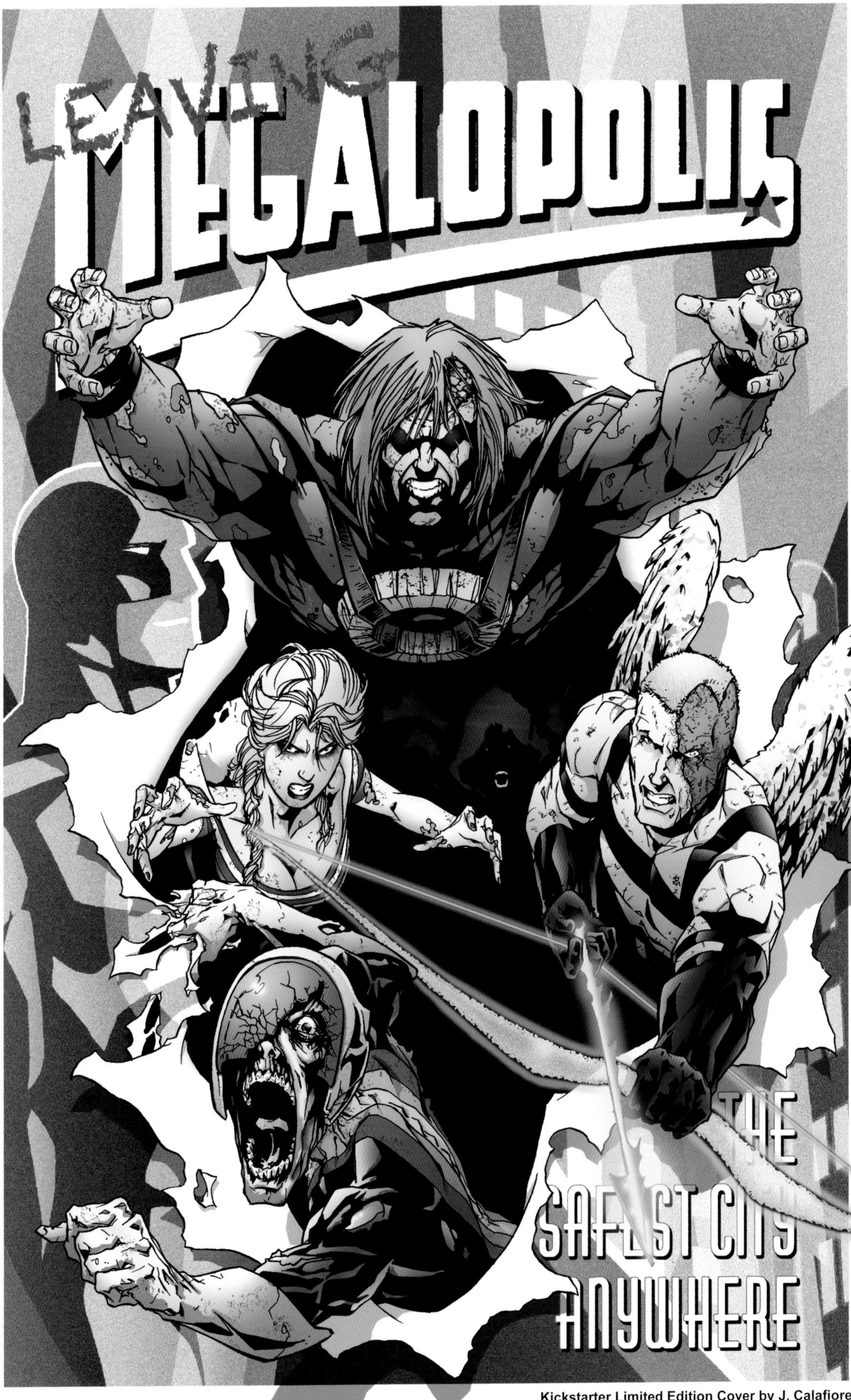
LEAVING
MEGALOPOLIS
THE
SAFEST CITY
ANYWHERE

Kickstarter Limited Edition Cover by J. Calafiore

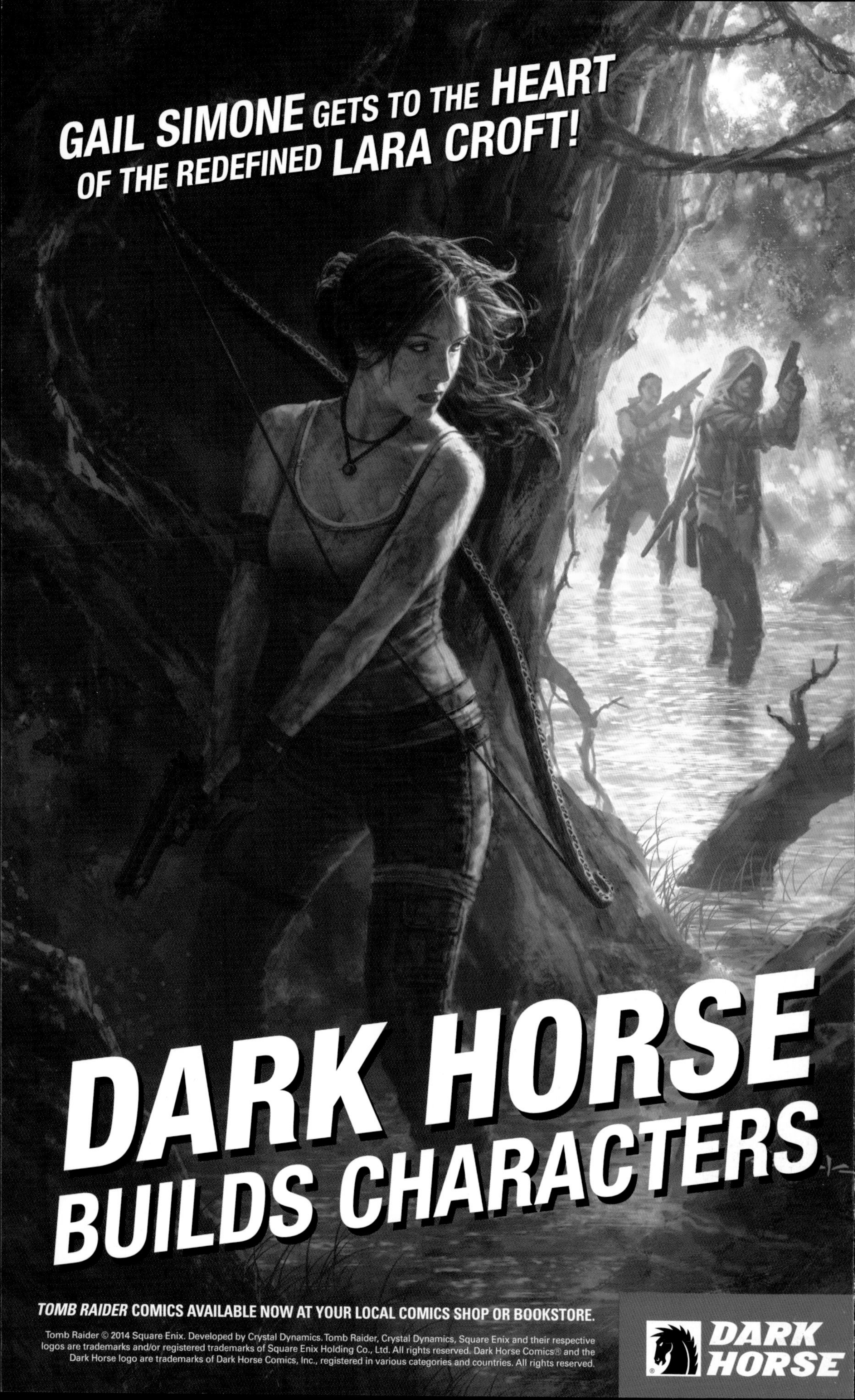
GAIL SIMONE GETS TO THE HEART OF THE REDEFINED LARA CROFT!
DARK HORSE BUILDS CHARACTERS
TOMB RAIDER COMICS AVAILABLE NOW AT YOUR LOCAL COMICS SHOP OR BOOKSTORE.
Tomb Raider © 2014 Square Enix. Developed by Crystal Dynamics. Tomb Raider, Crystal Dynamics, Square Enix and their respective logos are trademarks and/or registered trademarks of Square Enix Holding Co., Ltd. All rights reserved. Dark Horse Comics® and the Dark Horse logo are trademarks of Dark Horse Comics, Inc., registered in various categories and countries. All rights reserved.
DARK HORSE

SUPER:POWERED BY CREATORS!

"These superheroes ain't no boy scouts in spandex. They're a high-octane blend of the damaged, quixotic heroes of pulp and detective fiction and the do-gooders in capes from the Golden and Silver Ages." —Duane Swierczynski

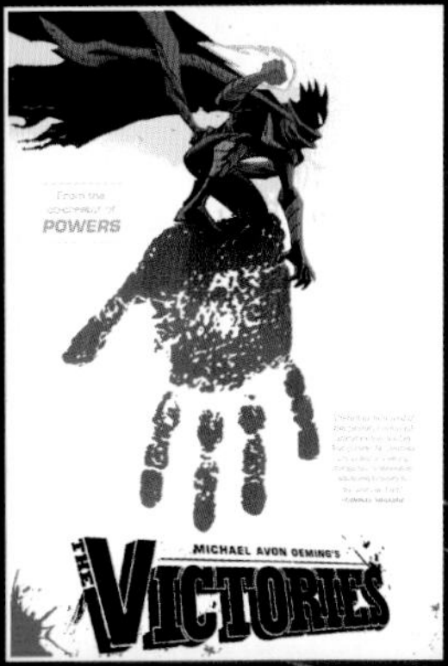
POWERS
MICHAEL AVON OEMING'S
THE VICTORIES

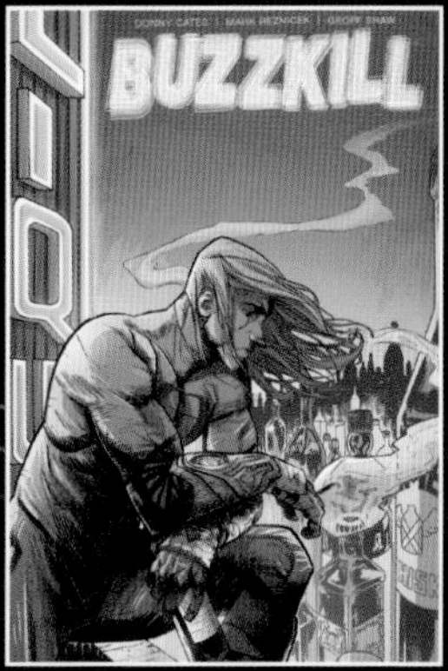
BUZZKILL

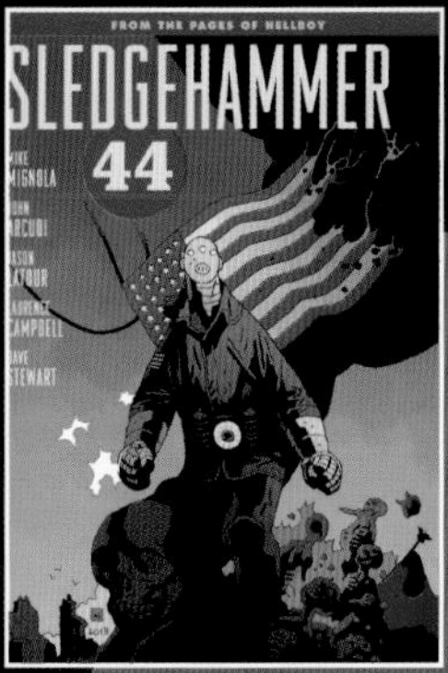
FROM THE PAGES OF HELLBOY
SLEDGEHAMMER
44

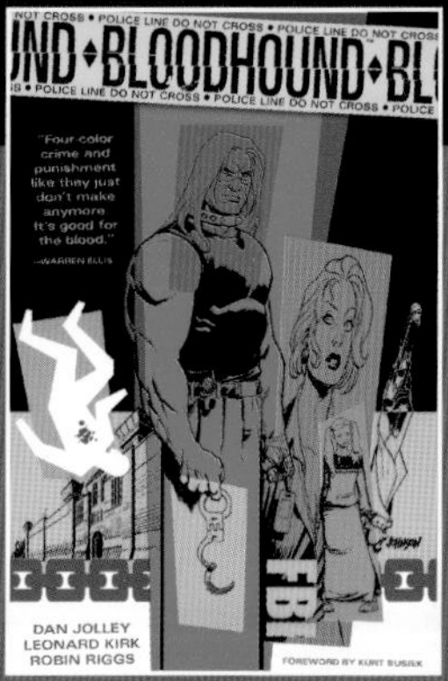
BLOODHOUND
"Four color crime and punishment like they just don't make anymore. It's good for the blood."
—WARREN ELLIS
DAN JOLLEY
LEONARD KIRK
ROBIN RIGGS
FOREWORD BY KURT BUSIEK
FBI

SLEDGEHAMMER 44
Mike Mignola, John Arcudi, and Jason Latour
ISBN 978-1-61655-395-1 | $19.99

DREAM THIEF
Jai Nitz and Greg Smallwood
ISBN 978-1-61655-283-1 | $17.99

BUZZKILL
Mark Reznicek, Donny Cates, and Geoff Shaw
ISBN 978-1-61655-305-0 | $14.99

THE BLACK BEETLE
Francesco Francavilla
VOLUME 1: NO WAY OUT
ISBN 978-1-61655-202-2 | $19.99

THE ANSWER!
Mike Norton and Dennis Hopeless
ISBN 978-1-61655-197-1 | $12.99

BLOODHOUND
Dan Jolley, Leonard Kirk, and Robin Riggs
VOLUME 1: BRASS KNUCKLE PSYCHOLOGY
ISBN 978-1-61655-125-4 | $19.99
VOLUME 2: CROWBAR MEDICINE
ISBN 978-1-61655-352-4 | $19.99

MICHAEL AVON OEMING'S THE VICTORIES
Michael Avon Oeming
VOLUME 1: TOUCHED
ISBN 978-1-61655-100-1 | $9.99
VOLUME 2: TRANSHUMAN
ISBN 978-1-61655-214-5 | $17.99
VOLUME 3: POSTHUMAN
ISBN 978-1-61655-445-3 | $17.99

ORIGINAL VISIONS— THRILLING TALES!

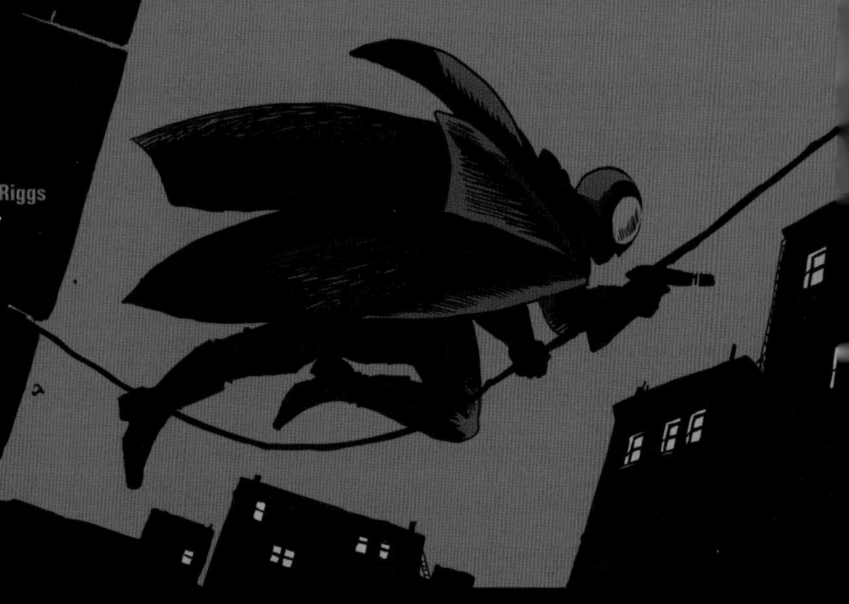

AVAILABLE AT YOUR LOCAL COMICS SHOP OR BOOKSTORE! • To find a comics shop in your area, call 1-888-266-4226.
For more information or to order direct visit DarkHorse.com or call 1-800-862-0052 Mon.–Fri. 9 a.m. to 5 p.m. Pacific Time. Prices and availability subject to change without notice.

CHECK OUT THESE OMNIBUS COLLECTIONS FEATURING CLASSIC DARK HORSE HEROES!

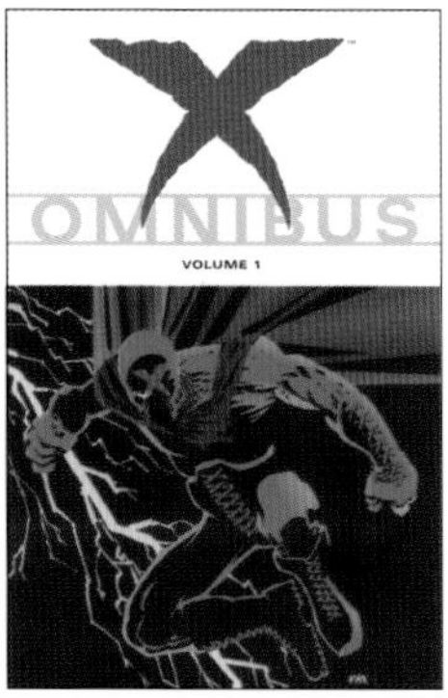
X
OMNIBUS
VOLUME 1

X OMNIBUS

X Omnibus collects the audacious, critically acclaimed Dark Horse series that made "grim and gritty" superheroes seem like cuddly plush toys. Violent and morally ambiguous, *X* walks the thin line between heroism and obsession and shows that sometimes the cure may be worse than the disease. The *X Omnibus* features incredible stories and arresting artwork from creators including Steven Grant, Doug Mahnke, Chris Warner, Jimmy Palmiotti, and Tim Bradstreet.

Volume 1
ISBN 978-1-59307-939-0

Volume 2
ISBN 978-1-59307-937-6

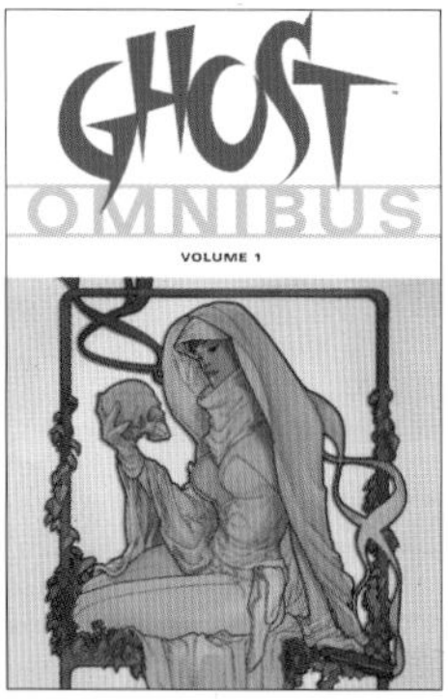
GHOST
OMNIBUS
VOLUME 1

GHOST OMNIBUS

Someone brutally murdered reporter Elisa Cameron, but back from the grave as the spectral avenger Ghost, Elisa intends to find out who killed her and why . . . and grab a double dose of .45-caliber retribution. But being a ghost is no protection from the dark forces of Arcadia, out to prove that even a ghost can be killed!

Volume 1
ISBN 978-1-59307-992-5

Volume 2
ISBN 978-1-59582-213-0

Volume 3
ISBN 978-1-59582-374-8

Volume 4
ISBN 978-1-61655-080-6

Volume 5
ISBN 978-1-61655-383-8

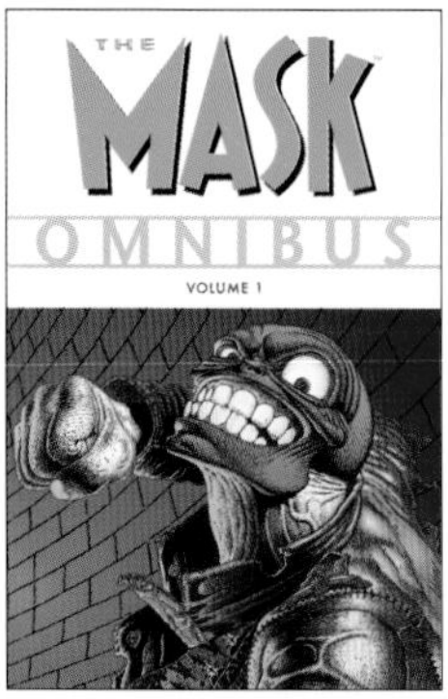
THE
MASK
OMNIBUS
VOLUME 1

THE MASK OMNIBUS

It has all the makings of an epic adventure: an ancient artifact is rediscovered—a mask of unknown origin with unforeseen power. But who knew that after donning this mask even the wimpiest geek would become an indestructible shape-changing super-tornado with a mind for mischief and an appetite for destruction? Equally adept with gun, knife, bat, bomb, pie, or bat-knife-gun-pie-bomb, the Mask cuts a crazed swath of cartoon mayhem! This omnibus edition collects *The Mask*, *The Mask Returns*, and *The Mask Strikes Back* (long out-of-print) for the first time in one volume.

Volume 1
ISBN 978-1-59307-927-7

Volume 2
ISBN 978-1-59307-937-6

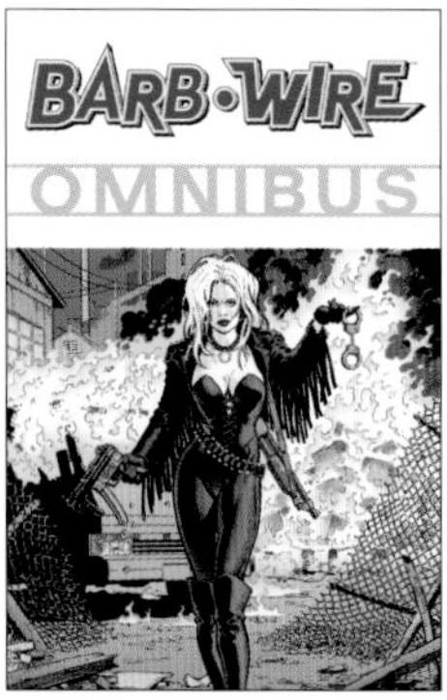
BARB WIRE
OMNIBUS

BARB WIRE OMNIBUS

Steel Harbor is a hell of a town, with the emphasis on *hell*, an urban wasteland of shuttered factories, decaying neighborhoods, and broken dreams. Crime and street violence are the soup of the day every day, but if you're a bounty hunter, every day in "Metal City" can be Christmas—assuming you survive, since the worst of the Harbor's most wanted can fly, summon up tornadoes, or tear cars in half with their bare hands. But manhunter Barb Wire is the best tracker in the business, and no super-gangster is too tough. Beautiful as she is lethal, Barb Wire really puts the "drop dead" in drop-dead gorgeous. The comics series that inspired the movie, *Barb Wire* is over-the-top action that opened doors for today's bad-girl characters.

ISBN 978-1-59307-993-2

$24.99 EACH

DARK HORSE BOOKS
DarkHorse.com

AVAILABLE AT YOUR LOCAL COMICS SHOP OR BOOKSTORE!

To find a comics shop in your area, call 1-888-266-4226

For more information or to order direct: • On the web: darkhorse.com • E-mail: mailorder@darkhorse.com

• Phone: 1-800-862-0052 Mon.–Fri. 9 AM to 5 PM Pacific Time